Notable Civil War Veterans of Oswego County, New York

Notable Civil War Veterans of Oswego County, New York

Natalie Joy Woodall

Published by State University of New York Press, Albany

© 2022 State University of New York

All rights reserved

Printed in the United States of America

No part of this book may be used or reproduced in any manner whatsoever without written permission. No part of this book may be stored in a retrieval system or transmitted in any form or by any means including electronic, electrostatic, magnetic tape, mechanical, photocopying, recording, or otherwise without the prior permission in writing of the publisher.

Excelsior Editions is an imprint of State University of New York Press

For information, contact State University of New York Press, Albany, NY
www.sunypress.edu

Library of Congress Cataloging-in-Publication Data

Name: Woodall, Natalie Joy, author.
Title: Notable Civil War veterans of Oswego County, New York / Natalie Woodall.
Description: Albany : State University of New York Press, 2022. | Series: Excelsior editions | Includes bibliographical references and index.
Identifiers: LCCN 2021055991 | ISBN 9781438489674 (hardcover : alk. paper) | ISBN 9781438489667 (pbk. : alk. paper) | ISBN 9781438489681 (ebook)
Subjects: LCSH: Oswego County (N.Y.)—Biography. | New York (State)—History—Civil War, 1861–1865. | Veterans—New York (State)—Oswego County—History—19th century. | Oswego County (N.Y.)—History—19th century.
Classification: LCC F129.O7 W665 2022 | DDC 974.7/670922—dc23/eng/20211117
LC record available at https://lccn.loc.gov/2021055991

10 9 8 7 6 5 4 3 2 1

This book is dedicated to the historians, genealogists, librarians, archivists, reporters, and photographers whose diligence ensures that the stories of notable Civil War veterans can be told.

Contents

List of Illustrations	ix
Acknowledgments	xix
Introduction	1
Chapter One: Oswego County, Slavery, and the Civil War	5
Chapter Two: Notable Civil War Veterans of Oswego County	17
John Barclay Alexander	17
Samuel B. Alger	22
James Barnes	29
Levi Bird	33
John H. Brockman	36
DeWitt Clinton Carpenter	41
Edward Austin Cooke	44
Dr. Samuel James Crockett	49
Freeman Henry Cross	53
Reverend Horace Melvin Danforth	57
Thomas DeWitt Deans	63
James Doyle	67
Gilbert C. Dutcher	72
William Dewey Ferguson	76
Delos Gary	81
Joseph M. Gould	86
Andrew J. Hirschbolz	89
Edwin Lester Huntington	95

Albert Lindley Lee	101
James H. Lee	107
Lucius V. S. Mattison	114
James A. McKinley	121
Daniel McSweeney	126
Oliver Burrill Mowry	131
Lawson Read Muzzy	137
Samuel Merwin Olmstead	142
Smith Parke	148
Francis M. Pease	153
Peter Pitcher	162
William C. Raulston	166
Dr. Lawrence Reynolds	171
Daniel Falley Schenck	177
Elmina Pleiades Keeler Spencer	181
Francis W. Squires	190
Dr. James K. Stockwell	196
John Wilson Sykes	200
William A. Tillapaugh	206
Edmund Underwood	211
Dr. Mary Edwards Walker	217
Granville Sharp Woodall	227
Notes	233
Bibliography	267
Index	277

Illustrations

I.1	Major George Hugunin, a veteran of the 147th Regiment, figured prominently in the National Guard after the Civil War.	2
1.1	Colonel Warren Douglas Smith was known in Oswego City for his devotion to the Presbyterian Church.	14
2.1	John Barclay Alexander was a longtime editor of the *Oswego Daily Times*.	21
2.2	Mary Place Alexander took a leading role in many Oswego City organizations.	22
2.3	Alger's dredge was a large and complex piece of machinery.	24
2.4	Little is known about Catherine Alger who died of unknown causes.	25
2.5	Samuel Alger was prominent in the development of complicated industrial machinery.	26
2.6	Anna Slauson Alger's reputation was marred by the scandal surrounding her marriage to William Waugh Jr.	28
2.7	James Barnes's occupation as a surveyor took him all the way to Panama.	29
2.8	Many members of the Barnes family are buried in Phoenix Rural Cemetery.	32

2.9	Levi Bird worked as a barber in Sandy Creek, New York, after the Civil War.	35
2.10	Lizzie Bird lies beside her husband in Woodlawn Cemetery, Sandy Creek, New York.	35
2.11	John H. Brockman duped an entire community with his impersonation of Charles Preuss.	36
2.12	Cartographer Charles Preuss hanged himself from a tree near Washington, DC, in 1854.	38
2.13	Brockman's deception is emblazoned on his gravestone. Author's collection.	40
2.14	DeWitt Clinton Carpenter led an active life in Orwell, New York. Courtesy of *Orwell Veterans' Memorial Souvenir*.	41
2.15	DeWitt and Abby Carpenter raised a large family while managing to be involved in local affairs.	43
2.16	Edward Austin Cooke was an officer in the 81st Regiment.	45
2.17	Edward Cooke bought this monument after Kittie's death.	46
2.18	Harriet Griswold Cooke lived quietly in Oswego for many years following her husband's death.	48
2.19	Dr. Samuel J. Crockett devoted his life to his patients and his community.	50
2.20	The Crockett family plot occupies a large space near the back of Woodlawn Cemetery, Sandy Creek, New York.	53
2.21	Freeman Cross's talents and skill permitted the physically impaired to walk.	54
2.22	Freeman Cross enlisted in the Union army as a musician.	55
2.23	Freeman and Delia Cross are buried in Pulaski Village Cemetery.	56
2.24	Reverend Horace M. Danforth was a dedicated Methodist minister.	58
2.25	Caroline Danforth died in Herkimer County and was buried in Riverside Cemetery, Scriba, New York.	59

2.26	A flag-draped coffin carried Rev. Danforth to his final resting place in Riverside Cemetery, Scriba, New York.	62
2.27	Sarah Danforth, who died in Massachusetts, was buried in Riverside Cemetery with her husband, Horace.	62
2.28	One side of Deans's prized watch fob carried the GAR logo.	63
2.29	The other side of Deans's watch fob is decorated with the Masonic square and compass.	64
2.30	Isabel Deans is buried in Cleveland Village Cemetery.	65
2.31	Ada Deans is also buried in the Deans family plot.	66
2.32	Thomas Deans was the last Civil War veteran in Cleveland, New York.	67
2.33	Colonel James Doyle's untimely death saddened the entire Oswego community.	71
2.34	Margaret McCanna Doyle was well regarded in Oswego City.	72
2.35	Gilbert Dutcher's regiment saw little battlefield action but he suffered from the effects of exposure and disease for the rest of his life.	75
2.36	Helen Forsyth Dutcher outlived her husband by many years.	76
2.37	William Dewey Ferguson had the distinction of serving in two Oswego County regiments.	78
2.38	William and Helen Monroe Ferguson were prominent residents of Sandy Creek, New York.	80
2.39	Delos Gary recruited an entire company for the 147th Regiment and became its captain.	82
2.40	Catherine "Kate" Martin Gary was the daughter of one attorney and the wife of another.	84
2.41	Due to a clerical error, Captain Gary's gravesite was unidentified for almost 150 years.	85
2.42	Sergeant Joseph Gould was the first Civil War veteran buried in Phoenix Rural Cemetery.	88

2.43	Andrew J. Hirschbolz was a colorful character in Oswego who won widespread recognition for his annual pilgrimage to Riverside Cemetery, Scriba, New York, to decorate the graves of Confederate soldiers buried there.	89
2.44	Aletha Kingsley Hirschbolz was the mother of four sons.	93
2.45	Andrew J. Hirschbolz served his adopted country in two different regiments and states.	94
2.46	Edwin Huntington lived his entire life in Mexico, New York, and was instrumental in bringing electricity to the village.	97
2.47	Edwin Huntington was an important supporter of the campaign to raise a GAR monument in Mexico, New York.	98
2.48	The Huntington monument stands in the middle of the large family plot in Mexico Village Cemetery.	100
2.49	Mary Turdot was Edwin Huntington's second wife.	100
2.50	General Albert Lindley Lee's monument stands on the highest point of Mt. Adnah Cemetery, Fulton, New York.	101
2.51	Albert Lindley Lee began his military career in Kansas.	102
2.52	The inscription on General Lee's gravestone reads: "Warm summer sun shine kindly here, / Warm summer winds blow softly here, / Green sod above lie light, lie light, / Good night dear heart good night, good night."	104
2.53	A. L. Lee Memorial Hospital served the greater Fulton community for over a century.	106
2.54	Victorine Lee is buried beside her husband in Mt. Adnah Cemetery, Fulton, New York.	106
2.55	The USS *Kearsarge* chased the CSS *Alabama* for months before sinking her off the coast of France.	108
2.56	James H. Lee never received his Medal of Honor.	109
2.57	The citation on the reverse of Lee's medal reads: "Personal Valor / James H. Lee / Seaman / USS Kearsarge / Destruction of the Alabama / June 19, 1864."	110

2.58	James H. Lee succumbed to tuberculosis acquired while serving in the US Navy.	111
2.59	Julia Place Lee took an active interest in the budding Grange movement.	112
2.60	James H. Lee's government grave marker memorializes his MOH.	112
2.61	James and Julia Lee are buried in the Place family plot in Rural Cemetery, Oswego Town, New York.	113
2.62	Lucius V. S. Mattison's fondest desire as a young man was to enter the military.	115
2.63	These keys are reputedly those taken by Colonel Mattison after the 81st Regiment liberated the Union prisoners in Castle Thunder.	116
2.64	Caroline Gillmore Mattison Search is buried with her parents in Riverside Cemetery, Scriba, New York.	118
2.65	Colonel Mattison and his second wife, Mary Sinclair Oliver, died within a short time of each other.	119
2.66	This collection of Mattison memorabilia once belonged to his only child, Elizabeth M. Scoville.	120
2.67	Veterans of the 147th Regiment raised the money to have this monument built and erected near the spot on the Gettysburg battlefield where they held the line against advancing Confederate forces on July 1, 1863.	124
2.68	James McKinley led an interesting and varied life in Oswego.	125
2.69	Jane Reid McKinley lies next to her husband and is surrounded by several of their children in St. Peter's Cemetery, Oswego.	126
2.70	Daniel McSweeney spent many months in Andersonville POW camp.	127
2.71	Although Mary Sheridan McSweeney died in Pittsburg, Pennsylvania, she was buried in her hometown, Oswego City.	130

2.72	After Daniel McSweeney was fatally injured when he fell down an elevator shaft, his body was returned to Oswego for burial.	131
2.73	Oliver Mowry was the last Civil War veteran in Oswego County.	133
2.74	Oliver Mowry's interests included membership in the Mexico Cornet Band. Courtesy of *Grip's Historical Souvenir of Mexico*.	134
2.75	Ella Calkins Mowry taught school for many years in addition to rearing a large family.	136
2.76	Oliver Mowry is buried next to Ella in Daysville Cemetery.	137
2.77	Lawson Read Muzzy was the long-time editor of the *Pulaski Democrat*.	140
2.78	Although Lawson and Alma Muzzy died elsewhere, their bodies were returned to Pulaski, New York, their home for many years.	142
2.79	Samuel Merwin Olmstead lay on the battlefield for three days before he was rescued.	143
2.80	A brokenhearted Captain Orimel B. Olmstead escorted his son's body to Orwell for burial.	145
2.81	Elizabeth Olmstead died after traveling to Baltimore to care for her sick husband. Her body was returned to Orwell, New York, for burial.	146
2.82	Orimel B. Olmstead was married three times. His last wife was Julia A. Gilbert.	147
2.83	Smith Parke was discharged from the army for "disability" and died shortly after returning to Amboy, New York.	150
2.84	Harriet Parke's death made her six children orphans.	151
2.85	Clark Stewart Parke, who enlisted in the 147th Regiment to support his siblings, succumbed to typhoid fever a few months later.	152

2.86	Danville Prison was a notorious Confederate POW camp.	156
2.87	Camp Sumter, located in Andersonville, Georgia, was the most reviled prison of the Civil War.	157
2.88	Union prisoners complained that conditions at Florence, South Carolina, were worse than at Camp Sumter.	158
2.89	Francis Pease's imprisonment during the Civil War resulted in years of physical suffering.	160
2.90	Catherine Lord Pease survived her husband by many years, subsequently marrying Himan P. Dutcher, another Civil War veteran.	161
2.91	When Peter Pitcher died, he was the oldest member of the GAR in New York State.	164
2.92	Margaret Blair Pitcher's grave marker contains only the word "Mother."	166
2.93	William Raulston was fatally wounded in an escape attempt from Danville Prison.	167
2.94	The inscription on the Raulston monument reads: "Died of wounds at Danville, Va. This distinguished soldier served during the war of 1861-5 as Capt., Major and L't Col. 81 Inf't'y and as Col. 24 Cavalry N. Y. Vol.	170
2.95	The Ratigan family was prominent in Oswego's construction industry.	172
2.96	Dr. Reynolds's grave lies somewhere in the Ratigan plot in St. Paul's Cemetery, Oswego. City.	177
2.97	The construction abilities of the 50th New York Engineers were crucial for the Union Army's success.	178
2.98	Daniel Falley Schenck is buried in the family plot in Mt. Adnah Cemetery, Fulton, New York.	180
2.99	Grateful veterans recommended that Elmina Spencer's likeness be carved into the staircase of the New York State Capitol Building.	186
2.100	The Woman's Relief Corps cared for Elmina Spencer in her later years.	188

2.101	This modest stone, on which her maiden name is misspelled, marks Elmina Keeler Spencer's grave in Rural Cemetery, Oswego Town.	189
2.102	Francis W. Squires, avid writer and statistician, was well known in Oswego County for his extensive research into local history and biography.	190
2.103	Sarah Rice Squires was the mother of four children.	191
2.104	It is ironic that the gravestone of Francis W. Squires, who compiled years of statistics and kept a diary for forty-three years, contains no biographical information.	195
2.105	James and Margaret Fleming Stockwell pose with members of the Fleming family in this 1895 portrait.	197
2.106	Margaret Fleming Stockwell took an active interest in Oswego Hospital.	199
2.107	Dr. James Stockwell was a tireless crusader in the struggle to improve the health of Oswego City residents.	200
2.108	John Wilson Sykes was a longtime soldier in the Salvation Army.	203
2.109	Only this gravestone provides evidence that John Wilson Sykes died in Fulton and was buried in Mt. Adnah Cemetery.	204
2.110	Elizabeth Slaver Moore Sykes and her daughter, Doris, are buried a short distance from John Wilson Sykes in Mt. Adnah Cemetery, Fulton, New York.	205
2.111	William and Harriet Tiffany Tillapaugh are buried in Mexico Village Cemetery.	210
2.112	Major Edmund Underwood was a career soldier in the US Army.	214
2.113	Mary Beardsley Underwood was instrumental in the construction and management of the Home for the Homeless (Ladies' Home) in Oswego City.	216
2.114	Mary Underwood is buried next to her husband in Riverside Cemetery, Scriba, New York.	217

2.115	Dr. Mary Walker's letter to her family described her position in the Patent Office Hospital in Washington, DC.	219
2.116	Two Union army generals recommended Dr. Mary Walker for the Medal of Honor. Courtesy of the Oswego County Historical Society.	220
2.117	The reverse of Dr. Walker's medal reads: "The Congress / To / Dr. Mary E. Walker / A.A. Surgeon, U. S. A. / Nov. 11th / 1865."	221
2.118	During the Civil War, Dr. Walker adopted a mode of dress intended to identify her as a military doctor.	222
2.119	Dr. Mary Walker's crusade for dress reform was personal, leading her eventually to wear only male attire.	223
2.120	Mary Walker was buried in the family plot in Rural Cemetery, Oswego Town.	227
2.121	Although only fifteen years old, Granville Woodall put on a Union soldier's uniform and marched off to war.	228
2.122	Thanks to the efforts of Elmina Spencer, John Woodall succeeded in having Granville's body shipped home for burial.	231
2.123	Granville's regiment and company are erroneously carved into the Soldiers' Monument in New Haven, New York.	232

Acknowledgments

I gratefully acknowledge the following persons and organizations for their assistance in the production of this book: James Gandy and the New York State Military Museum for permission to use the photographs of Edward Austin Cooke, Delos Gary, William Dewey Ferguson, Elmina Spencer, Samuel Merwin Olmstead, Warren Douglas Smith, and Daniel McSweeney; Dr. Jesse Kraft and the American Numismatic Society Museum for permission to use the photographs of James H. Lee's Medal of Honor; Michael Pittavino and the H. Lee White Maritime Museum for permission to use the portraits of James H. Lee and Julia Place Lee and for permission to quote Lee's diary; Gulfport Bob (Find a Grave) for permission to use the photograph of Clark Stewart Parke's gravestone; Shawn P. Doyle and the Half-Shire Historical Society for permission to use the photograph of Dr. Samuel Crockett and for innumerable kindnesses during the writing of this book; Charles Young, Scriba town historian, and the Scriba Historical Society for permission to use the photograph of Lucius V. S. Mattison; Joni Hinds, Cleveland village historian, and the Cleveland Historical Society for permission to publish photographs of Thomas Deans's watch fob; Susan Mitchener, national archivist, Salvation Army National Archives, for permission to use the photograph of John Wilson Sykes; Debra Allen, Volney town historian, for permission to use Francis Squires's diary; Theresa Jones and the Friends of Fulton History for permission to use a photograph of A. L. Lee Memorial Hospital; Keith O'Connell for permission to use the photo of Dr. James and Margaret Fleming Stockwell; Mary Kay Stone and the Oswego County Historical Society for permission to reproduce Dr. Mary Walker's letter dated November 13, 1861, and the images of her Medal of Honor; Library of Congress for the portrait of Freeman

Cross, the picture of the battle between the USS *Kearsarge* and the CSS *Alabama*, the painting of 50th New York Engineers at Fredericksburg, and photographs of Danville Prison, Andersonville Prison, Florence Prison Pen, photograph of William C. Raulston; Gary Heinmiller for countless kindnesses; Seth Wallace, editor of the *Palladium-Times*, for permission to use material previously published in that newspaper; Dr. Richard Carlin and SUNY Press for the opportunity to write this book; Elaine DeLong for her "eagle eyes" in locating soldiers' graves in old cemeteries; Darlene Woolson for permission to use her photograph of the 147th Regiment's Gettysburg Monument and especially for her company as we wandered through cemeteries in pursuit of long forgotten Civil War soldiers; and Joanne Paino for sound editorial advice and amazing computer wizardry. If I have omitted anyone, please know that I am thankful for each and every scrap of information and picture provided to me in the course of writing this book.

Introduction

The thirty-nine stories contained in this book were gleaned from a larger project concerning the Grand Army of the Republic (GAR) in Oswego County. Having learned that many of the original descriptive books had disappeared, I set out to recreate the missing membership lists for those posts, utilizing articles, notices, and obituaries published in local newspapers. For them and for the few posts whose members were identified, my goal was to provide birth and death dates; provide names of parents, wives, and children; note the military unit in which each man served; and add biographical material through references to published material. Along the way I discovered that many of these veterans had served in regiments outside of Oswego County or, indeed, outside New York State.

They may have been native New Yorkers working or attending school in another state when the war broke out, such as John B. Alexander. They may have been immigrants desirous of supporting their new country, as was the case of Dr. Lawrence Reynolds. Still others moved to Oswego County from parts unknown after the war, including John B. Brockman.

This investigation uncovered the truly notable lives of men who were, among others, politicians, farmers, ministers, and teachers. Edward Austin Cooke and Thomas DeWitt Deans are only two examples of veterans who devoted years to improving their communities.

Previous study had already revealed stories of soldiers who had not been members of the GAR but who were notable for their sacrifices on behalf of the nation. William C. Raulston, Smith Parke, and Samuel Merwin Olmstead belong to this group.

Women played an important role in the Civil War. They held families together while their menfolk were at the front. They tended cattle, grew crops, and cared for children and elderly relatives. Women formed relief societies to assist soldiers' destitute families, sent food and clothing to soldiers, and wrote letters to boost the morale of those hungering for hometown news. After the war they founded the Woman's Relief Corps, which participated in the various activities of local GAR posts. A few women, such as Elmina Spencer and Mary Walker, overcame male prejudices and contributed directly to the war effort by caring for wounded and sick soldiers on the battlefield and in the hospital.

The men and women appearing in this book represent only a fraction of the millions who put aside personal endeavors to unite in a common cause: preserving the Union. In a larger sense, however, every person so engaged was notable, even if only to family and friends.

Figure I.1. Major George Hugunin, a veteran of the 147th Regiment, figured prominently in the National Guard after the Civil War. Author's collection.

The political and cultural atmosphere in which these people lived was influenced by the great social issues of the time, notably that of slavery. Men enlisted to preserve the Union, not to free slaves. Yet that debate was the catalyst for the secession of eleven southern states following Abraham Lincoln's election to the presidency in November 1860. The attack on Fort Sumter in April 1861 catapulted the nation into a conflict whose effects are still felt in twenty-first-century America.

Oswego County was a microcosm of nineteenth-century American society. Abolitionists called for the immediate liberation of slaves everywhere, arguing that perpetual bondage was legalized robbery. Pro-slavery advocates referred to biblical texts which, they surmised, confirmed one man's right to own another. Both groups vehemently claimed God was on their side. Accommodations made by either were pleasing to none—and so the war was fought.

Out of the conflict, which consumed the lives of more than 620,000 soldiers and sailors, emerged the thirty-nine people featured in this narrative. Not all survived the war, and those who returned to civilian life were changed forever. Despite hardships, trauma, and loss, however, each contributed to improving the situation of family, friends, Oswego County, and, indeed, the entire country.

Chapter One

Oswego County, Slavery, and the Civil War

Situated on the southeastern shore of Lake Ontario, Oswego County was largely an agricultural community during the nineteenth century. Most inhabitants had never seen a dark-skinned person, and the slave "problem" plaguing other places was only a topic to read about in the newspaper. Therefore, that this area should become embroiled in the controversy is somewhat surprising. Nevertheless, Oswego figured heavily in the abolitionist movement and in the war which ultimately forced the nation to face the problem directly.

Slavery, which made its first appearance in the New World as early as the sixteenth century, came to the area now known as New York State in 1626 when a Dutch East India Company ship arrived in New Amsterdam (New York City) carrying eleven African captives whom the crew exchanged with the locals for food. By 1703, more than 42 percent of households in New York City held enslaved persons. Slave labor in construction and farming was crucial to the development of largely populated areas. It is estimated that by 1790, only one-third of Africans residing in New York State were free.

In addition to manual labor, slaves were recruited to serve in the armies of both the British and the Americans in the Revolutionary War. British officers enticed slaves to run away from their owners with a promise of freedom at war's end. The American military acted similarly, offering money to owners who assigned slaves to the military. They too promised freedom to those who would support the Revolution.

The slavery problem vexed the writers of the United States Constitution, many of them slaveholders. If all men were "created equal," how could the enslavement of hundreds of thousands of people be justified? The unhappy compromise of considering a black person to be three-fifths of a white person satisfied no one and continues to torment twenty-first-century Americans.

New York State made inroads into the emancipation of its enslaved population in 1799 with the passage of a law which freed slaves born after 1799. Henceforth these persons would be considered indentured servants, owing many years of service to masters. Males were required to work until they reached the age of twenty-eight, and females, until they were twenty-five. Another provision of the law stated that slaves born before 1799 would henceforth be considered indentured servants who must continue working without pay.

In 1817 the state legislature enacted another law covering slaves born before 1799. They would be freed but not until July 4, 1827, thus ensuring that owners could exact another ten years' labor from them. Nevertheless, in consequence of the law, no slaves were enumerated in New York City in 1840.

Despite the "enlightened" albeit slow actions taken by the New York State Legislature, many citizens came to believe that slavery was inherently evil and had to be abolished in every state and territory. The American Anti-Slavery Society was formed in Philadelphia, Pennsylvania, in 1833, the first of many such organizations. One was created in Central New York when a group of abolitionists gathered in Utica on October 31, 1835. Their plans to create a state anti-slavery society were temporarily thwarted when a pro-slavery mob broke up the meeting. In attendance that day as an observer was Gerritt Smith, a wealthy businessman, who became so angry that he invited the participants to reconvene the next day at his home in Peterboro, Madison County.

Oswego County's efforts at establishing an anti-slavery society antedated state efforts by a month. Residents of Mexico, New York, had, at some point between 1834 and 1835, held the county's first abolitionist meeting at the Colosse Baptist Church.[1] Subsequently, a notice was published in a local newspaper inviting residents to assemble for the purpose of forming an Oswego County anti-slavery society:

> One of the greatest evils, both natural and moral, with which our beloved country is afflicted, is slavery. That it is an increas-

ing and threatening evil, is generally admitted . . . When this engrossing subject shall have been fully discussed, and then only, will the people be prepared to act, and act right in relation to it . . . Therefore the undersigned in the exercise of their rights as members of this community, without presuming to dictate to others, would respectfully invite a Convention of the citizens of the county of Oswego, who are friendly to the "Immediate Emancipation of the Slaves," to be held on Thursday, the 8th of October next, at 10 o'clock A. M. at Mexicoville, to consider the propriety of forming a County Anti Slavery Society, and adopt such other measures in relation to this subject as may be thought expedient.[2]

Fifty-five locals signed the notice, which was dated September 28, 1835. In that same newspaper was an editorial criticizing the men for their plans:

We regret to find that the few abolitionists among us have resolved upon calling a meeting in this county–not that we have any fears that their meeting will tend to promote their principles, or add converts to their cause, but that it is calculated to stir up a spirit in this community which will not be quieted until much ill feeling is engendered among our citizens. And what, let us ask, is the object of this meeting? Do the abolitionists expect that by assembling the people together and adopting resolutions denouncing the institution of slavery among our southern brethren, that they are in any measure loosening the chains of slavery, or hastening the period of emancipation of that unfortunate race of human beings . . . They know that all they can do for the slaves will avail nothing without the consent of the slave-holder–and yet they are determined to persevere in feeding an excitement, which already threatens the existence of the Union, and is tending to strengthen the chains of slavery. Verily these men are assuming a dreadful responsibility; and we hope every citizen who has one spark of humanity, or who would save this Union from dissolution, will pause and reflect before he gives his aid in the work of destruction.[3]

From that historic meeting came the first petition ever sent to Congress regarding slavery. Signed by seventy-nine men, the petition called upon Congress to abolish slavery and the slave trade in the District of Columbia. Chief among the signers was Starr Clark, whose tin shop in the village of Mexico served as a gathering place to discuss the latest news and to plan abolitionist activities. Clark and his wife, Harriet Loomis, had experienced a religious enlightenment several years earlier and had dedicated themselves to eradicating slavery. Other activists included Asa Beebe and Leonard Ames, described by author Crisfield Johnson as "an uncompromising abolitionist, having in him the inherent love of freedom and a natural hatred of oppression."[4] James Caleb Jackson, known for his views on dress reform, figured prominently in the local movement on account of his oratorical abilities.[5]

On February 13, 1839, the society held its annual meeting at the Presbyterian (now Congregational) Church in New Haven, New York, located a short distance from Mexico. Reverend Ralph Robinson chaired the convention and was reelected president. Elected vice presidents were T. C. Baker, Hiram Gilbert, and Hamilton Littlefield. Lewis Falley was elected secretary, and Seth Johnson, treasurer.

The significance of this session lies in the resolutions passed by the participants. According to the first resolution, slavery was wrong because it was sinful "and we view it of especial importance that in all of our operations, we act in accordance with the principles of our holy religion." Secondly, the conventioneers avowed that "a man's right to himself is the foundation of all his other rights; slavery, which deprives him of this, deprives him of all his other rights & is a system of legal robbery, and ought to be immediately abolished." The third resolution was perhaps the most significant for subsequent political campaigns because members were encouraged to refuse "to vote for any but sincere practical advocates for immediate emancipation." Thus a political litmus test was born to which every candidate for local and state office would be subject.[6]

The movement from "moral suasion" to political pressure and candidates' reaction to it was exemplified by the response of William H. Seward, who was running for governor in 1838. When asked about his stance on slavery, he cannily replied: "Persons selected as the representatives of political principles, can have no right to compromise their constituents by the expressions of opinions on other subjects than those in reference to which the selections were made."[7] His purposefully vague response demonstrates how seriously candidates considered this question and how much they resisted being brought into the controversy.

Henry Clay, a proponent of the American Colonization Society, founded in 1817, responded to the abolitionists' growing political power in a speech delivered in Congress on February 7, 1839. Clay divided abolitionists into three categories: humanitarians, apparent abolitionists, and ultra-abolitionists. Humanitarians, according to Clay, were "honest philanthropists." Apparent abolitionists were motivated by "sinister purposes" and "sought to convince the first group that a proslavery South was intently conducting a campaign to abridge the civil and constitutional rights of the nation." Ultra-abolitionists were the most dangerous because they "determined to overthrow slavery by any means, regardless of consequences, and were motivated by feelings devoid of honor, patriotism, or respect for the rights of property." Specifically referring to the "litmus test" he said: "It is because these ultra-abolitionists have ceased to employ the instruments of reason and persuasion, have made their cause political, and have appealed to the ballot-box, that I am induced upon this occasion to address you."[8]

Despite Oswego County's growing awareness of and sympathy for enslaved peoples, subtle forms of discrimination existed, as Reverend Samuel Ringgold Ward (1817–1864) discovered when, in October 1849, he bought a ticket to travel from Oswego City to Watertown, Jefferson County aboard the steamer *Ontario*:

> The citizens of Oswego are liberal towards the anti-slavery cause, and prejudice is not so controlling here as in some cities. But there is enough of it remaining, to sink a thousand cities. It is partly on this account *that the Steamer Ontario prohibits negroes going into any cabin or saloon even at night*. So the clerk (a very handsome young man) told me on the 26th October 1849. I was compelled, therefore, to spend the night on deck, exposed to such wind and weather as Providence might direct, no other than a deck passage being allowed me.[9]

The passage of the Fugitive Slave Act in 1850 angered Oswego County abolitionists, as it did elsewhere. This was not the first time attempts were made to prevent runaway slaves from obtaining their freedom. According to Article IV, section 2, clause 3 of the United States Constitution, slaves did not become free simply by escaping to a free state. The Fugitive Slave Act of 1793 reinforced that prohibition, authorizing local governments to capture and return fugitives. Owners or their agents had a legal right to enter non-slave states to hunt for runaways, and anyone aiding them in their flight was liable to criminal prosecution. In 1850, however, the law stripped northern courts of their authority to handle fugitive slave cases, instead placing that power in the hands of federal commissioners who were encouraged to find in favor of slave owners with a ten-dollar bounty paid for each returned slave.

Heedless of consequences, abolitionists in Oswego County increased their efforts to enable fugitives to seek freedom in Canada via a system of transportation loosely known as the Underground Railroad. Starr Clark's secret room in his tin shop was only one location on the route. William Schenck, a prominent Fulton businessman, was so secretive about his efforts to assist fleeing slaves that his own wife allegedly did not know what he was doing. Oswego City residents Edwin and Charlotte Clark were credited with helping approximately 125 runaways make their way across Lake Ontario to Canada. Others who helped fleeing slaves include Silas Brewster, Arvin Rice, and Dr. Amos Kent of Hannibal.

While Oswego County residents were marshalling their efforts to aid fugitives, Dred Scott was using the federal judicial system to escape enslavement. He formally sued his owner, claiming that since he had been taken to a free state not once but twice, he was therefore free. The case made its way to the United States Supreme Court in 1857, where Scott ultimately lost in a 7–2 vote. Significant for the cause of abolition was the decision penned by Chief Justice Roger Brooke Taney. Writing for the majority, Taney held that slaves were not citizens of the United States and were thereby legally prevented from bringing suits of any kind. They were in fact property, not humans. Second, the court struck down the 1850 Compromise, which had permitted Missouri to join the Union as a slave state and California as a free state. In other words, held the court, Congress had no power to prevent the spread of slavery.

American churches also became embroiled in the abolitionist debate. Using both the Old and the New Testaments as their rationale, many church leaders avowed that if God did not disagree with enslavement, why should nineteenth-century Americans? This issue led the Presbyterians to split in 1838, followed by the Methodists in 1844. The Baptist Church splintered in 1845 after northern Baptists refused to allow slaveholders to become missionaries.

The "white man's burden" to "civilize" slaves by converting them to Christianity was used as an excuse to perpetuate the institution of slavery. Such was the rationale of Bishop Stephen Elliott of Georgia, who explained that God "has caused the African race to be planted here under our political protection and under our Christian nurture, for his own ultimate designs, and he will keep it here under that culture until the fulness of his own times."[10]

Senator Jefferson Davis of Mississippi saw nothing wrong with slavery and repeated the current southern religious view during the debate on the Missouri Compromise: "It is enough for me to know . . . that it [slavery] was established by decree of Almighty God, that it is sanctioned in the Bible, in both testaments . . . that it has existed in all ages, has been found among the people of the highest civilization, and in nations of the highest proficiency in the arts."[11]

It was inevitable that the opposing views would be voiced in Oswego County churches. Reverend Mason Gallagher, priest of the Episcopal Church of the Evangelists in Oswego City, firmly supported the abolition of slavery. A series of anti-slavery sermons caused considerable uproar among his congregants: "I have given offense to all the so-called conservatives in town, but I believe there is virtue enough in the place to sustain the untrammeled and fearless preaching of the gospel. I will persevere with the help of God."[12] So great was Reverend Gallagher's devotion to the cause that he volunteered to serve as chaplain for the 24th Regiment.

Conversely, Reverend Anthony Schuyler, priest of the city's other Episcopal congregation, Christ Church, asserted that slavery was not sinful. In a fiery, controversial sermon delivered on February 3, 1861, he stated:

> They [southern Christians] do not ask us to concede what some of them, and only some, claim for themselves, the Divine right of their peculiar institution. But they do ask, and that too with a sternness as rigid, and a feeling as lofty as that of the most uncompromising abolitionist, that we *yield*, wholly and completely, the postulate that slaveholding is a crime . . . We believe all the South asks at our hands, is our toleration of which the New Testament tolerates *beyond the possibility of a doubt*—that our ministers and Christian people should treat it as the Saviour and his apostles treated it and that was to let the *relation* alone . . . Among all the laws of God, there is no law against the domestic relation of master

on one side, and slave on the other. No woe nor curse, among all the woes and curses of God, can be found lighting upon the slaveholder because he *is* a slaveholder.[13]

Reverend Edward Lord, minister of Fulton's Presbyterian Church, encountered considerable resistance to his support of the war and opposition to slavery.

Reverend Lord served as chaplain for the 110th Regiment from 1862 to 1863. Upon returning to Fulton he gave several sermons eliciting a decidedly negative reaction. His son Chester remembered one particular service:

> Alive with patriotic fervor as a result of his army experiences, he began a fiery sermon urging the prosecution of the war and demanding united support for Lincoln. He had not preached more than two minutes, before one of the "pillars" of the church arose, flung his overcoat over his arm, and stamped down the aisle. Two other members walked out of the other aisle, and then six more in rapid order. Before Rev. Lord had finished his sermon, 15 members of the congregation had departed in anger. So bitterly set in their views were these men that they refused to listen to arguments against their cause.[14]

Partisan debates about slavery permeated all aspects of American politics throughout the 1850s, exploding in November 1860 with the election of Abraham Lincoln to the presidency and the subsequent secession of eleven southern states, led by South Carolina. Centuries of cultural and political strife culminated with a four-year struggle claiming an estimated 620,000 soldiers and sailors and devastating a vast amount of the American economy.

New York State contributed 450,000 men to the Union cause, the largest number of any state. Of that figure, Oswego County contributed approximately 12,000 or 75% of the voting population.[15] Oswego County citizens were repeatedly exhorted and cajoled into furnishing troops for the infantry, navy, cavalry, and artillery. Initial patriotic fervor leading to the formation of the 24th and the 81st Regiments in 1861 was quickly replaced by hesitation to send husbands, sons, and brothers to a protracted war which might or might not end in a northern victory.

A draft announced in July 1862, considered scandalous and unpatriotic in Oswego County, was employed to encourage enlistments, resulting in the formation of the 110th and the 147th Regiments, as well as the 21st New York Independent "Barnes" Battery Light Artillery. The passage of the Enrollment Act of March 3, 1863, legalizing conscription, resulted in riots, and whole communities in New York State used the law's loopholes to buy their menfolk's way out of the obligation to serve.

Nevertheless, soldiers' letters to loved ones at home, which found their way into the pages of the local press, spoke volumes about the desire to put down the rebellion. For example, Horace Snow, a member of Co. E, 110th Regiment, wrote, "It is generally believed that we are enjoying our best times, and that the worse is yet to come. But no matter; we have come to put down this wicked and cruel, yes, inhuman rebellion, and sink it into oblivion so far that it will never have a chance to revive on this continent."[16] Other letters reveal changing perceptions about the South. John Wilder, another soldier in the 110th Regiment, wrote to his father:

> Before I came to this part of the country [Louisiana], and not knowing the disposition of the natives here, I had some feeling for them, thinking they must be sincere in the belief that they were in the right; but since I have had the chance to see them and talk with them, my mind is greatly changed, as they are a miserable, mean, low, ignorant set, and know nothing but "nigger" . . . I thought that we were fighting brothers, but I must say that I disown them. I do not consider them brothers or Americans. They are so blind and strong headed in rebel belief that it is vain to reason with them . . . This is the kind of people we are fighting . . . Now then, such people, I say, ought not to be allowed to hold an inch of our soil without being under the most strict laws of the United States. And for my part, I will stick to them until they rue the day that they seceded.[17]

In the autumn of 1863 and the summer of 1864, the federal government again came to Oswego County calling for troops, snatching up through enlistment or conscription recruits who were too young to serve in the war's early years. From these campaigns the 24th Cavalry and the 184th Regiment were filled.

Although men originally enlisted to preserve the Union, not to end slavery, the situation changed with the publication of the Emancipation Proclamation, which, willy-nilly, recast the conflict's rationale. While Union soldiers were aiming at outright victory, anti-war Democrats, dubbed Copperheads, were agitating for a swift conclusion, no matter the consequences. In 1864, war-weary Oswego residents were beginning to listen. Colonel Warren Douglas Smith of the 110th Regiment, a normally genial and even-tempered man, vented anger and disgust at the news that Clement Laird Vallandigham, notorious Copperhead and pro-slavery advocate, was scheduled to speak at a peace rally in Syracuse on August 18, 1864:

Figure 1.1. Colonel Warren Douglas Smith was known in Oswego City for his devotion to the Presbyterian Church. Courtesy of the New York State Military Museum.

Those who remain at home must keep up this patriotic spirit and it should run so high that no traitor like Vallandigham would dare take the stump within thirty-five miles of Oswego . . . When I saw it announced that he was to speak in Syracuse I had feelings I never again wish to have. God forgive me, but I hate a man who hates his country, and I hope his mouth was shut before he spoke a word in that loyal city . . . a northern traitor of the Vallandigham . . . stripe should have no place on the soil of this fair land.[18]

The incompetent or indecisive generals selected to guide the North to victory did little to advance the Union cause: Irvin McDowell, George McClellan, John Pope, Ambrose Burnside, Joseph Hooker, and George Meade all failed. Not until President Lincoln appointed General Ulysses S. Grant as commander of Union forces in March 1864 was the fate of the southern states sealed. General Grant's tactics may have been considered extreme, but he recognized that only a sustained, aggressive campaign would achieve peace. When General Robert E. Lee surrendered on April 9, 1865, it was because he could no longer withstand the North's superior ability to produce men, weaponry, and other materiel.

Oswego County residents rejoiced at the nation's reunification and welcomed the survivors home. Although all were forever altered by their experiences, many, as will be seen in the following pages, employed the same grit and determination displayed during the war to undertake causes resulting in improved lives for succeeding generations.

Chapter Two

Notable Civil War Veterans of Oswego County

John Barclay Alexander

The son of Samuel Alexander (October 21, 1799–February 28, 1871) and Mary Ann Ryan (May 27, 1811–January 27, 1894), John Barclay Alexander was born in Constantia, New York, on February 28, 1841. While still a child he moved with his parents to Southwest Oswego. After attending the local schools he enrolled in the Collegiate Institute in Baraboo, Sauk, Wisconsin. He had graduated and was enrolled in the University of Michigan when the Civil War began. He left his studies, returning to Wisconsin, where he enlisted and was mustered into Co. F, 23rd Volunteer Regiment.[1]

The 23rd Wisconsin Regiment, mustered on August 30, 1862, was composed of 1,134 officers and enlisted men.[2] The regiment participated in, among others, the siege of Vicksburg (March–May 1863) and the Red River Campaign (March–May 1864). It was part of the occupying force at Mobile, Alabama, and was there in April 1865 when the war ended. On July 4, 1865, the soldiers mustered out.[3] Alexander, however, was discharged on November 1, 1864, after contracting enteric fever.[4]

After his discharge, Alexander reentered the University of Michigan, earning a law degree in the late 1860s. He then returned to Oswego and practiced his profession until 1879.

Mary I. Place (July 7, 1852–January 28, 1928), daughter of John Albro Place (February 25, 1822–October 4, 1902) and Julia Anna Lewis (July 9, 1830–January 22, 1921), was to play an influential part in Alexander's life. Her father owned the *Oswego Daily Times*, which served as the local Republican Party's voice for decades. He also was also postmaster for years with Mary as his deputy. Thus this extraordinary woman was well versed in city affairs, local politics, and a business' day-to-day operations.

John and Mary were married in Oswego on January 20, 1875, and were the parents of three children. Laura (December 1875–September 19, 1959) married her first husband, Alfred Harden (1873–January 30, 1910), on October 17, 1901. Her second marriage to Platt P. Gibbs (1853–November 12, 1935) took place on March 24, 1920. Henry Hermon (October 24, 1882–August 26, 1954) married Edna R. Speir (September 16, 1883–September 24, 1956) on February 15, 1913. Julia Mary (September 6, 1886–June 16, 1969) married Armin George Kessler (August 18, 1886–May 30, 1961) on September 30, 1913.

By 1879, John Alexander owned the majority share of the *Oswego Daily Times*. He discontinued his law practice to concentrate on writing for the newspaper. When his father-in-law was appointed canal auditor in 1880, he assumed the editorship, a position he held until he sold the newspaper in 1922.[5] As late as 1921, when he celebrated his eightieth birthday, John Alexander could be seen walking to the newspaper office every day: "There are few older active newspaper men in the State, and Mr. Alexander, following his custom of years, was one of the first men down this morning and will be one of the last to leave this evening."[6]

Alexander was part of the machine which dominated Oswego County politics for decades. An ardent Lincoln Republican, he used his newspaper to promote his party's candidates. Through the pages of the *Times* he supported such luminaries as Congressman Thaddeus Sweet, Governor Charles E. Hughes, and Justice Maurice L. Wright.[7] In 1898, no doubt in return for that support, President William McKinley named him postmaster of Oswego City, replacing Louis C. Rowe, who was retiring.[8] He wasted little time appointing Mary his deputy, a move generally approved by the Oswego community: "Her administration of the affairs of the office was also excellent and aside from those who may be looking for the place, the appointment would give general satisfaction."[9]

While ordinarily satisfied with kingmaking, Alexander did attempt once to run for public office. His unsuccessful candidacy for Oswego county clerk led to derisive commentary in a rival newspaper and simultaneously revealed the frequently ugly nature of local politics:

> As they [John A. Place and J. B. Alexander] drove home from Fulton Friday night, though the moon was at its full it

gave them no light nor hope. The grim spectre of defeat, of repulse, of caucuses to be lost, of conventions against them of delegates unpurchaseable, rose up on every side, while the remembrance of their own treacheries, of their falsehoods, of their slanders came sweeping down upon them and what its effect this Fall would be on Alexander's candidacy, until it enveloped them like a fog; it rested like a pall upon them and shut out by the myriad of stars that studded the blue vault and veiled the brilliancy and loveliness of the fair and silvery moon, making the glorious Summer night a lonely, gloomy dismal time, full of horrors and dread anticipation, until their own heads buried in the sand, they thought the moon and all the earth were in eclipse. It was simply the reflection of Alexander's prospects for County Clerk.[10]

It is interesting to note that John Alexander declined to run for mayor of Oswego City in 1893.[11]

Being the editor of a local newspaper could be dangerous in the late nineteenth century, as Alexander discovered during the notorious Frost divorce case. Edgar E. Frost, a local lawyer, was determined to divorce his wife, Mary Jane Ryan, for adultery. Mary Jane countersued, accusing him of infidelity. The legal wrangling culminated in two trials producing many witnesses for both sides. Alexander ran into trouble when one of his reporters wrote that William W. Harman, Esq., a prosecution witness, had been observed with the arms of Miss Mary Kanouppe, a defense witness, encircled about his neck.[12] Harman had Alexander, John Place, and the city editor Ben Ketcheson arrested for criminal libel and marched off to court under police guard.[13] When the *Oswego Daily Times* published a retraction on May 17, 1890, pointing out that the offending article stated Miss Kanouppe had embraced Harman, he complained that the editorial was even more libelous: "When Counsellor [sic] Harman was reminded of this fact this morning he very ungenerously declared that he did not consider the retraction was ample by any means. In fact he intimated that the retraction was a greater shock to his feelings than the original statement. It is queer how particular some people are."[14] Harman did not help his case by stating that "he would not have been offended if one of the other ladies in the party had been cited as the one bestowing the caresses . . . But Kanouppe he must draw the line on Kanouppe."[15] In August the grand jury refused to indict the *Times* men and the case was dismissed.[16] While it is impossible to state with certainty, this scandal may have contributed to Alexander's decision not to run for mayor in 1893.

While Alexander was busy with the newspaper and politics, Mary, a graduate of Vassar College, was involved with Oswego's civic life. She was one of the founders of Oswego Hospital in 1881 along with Louise McFarlane and other concerned women. She was president of the hospital's board of directors for several years.[17] Her name frequently appeared in the local newspapers as a donor to the hospital and the Orphan Asylum.

Mary was a charter member of West Baptist Church, serving on its board of trustees. In 1892 she was president of the Woman's Baptist Union and led the celebration exercises for the sixtieth anniversary of the Oswego Baptists' Association.[18] She was active in clubs associated with her church, such as the Whatsoever Circle of the King's Daughters, which met one night at her home to hear Anna Randall-Diehl, founder and longtime president of the American Shakespeare Club.[19]

As a mother, Mary was concerned with the city's children. When the Oswego Municipal Playground Association was organized, she was elected to its executive committee.[20] She was also a member of Winter Club, a women's literary organization which met from January to March and whose active membership was limited to twenty-five at any one time.[21]

Lastly, Mary belonged to the Fort Ontario chapter of the Daughters of the American Revolution. She was elected regent for 1917 and 1918,[22] and later she was chapter secretary.[23]

John Alexander was also active in Oswego's social life. In addition to his church affiliation, he belonged to John D. O'Brian Post No. 65 Grand Army of the Republic (GAR). He was a member of the Oswego City Bar Association and the Chamber of Commerce. When the New York State Historical Association decided to hold its annual meeting in Oswego from September 29 to October 2, 1913, he was named to the reception committee.[24]

As a prominent citizen, he was frequently asked his opinion on current events. Sometimes he was right and sometimes he was wrong. His opposition to improving the city's sewer system was soundly criticized.[25] He undoubtedly ruffled some feathers when he, along with 1,207 other men, signed a petition to make Oswego a "dry" city.[26] On the bright side, he supported an effort by the Knights of Columbus to provide assistance to Ireland and was a member of the honorary local general committee.[27]

Alexander participated in successful campaigns to keep the Ames Iron Works in Oswego and to construct a new building on the campus of the Oswego Normal School.[28] He supported women's suffrage. When asked to opine on the subject, he stated that there was "no more ardent worker in the cause . . . when it comes to a question of their rights I can see that they are just as earnest as men, and rightly so."[29]

When Alexander sold the *Oswego Daily Times* to Clifford L. Snowden from Bridgeton, New Jersey, in 1922, he was eighty-one years old and wanted to retire. Noted a sister newspaper: "Mr. Alexander has invariably aimed in his newspaper to reflect the best public sentiment of his community and in this he has succeeded well. He is a vigorous writer, and when he devoted himself to his editorial page it was a much respected medium of expression and its views have always been highly respected."[30]

In December 1924 Alexander suffered a massive stroke from which he never recovered. His death on March 19, 1925, was widely reported and he was eulogized by longtime friends and colleagues. John Mott reflected: "Courage never failed him in the face of a call that he considered right."[31] Byron G. Seamans, editor of the *Pulaski Democrat*, added: "He was a man of cordial manner and the editor of the *Democrat* always enjoyed to sit with him in his sanctum and chat when occasion permitted such a privilege."[32] Even the *Oswego Daily Palladium* expressed

Figure 2.1. John Barclay Alexander was a longtime editor of the *Oswego Daily Times*. Author's collection.

Figure 2.2. Mary Place Alexander took a leading role in many Oswego City organizations. Author's collection.

grudging esteem: "John B. Alexander, whose death occurred today was of a type of militant citizenship. Of strong convictions and deep-seated prejudices that were perhaps an inheritance of the times in which he lived his prime, he had the courage of those convictions and always was willing and anxious to show his continued and undying interest for his creed and life and living. His was a strong character, and a strong will, unbending and unwavering."[33]

Mary died in Buffalo three years later. Her body was returned to Oswego and interred next to her husband's.[34]

John Barclay Alexander and Mary Place Alexander are buried in Riverside Cemetery, Scriba, New York, section O.

Samuel B. Alger

Samuel B. Alger's career was one of industry and creativity. Although his life was cut short by mental illness, his inventions nevertheless helped move the United States into the Industrial Revolution.

Little is known of his early life. His muster card indicated he had been born in 1832 in Schoharie County, New York, a fact confirmed by state census records. It is probable that Jared Alger (October 12, 1792–February 5, 1867) and Deborah Olmstead (October 25, 1797–May 17, 1851), who resided in Middleburgh, Schoharie, New York, in 1850, were his parents. In that year a daughter, Harriet, fifteen, resided with them. In 1855 Harriet, identified as Samuel's sister, lived with him in Fulton, New York.

In 1850 Samuel Alger lived in Fulton with Ransom P. and Lydia Alger, his brother and sister-in-law. Both men were carpenters and joiners. By 1855 Samuel had married Catharine _____ (1834–March 19, 1870), a native of Madison County.

Alger enlisted as a private in the 110th Regiment on August 11, 1862, mustering into Co. A on August 12. He was promoted to first sergeant on October 1, 1862. After a stay in Baltimore, Maryland, the regiment boarded the transport *Ericsson* and headed for Louisiana.[35]

Although living deep in secessionist territory, many people residing in Louisiana, especially the foreign-born or those born in other states, supported the Union cause and were collectively called "Unionists."[36] General Benjamin Butler obtained permission to enroll these people in the Union army, one regiment of which, organized in August 1862, became known as the 1st Louisiana Cavalry. On February 6, 1863, Alger was discharged from the 110th in order to receive a commission as first lieutenant in the cavalry unit. Before his term expired, he had served in Cos. E and D and had risen to the rank of captain.

The 1st LA Cavalry saw much of the same action as the 110th: the battle of Fort Bisland, the Port Hudson Campaign, and the battle of Vermillion Bayou. The 110th Regiment, however, was ordered to Fort Jefferson in the Dry Tortugas, Florida, in February 1864, thereby missing the ensuing bloody warfare in that part of the South.

Alger's new unit was less fortunate, taking part in the Red River Campaign, Mansura, and Morganza, where it served until November 1864 when ordered to Baton Rouge. In February 1865 the regiment traveled to Barrancas, Florida. That spring it moved to Mobile, Alabama, to join the fighting there, ultimately seizing control of the fort at Blakely, Alabama. Not until December 18, 1865, were the soldiers mustered out.

After the war, Alger returned to Fulton. During the next few years he was in the construction business with Colonel Clinton H. Sage, formerly regimental commander of the 110th Regiment. Together they developed

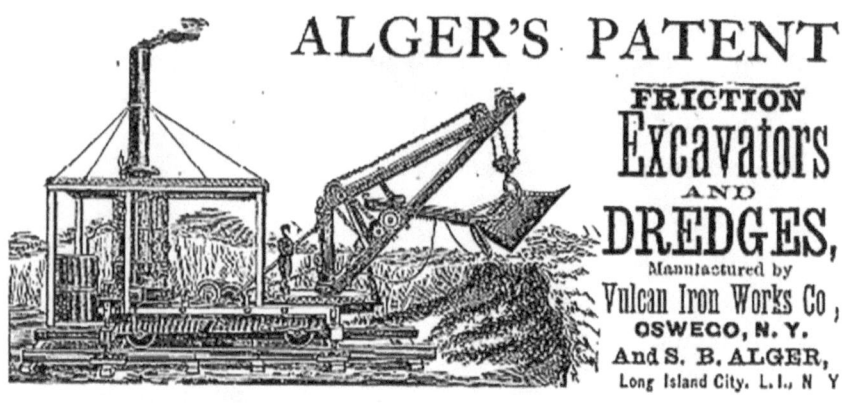

Figure 2.3. Alger's dredge was a large and complex piece of machinery. Courtesy of the *Chicago Railway Review*.

and patented in 1870 the "Oswego Boom Machine," an excavator built in the Vulcan Iron Works in Oswego City.[37] Alger held several patents, among them one for "rotary elevating buckets in an excavator."[38] Later that year he obtained a patent on a friction clutch for his excavator.[39]

Called to testify in a criminal case in New York City in 1876, Alger listed his contracting experience: "A contractor, named S. B. Alger, of Fulton, New York, was the first witness, and testified that he was now engaged in filling up the streets of Long Island City; the excavation there consists of 2,000,000 cubic yards; he had been for the past ten years engaged in manufacturing steam excavators and shovels; . . . he had been a contractor on the New York, Oswego Midland Railroad, and on the St. John's River, in Florida."[40]

Alger's name appeared in newspapers several times in 1878. In January the following was reported:

> Mr. Samuel B. Alger has just sent the plans and the cost of furnishing four large-sized excavators to the agent of the Russian Government, now in New York, and will doubtless be offered the contract for building and going with them to Russian waters and setting them to work. Mr. Alger is the inventor and owner of valuable patents connected with these dredges. He is at home presently here [Fulton] with his family, having stopped work for a few winter months on the Long Island contract.[41]

Simultaneously he was planning to travel to Florida "in a short time to set in operation a dredge sold to the Santa Fe canal company. They propose to construct a canal from Waldo to Lake Santa Fe, which will give access to 100,000 acres of rich lands which are especially adapted to the growing of early vegetables, and the raising [of] oranges and lemons and farming lands generally."[42] Alger reportedly sold that dredge for $5,000.[43]

That he actually went to Florida is known: "Mr. S. B. Alger has arrived at Waldo, Fla., with his dredge and will soon have it at work for the Santa Fe Canal Company. He reports May weather, the orange crop nearly gathered, and people generally poor."[44]

Samuel and Catherine Alger had no children. She died in 1870, cause unknown.

Samuel Alger next married Anna Slauson (January 19, 1853–June 19, 1931) some time before the 1875 New York State census. She was

Figure 2.4. Little is known about Catherine Alger who died of unknown causes. Author's collection.

the daughter of Jonas Slauson (November 26, 1817–May 12, 1898) and Emeline "Emily" Darrow (1824–February 12, 1885). Emeline, who was separated from Jonas, lived with the Algers throughout their marriage.

Alger was in Florida in 1881 when he suffered some sort of mental breakdown. The newspapers were filled with statements to the effect that he had been "adjudged insane" and taken to the insane asylum in Utica, Oneida, New York.[45] He died in the asylum on September 5, 1881, and his body was returned to Fulton for burial: "Sept. 8.–Major Samuel Alger, who died in the Utica insane asylum on Monday, was buried with Masonic honors yesterday. He was a talented man and his loss will be deeply felt."[46]

Figure 2.5. Samuel Alger was prominent in the development of complicated industrial machinery. Author's collection.

A lengthy, somewhat fanciful obituary provided more information about Alger's life and career:

> Samuel B. Alger, who was recently buried in Fulton, had an army and civil record that deserved to be preserved and remembered. He was by trade a carpenter and joiner and first enlisted in the volunteer forces during the Mexican war, and served till the close of that war, when he returned to Fulton and resumed his trade. During the rebellion he enlisted as a private in Co. "A." . . . When the 1st and 2d Louisiana cavalry were raised by volunteers from all regiments, he was promoted to first lieutenant in the 2d cavalry, and afterwards to captain and then to major of the same regiment for gallant conduct in the field . . . Afterwards he took the contract to dredge the St. John's river 26 miles, performing it successfully. He was the inventor of the Alger railroad dredge, self-filling cart and other machines used in public works. In company with Col. O. S. [sic] Sage he was engaged on a large contract of earth cutting and filling on Long Island . . . He was twice married, and leaves a wife, but no children . . . He was a prominent Free Mason and highly respected.[47]

There is no evidence that he served in the Mexican War or that he attained the rank of major. He did not serve in the 2nd Louisiana Cavalry, although that unit was eventually consolidated with the 1st.

Anna made news herself when she married William E. Waugh on April 9, 1884. Waugh, twenty-three, was the son of William Waugh (1831–February 12, 1904), Fulton village president, and his wife, Jane (1834–1911). The marriage led to a scandal since Waugh Jr. was already married to Della Roberts and the father of a four-year-old daughter, Eva.[48]

Newspapers far and wide carried the story because of the family's prominence in local society.[49] Young Waugh reportedly "became addicted" to liquor and to satisfy that addiction began living at a local hotel to be near his supplier. During this period he met Anna Alger, described in the press as "a dashing widow."[50] Anna and her mother, both either naïve or just plain stupid, believed Waugh when he told them the "Mrs. Will Waugh" living in his father's household was a cousin's wife. Anna even had him swear on a Bible that he was single.[51] After knowing each other roughly two months, the couple married. About the only intelligent thing Anna did was obtain a marriage certificate from Dr. Tully, the officiating clergyman.[52]

When the deception was revealed, Waugh was arrested for bigamy. He did not deny the fact but used intoxication as his excuse. If he had been sober, he claimed, he would not have gone through with the wedding. Dr. Tully refuted Waugh's allegation.[53] Had the man been intoxicated, he told a reporter, he would have refused to perform the ceremony. He produced the marriage register, maintaining that Waugh's steady signature proved he had been sober.

Blame was also attached to Anna because, as was reported, she should have been aware of Waugh's marital status since the village only had six thousand inhabitants. Her mother claimed Anna "seldom went into society . . . [and] was the more easily deceived by Waugh's professions."[54] Emeline herself initiated the inquiry by approaching one of Della's brothers. Her discovery that Will Waugh was the young man's brother-in-law led to the arrest and attendant scandal. Della immediately began divorce proceedings.

Waugh posted $800 bail and very quickly disappeared. His father disinherited him and Anna and Della were both humiliated by the affair.[55] Della never remarried.

Figure 2.6. Anna Slauson Alger's reputation was marred by the scandal surrounding her marriage to William Waugh Jr. Author's collection.

Anna's story ended more happily. On May 29, 1887, she married Edward J. Davis (1863–July 4, 1946) in Granby. She and Davis, an immigrant from England, lived for many years in Syracuse, where she died on June 19, 1931.[56]

Samuel and Catharine Alger, Anna Slauson Alger Davis, and Edward J. Davis are buried in Mt. Adnah Cemetery, Fulton, New York, section 4.

James Barnes

As a pioneer settler in Phoenix, New York, James Barnes must be considered a notable veteran of Oswego County. His numerous endeavors effected significant, positive change in Oswego County.

Barnes was born in Charlotte, Chittenden, Vermont, in 1816, the child of Hezekiah Barnes Jr. (November 27, 1784–August 25, 1849) and Caroline Olmsted (1793–1858). When he was eighteen, he and his father traveled from Syracuse, New York, to the tiny hamlet of Phoenix. Hezekiah purchased several hundred acres of land and built several mills along the Oswego River.

Figure 2.7. James Barnes's occupation as a surveyor took him all the way to Panama. He is number eight in this photo of early settlers of Phoenix, New York. Courtesy of *Grip's Historical Souvenir of Phoenix*.

Barnes became a civil engineer and surveyed much of the land in and around Phoenix. Notices of land records published in local newspapers frequently mentioned him as the original surveyor.

Much of Barnes's work dealt with surveying areas under consideration for railroad construction. In the 1840s he was the superintendent and engineer for the Western Railroad which ran from Boston to Albany.[57] In 1848 he and two other men contracted to construct a railway line from Rome, Oneida County, to Watertown, Jefferson County.[58] In 1866 he was appointed deputy state engineer and surveyor for New York State.[59] Throughout the 1870s and 1880s he was actively employed in surveying land for possible railroad service in central and northern New York. Many meetings about routes, financing, and related matters were conducted during which Barnes was consulted. He was particularly interested in the proposal to bring rail service to Phoenix. Although few of these schemes were successful because of limited financial backing and inability to secure rights to tracks owned by other companies, Barnes's work was consistently praised.[60]

Perhaps Barnes's most adventurous surveying opportunity occurred in 1871 when he was appointed chief civil engineer for the Darien Expedition to Panama under the command of Colonel Thomas Oliver Selfridge. Interest had long been expressed in finding a way to cut a canal across the Isthmus of Panama to permit shipping from the Atlantic to the Pacific. Colonel Selfridge, along with engineers, sailors, and photographers, set sail in late December 1870 to survey the area on both coasts and locate possible routes for a canal. For the next seven months, newspapers all over the United States reported on their findings. The venture ultimately failed, but the completed surveys would eventually facilitate the construction of the Panama Canal.[61]

Barnes's civilian career was temporarily halted with the outset of the Civil War. In response to President Lincoln's call for three hundred thousand men in the summer of 1862, Barnes raised the 21st New York Independent Battery Light Artillery, which was mustered into service in September 1862 and left New York State on December 2. The men arrived in Louisiana in January 1863 and participated in operations near Port Hudson, a fortification on the Mississippi River occupied by the Confederates. On May 27, the 21st took part in the first major assault on the fort. Commented one observer, "We have had a very hard and bloody battle."[62] Another observer noted, "It has been one of, if not the bloodiest battle, that has yet been fought on this continent."[63]

Two of Captain Barnes's letters found their way into the local press. He offered sympathy to Horatio Holden, father of Wallace Holden, who had dropped dead while performing his duty as a soldier on July 25:

> I condole with you most sincerely, my dear sir, in this your great affliction. It is another added to the great multitude of private calamities which have filled this land with mourners, while the public are rejoicing over the great successes which our armies are achieving. Your son died while doing his utmost to serve the cause of his imperiled country, of human liberty, and, as I do not doubt of God, he was in the path of duty; and your loss, though grievous, is his great gain.[64]

The 21st remained at Port Hudson for about a year after General Nathaniel Banks succeeded in starving out the defenders in July 1863.[65] Captain Barnes described in another letter how members of his battery were sent out to repair telegraph wires destroyed by the Confederates. He noted that seven men had been taken prisoner when suddenly attacked.[66]

Captain Barnes mustered out with his unit on September 8, 1865, at Syracuse. His association with military comrades, however, did not cease. An active member of the Oswego County Veterans' Association, he held various offices. On March 19, 1880, he and fifteen other veterans became charter members of Joseph Gould Post No. 145 GAR. Barnes was elected its first commander.[67] This post was active until 1926, when, with only six members still alive, the charter was surrendered.

James Barnes married Frances Caroline Morse (?–November 28, 1889) on January 7, 1850.[68] To them were born six children, four of whom survived to adulthood. Frank Morse Barnes (November 23, 1851–October 29, 1924) apparently never married. He died in Taunton, Massachusetts. Caroline Frances Barnes (January 14, 1853–September 15, 1934) also remained single. She was a longtime mathematics teacher in the Phoenix area. Cornelia C. "Nellie" Barnes (April 1, 1855–March 13, 1940) married Fred A. Carrter (June 23, 1855–December 19, 1918). She too died in Taunton. Catherine "Kate" Barnes (March 31, 1857–March 6, 1868) died in Phoenix, as did Edward Dennis Barnes (September 28, 1859–March 11, 1860). The Mortality Schedules for the 1860 census reported he had succumbed to "inflammation of the lungs." The birth date of Charles Edward Barnes (?–February 13, 1921) is unclear. According to the family gravestone, he was born in 1863. Nevertheless, when the

1865 New York State census was taken, he was four years old. Charles, sometimes known as Charlie or Edward, was married twice. His first wife was Cora Glenn Perry, whom he married *ca.* 1890. The couple had a son, Harold "Harry" Gordon, born in Granby, New York, on October 28, 1891. It appears that Barnes abandoned them because on August 19, 1894, Cora G. Perry Barnes married John N. Elmer at Fair Haven, Cayuga, New York. Born *ca.* 1870, Cora died in Onondaga County on July 8, 1909, and was buried in Fairdale Cemetery in Hannibal, New York. Charles's second wife was Marguerite Irvine, born in Toronto, Canada, in 1882. The couple, who married on December 23, 1908, both worked at the Monson State Hospital in Massachusetts. They were living together in 1910, but what happened subsequently is unknown. In 1920 Barnes claimed to be a widower. He died in Lakeville, Plymouth, Massachusetts.

Frances succumbed to pneumonia. Her passing was noticed by two short announcements appearing in local newspapers.[69] No evidence of

Figure 2.8. Many members of the Barnes family are buried in Phoenix Rural Cemetery. Author's collection.

community activities has been located. It is possible that she had little time for such activities since her husband was away so often and she had a house and five children to care for.

After Frances's death, James Barnes lived with Cornelia. Near the end of his life he was interviewed about his recollections of early days in the village and the activities of his father, Hezekiah.[70]

James Barnes died in Phoenix on July 8, 1905, after a long illness. He was at the time one of the village's oldest residents. Obituaries reviewed his long career as a surveyor and captain of the 21st Independent Battery. It was reported that Gould Post would attend the funeral "in a body."[71]

James Barnes and Frances C. Morse Barnes, *together with Caroline, Kate, Edward Dennis, and Charles Edward, are buried in Phoenix Rural Cemetery, section 50. Cornelia and Fred Carrter are buried in section 28.*

Levi Bird

Born a slave and died a Union veteran, Levi Bird deserves a place among Oswego County's notables for his desire to be a free man and his courage to fight to make that dream a reality. It is uncertain whether he ever held a rifle, but had he been captured wearing a Union uniform, his life would have likely been forfeit since Confederate soldiers seldom spared black soldiers' lives.[72]

Little is known about Levi's early life. In 1864 he claimed to be eighteen, suggesting a birth date of 1846. His gravestone inscription provides an age of fifty-three at the time of death, also suggesting that he had been born in 1846. In 1875, however, his age, twenty-six, intimated he had been born in 1849. That date also found its way into his obituary.

His birth place is also something of a mystery. In 1875, the only year he apparently was ever enumerated, he was supposed to have been born in Virginia. His obituary states he was born in Maryland and sold to a planter in Georgia.[73]

Bird's story begins in January 1864 when the 159th Regiment NYSV was stationed at Thibodaux, Louisiana, as part of General Nathaniel Banks's 19th Corps. Organized in Dutchess County, New York, in the summer of 1862, this regiment had already seen hard fighting, particularly during the Port Hudson Campaign of March–July 1863. According to his muster card, Levi Bird, eighteen, was enrolled at Thibodaux on January 1, 1864, as a "colored cook" for Co. G. No other identifying details were provided.

The 159th became part of General Philip Sheridan's Shenandoah Valley Campaign and fought its last battle at Cedar Creek on October 19, 1864. Later that year, the unit was sent to Savannah, Georgia, and in March 1865, to North Carolina. The soldiers mustered out in October 1865 at Augusta, Georgia. Egbert E. Covey, also a member of Co. G, allegedly persuaded Bird to move to New York State after mustering out.[74]

Bird, whose name was frequently mentioned in the *Sandy Creek News*, was running a barber shop in Lacona in 1882 when it was announced that George Hydorn Jr. was buying his share of the business.[75] In September 1885 Levi "and wife" were residing in Syracuse. By October they had moved to Belleville, Jefferson, New York.[76] In fact, he moved frequently, usually in the Ridge Road area of Sandy Creek.[77] Not everyone accepted Bird: "Levi Bird has shaken the dust of Lacona from his feet and gone to Syracuse. Thus a dark cloud that has hung around our usually bright place has passed away for a season."[78] Generally, however, no mention was made of his race.

Bird was a member of Andrew Jackson Barney Post No. 217 GAR but it is unknown how active he was. On July 29, 1890, he initiated a successful application for an invalid's pension.

Levi's death on May 22, 1899, was noted in a lengthy obituary:

> In the death of Levi Bird, colored, which occurred Monday morning, May 22, our village has lost one of its old landmarks. He was born in Maryland about the year 1849 and in infancy was sold with his mother to a planter in Georgia . . . In his early days he was noted for his activity and intelligence and always commanded the highest wages for his labors. Several years ago he had a stroke of paralysis which greatly affected his speech and walking, and it was another stroke of the same disease that ended his life . . . Members of Post Barney of G. A. R. and friends from Mexico, Pulaski, and here were in attendance at the funeral, Rev. T. T. Davies officiating. A widow survives him who has the sympathy of the community in this hour of sadness and sorrow.[79]

Little is known about Lizzie E. Bird, except that she was African American. Her birth date is unknown and she apparently had no children. Their marriage date is unknown, but the wedding must have occurred after 1875 when Levi was enumerated as a single man.

Figure 2.9. Levi Bird worked as a barber in Sandy Creek, New York, after the Civil War. Author's collection.

Figure 2.10. Lizzie Bird lies beside her husband in Woodlawn Cemetery, Sandy Creek, New York. Author's collection.

Lizzie applied for a widow's pension on June 13, 1899, but died on March 10, 1900, before the process could be completed: "Mrs. Levi Bird died at the home of Mrs. John Packwood last Friday and her remains were laid at rest beside her husband in Woodlawn cemetery Saturday, Rev. T. T. Davies officiating. Mrs. Bird was one of the handsomest women of her race (colored) twenty years ago but intense suffering and long continued illness had wasted her once handsome form."[80]

Levi and Lizzie E. Bird are buried in Woodlawn Cemetery in Sandy Creek, New York, plot L 32.

John H. Brockman

Although John H. Brockman was a successful businessman in the village of Pulaski, New York, in the years following the Civil War, he is most notable for the big lie he perpetrated on his fellow citizens. That he was able to pull off the deceit borders on the unbelievable.

Figure 2.11. John H. Brockman duped an entire community with his impersonation of Charles Preuss. Courtesy of *Grip's Historical Souvenir of Pulaski*.

Brockman's antecedents are unknown. He allegedly was born in 1820 in Hamburg, Germany. When he arrived in the United States is unknown but he enlisted in the 41st Regiment NYSV on June 6, 1861, at New York City and was enrolled in Co. B. This organization was primarily composed of German immigrants from New York City and Philadelphia, Pennsylvania. The 41st Regiment left New York State in July 1861 and, in the three years that Brockman was a member, participated in battles at Groveton, Virginia; Second Bull Run, Chancellorsville; and Gettysburg. Later it was stationed in South Carolina and participated in the battles of Fort Wagner and Charleston Harbor. In June 1864 the unit was reconstituted as a veteran regiment. Brockman, however, was discharged on June 20, 1864, having completed his tour of duty.

John was wounded at Gettysburg in July 1863 and in 1890 told the enumerator he had been shot in the leg and belly. He also apparently lied about having a pension. The enumerator wrote, "Should have pension," implying the veteran did not have one. That, however, was untrue since his application for a pension on April 11, 1881, was successful.

When the 1865 New York census was taken, Brockman lived in the town of Richland. He was unmarried and was a mason. He was still unmarried in 1870 when enumerated living at a hotel in Pulaski, this time claiming to be a pipe maker. He, Charles Tollner, and C. C. F. Otto formed a company in Pulaski which made roof tiles and tobacco pipes.[81] The business provided work for local men for many years.

On March 12, 1871, John married Anna McNamara, whose own antecedents are sketchy. Depending on the year and the circumstance, she was born either in Quebec, Canada, or Limerick, Ireland. According to her obituary, she was the daughter of John McNamara and an unnamed mother.[82] Her actual birth year was variously reported as 1833, 1836, and 1839. While the obituary claimed she was eighty-nine, her gravestone bore an age of ninety, which may be correct since the body was placed in the vault until spring burial was possible. She provided a birth date of April 15, 1836, when applying to enter the WRC home in Oxford, Chenango, New York, perhaps in a ploy to appear older than she actually was and thus more easily gain admittance.

If, as claimed, Anna had been in the United States for seventy years, she would have arrived in 1859, at approximately twenty years of age. Her whereabouts between that date and 1871 when she married Brockman are unknown. When the 1875 New York census was taken, she was the mother of Frank I., born July 4, 1874. Years later, when she applied for admission to the WRC home, she also claimed to have a daughter, Mrs. William Towsley of Syracuse, New York, whom she had disowned. Her obituary revealed that the daughter, Jennie Towsley, still lived in Syracuse. The problem is that no one named Jennie Towsley living in Syracuse at that time could be her child. No one named Jennie ever lived with John and Anna, leading to the conclusion that she was Anna's child by an unknown father.[83]

John H. Brockman was an "honored member" of J. B. Butler Post No. 111 GAR in Pulaski and it is here that his big lie comes into play. Numerous articles repeated the story that Brockman was a friend of Colonel John C. Fremont, an early explorer of the American West. He supposedly assumed the name of Charles Preuss and was the first person to pitch a flag on Pike's Peak. It wasn't true.

Charles Preuss, an alias for George Karl Ludwig Preuss, was born in Hohscheid, Prussia, in 1803. He and his wife Gertrude _____ (1819–August 4, 1886) arrived in the United States in 1834. They were the parents of five daughters, the eldest born in Pennsylvania in 1840. Preuss did indeed accompany Fremont on several surveying expeditions in the 1840s and was present when the flag was hoisted on Pike's Peak.

Figure 2.12. Cartographer Charles Preuss hanged himself from a tree near Washington, DC, in 1854. Public domain.

According to contemporary news reports, Preuss went insane because of harsh conditions and a possible sun stroke suffered during the expeditions. He hanged himself near Washington, DC, on September 1, 1854.[84] He is buried in Congressional Cemetery in Washington, DC.

Whatever possessed Brockman to perpetrate this deception is unknown, yet every article and obituary written about him alluded to his fictitious exploits in the far western territory of North America.[85] His fanciful tale included deserting from the Prussian Army and taking part in the Danish War and the Mexican War, as well as the Civil War, only the last of which is confirmed.[86] One article reported,

> Mr. Brockman was a native German, left the Prussian army without permission and came to this country. When John C. Fremont formed his expedition Brockman joined him under the assumed name, Charles Preuss. He was well educated and passed the examination as topographical engineer. Preuss (Brockman) was the first to plant a flag on the top of Pike's Peak . . . He spent a good part of his life in the west before the civil war, going into California at the time of the gold fever.[87]

It may be true that he was in California during the gold rush, but little real evidence exists to support the allegation. One may also ask why an expert topographer would settle in the tiny village of Pulaski and turn to making tiles and pipes for a living, and act as the sexton for Pulaski Village Cemetery.[88]

When Brockman died on May 12, 1901, he was eulogized not only in the local papers but also across the state: "Oswego, N. Y., May 15.—John H. Brockman has just died at Pulaski, this county, aged 82. He was born in Germany and served in the Mexican, civil and Danish wars. He was a personal friend and companion of General John C. Fremont, and assisted in conducting Fremont's campaign for the presidency in 1856. He refused a commission and staff appointment during the civil war, saying he went to fight. He was wounded at Gettysburg."[89] J. B. Butler Post published highly complimentary "Resolutions": "Whereas, Comrade Brockman, a true soldier of the first type, always ready at first call, was born in Germany, served in the Danish, Mexican and late civil wars, discharged with honor, he was wounded twice at Gettysburgh, Pa. Resolved, that the Post has lost a noble and true comrade, worthy of

Figure 2.13. Brockman's deception is emblazoned on his gravestone. Author's collection.

all credit, a respected citizen, always cheerful, extending a hand to all comrades. His history in military service is unparalleled in his rank."[108]

Anna resided in Pulaski as late as 1905 but by 1910 she was living in Oakland, Alameda, California. In 1910, she said she had been born in Canada and had immigrated to the United States in 1862. In 1920, however, she said she was a native of Ireland, had immigrated in 1849, and had been naturalized in 1909.[91] She returned to New York State in 1923 and entered the WRC Home in December, remaining there until 1926 when she voluntarily left the facility. She died in Watertown, New York, on January 13, 1929.

John Brockman and Anna McNamara Brockman are buried in Pulaski Village Cemetery, section 3. She lies in an unmarked grave.

DeWitt Clinton Carpenter

Born in obscurity, DeWitt Clinton Carpenter became one of the town of Orwell's most prominent residents. His role as a civic leader places him firmly among the notables of Oswego County.

DeWitt Carpenter was born in German Flats, Herkimer, New York, on June 4, 1848, the son of Artemas Carpenter (1820–June 13, 1897) and Nancy Keller (1822–July 13, 1913). The family moved to Orwell in 1849. Working on the family farm meant he received very little formal education.[92]

Too young to enlist in the Union army for much of the war, Carpenter enrolled in Co. G, 24th NY Cavalry on February 23, 1865. When that unit was discharged he transferred to Co. G, 1st Provisional NY Cavalry on June 17, 1865, and mustered out on August 5, 1865.[93] The 24th Cavalry was heavily involved in the siege of Petersburg, Virginia, and he may have participated in the closing events of that campaign.

Figure 2.14. DeWitt Clinton Carpenter led an active life in Orwell, New York. Courtesy of *Orwell Veterans' Memorial Souvenir*.

At the end of his military service, Carpenter returned to Orwell. He joined Merwin Olmstead Post No. 387 GAR and served as commander numerous times. His name appeared frequently regarding the annual ceremonies for Memorial Day. He also participated in other GAR activities. For example, one evening he delivered a speech on New York State's role in the Civil War.[94]

Carpenter took an active role in local politics. For many years he was a county Republican committeeman. He held the office of town supervisor in 1891. An interesting description of him appeared at the end of his first year: "DeWitt Carpenter represents the town of Orwell for the first time. He is a Republican, 43 years and a farmer. Was born in Herkimer County but came to Orwell when a child. He is a married man, five feet eleven inches, and weighs 198 lbs." He was included in the "go ahead group," which had been "remarkably active in their first year on the board."[95] As town supervisor he was also a member of the local board of health.[96]

In 1898 Carpenter declared his intention to challenge incumbent Republican Thomas Costello for a seat in the state assembly: "He is a farmer, a veteran of the late war, has served five years as supervisor, a number of years as justice of the peace and it is upon this record that his ambition to move a step higher politically is based."[97] His bid was unsuccessful.

Carpenter was elected justice of the peace numerous times. He was a county notary public, and even served as trustee for School District No. 7 in Orwell.[98] Despite operating a farm, he found time to belong to Orwell Grange No. 66 and Pulaski Lodge No. 415 F&AM.

On September 12, 1867, Carpenter married Abigail "Abby" Stevens (July 13, 1852–April 14, 1925), daughter of Ezra Fairchild Stevens (1819–May 9, 1863) and Huldah D. Bonner (1825–May 30, 1917). Ezra was killed by a falling tree, leaving Huldah with five children living at home. This fact may explain why Abby married so young. She and Carpenter were the parents of six children, all of whom survived to adulthood. Flora A. (September 8, 1868–*post* 1939) m1 George W. Richards (?–?) on December 5, 1888, in Orwell; m2 Edward Lucius Roach (April 24, 1860–April 23, 1907) ca. 1904 in Charleston, South Carolina; m3 William J. Edge (March 30, 1868–March 27, 1938) on October 21, 1941, in Fulton County, Georgia. Charles Ezra (October 15, 1871–November 25, 1950) married Rosa Belle Stevens (1884–September 15, 1922) in 1897. Cora (July 30, 1873–December 2, 1957) married Charles B. Eastman (March 18, 1871–October 2, 1960) on January 28, 1894. Ralph Warren (August 17, 1879–June 14, 1959) m1 Lydia Samantha Paddock (January

10, 1877–November 24, 1960) on April 18, 1898; m2 Annie Frances Devine (December 2, 1888–February 6, 1969) in 1920. Lillian (June 24, 1883–November 9, 1955) m1 Max Burton Himes (June 15, 1877–July 24, 1961) on January 7, 1899; m2 John Hammond (October 6, 1870–February 7, 1945) *ca* 1941. Edith Mae (December 14, 1894–October 4, 1939) married Charles S. Rippen (March 25, 1890–June 28, 1954) on November 1, 1917.

Abby organized the first Sunday school at the Orwell Union Church.[99] She took an active role in Orwell's Woman's Relief Corps Post. In 1897 she was secretary and in 1901 she was a color bearer.[100]

DeWitt succumbed to cancer on April 11, 1908. An obituary recalled his civic activities: "Mr. Carpenter was a Republican in politics and was prominently connected with all matters of interest to his town and always ready to help any good cause and to oppose anything not good for the community."[101] The Orwell town board issued Resolutions which stated, in part,

> Whereas, Death has entered our town board and removed from us our most worthy brother, DeWitt Carpenter, who has been a member of our board so many years and served

Figure 2.15. DeWitt and Abby Carpenter raised a large family while managing to be involved in local affairs. Author's collection.

his town faithfully as a member of the town board. We feel our great loss in the death of our brother, and while we realize that to him death means gain and unspeakable joy as one who so closely followed the Master, Yet to us it seems we need his help and our hearts are heavy and we need the sympathy that we as a town board would offer to those to whom he was still dearer.[102]

Members of Pulaski Lodge No. 415 performed the graveside services.[103]

Abby married Harvey Sylvester Hilton (June 17, 1859–September 11, 1933) on November 6, 1914. They lived together until her death on April 14, 1925.[104]

DeWitt Clinton Carpenter, Abby Stevens Carpenter Hilton, and his parents are buried in Evergreen Cemetery, Orwell, section 8. Abby's parents are buried in Stevens Cemetery in Lacona, New York.

Edward Austin Cooke

Edward Austin Cooke worked for the City of Oswego for almost fifty years and had the distinction of being its longest serving employee. Born on November 28, 1834, in Holyoke, Hampton, Massachusetts, he was the son of Shubael Cooke (October 23, 1803–February 1881) and Harriet "Hattie" Collins (June 2, 1812–September 27, 1904). He moved to Oswego in 1853 and was for many years associated with Burrit D. Barnes's jewelry business.[105] Barnes (*ca.* 1826–December 20, 1893) was married to Cooke's sister, Harriet (February 20, 1831–December 21, 1908).

Cooke enlisted in the 81st Regiment, Oswego County's second Civil War unit, on September 14, 1861, for a term of three years, mustering in as first lieutenant on September 26.

On December 20 he was appointed regimental adjutant.

The 81st Regiment participated in the battles of Yorktown, Williamsburg, Fair Oaks, and Malvern Hill, Cold Harbor, siege of Petersburg, and surrender of Richmond. Cooke sent a letter to Harriet shortly after the battle of Cold Harbor, remarking that the 24th, 81st, and 147th were all in the same area.[106] In another letter he revealed he was the brigade's acting adjutant-general.[107] He mustered out of the 81st on November 18, 1864, at the end of his tour of duty and returned to Oswego where he resumed living with his sister and brother-in-law and working in the jewelry store.

Figure 2.16. Edward Austin Cooke was an officer in the 81st Regiment. Courtesy of the New York State Military Museum.

His interest in the military continued. On November 27, 1872, he joined the 24th Brigade of the New York National Guard with the rank of lieutenant colonel. General Timothy Sullivan named him assistant adjutant-general.[108] For the rest of his life, he would be known as Colonel Cooke. One of his early duties was to serve on a board of examiners to "examine into the 'physical ability, moral character, capacity, attainment, general fitness'" of candidates seeking commissions in the National Guard.[109]

Cooke was involved with the county's Veterans' Reunion Association and in the 81st Regiment reunions, held annually near the unit's mustering out date of August 15. He served two terms as president of the latter organization.[110] In 1917 only 150 veterans of the 81st were alive and Cooke was the sole surviving original officer.[111] He was involved with John D. O'Brian Post No. 65 GAR from its earliest days.[112]

By 1874 Cooke had left the jewelry store and begun his long service to Oswego City's citizens as deputy city clerk. The city established various governmental departments in 1877, and he was appointed clerk of Public Works on May 8, 1878. He was also registrar of vital statistics and each January issued a report on the number of births and deaths occurring the previous year. He was a long-time commissioner of deeds. Cooke was a tireless municipal employee, and it was once remarked upon that for many years he even worked on holidays.

Cooke was a congregant of Christ Church (Episcopalian) in Oswego. He was a member of Frontier City Lodge No. 422 F&AM and of Oswego's Old Volunteer Fire Department. In 1894 he was named to the entertainment committee when the organization was planning a convention.[113]

Cooke and his first wife, Catherine "Kittie," were married in August 1869. Little is known about her except that she was born in Oswego County *ca.* 1848 to immigrant parents. It is possible she was the daughter of Michel and Nancy Ann Sanford, both born in Ireland. Kittie died on February 6, 1889, of unknown causes. A short article noted, "A handsome Scotch granite monument has been erected by A. Salladin & Son to mark

Figure 2.17. Edward Cooke bought this monument after Kittie's death. It also memorializes his sister, Harriet, and her husband, Burrit Benton. Author's collection.

the last resting place of the late Mrs. E. A. Cooke. It is as handsome as any in Riverside cemetery and attracts much attention from visitors."[114]

Cooke's status as widower was short-lived. On November 26, 1889, he married Harriet "Hattie" W. Griswold: "Mr. E. A. Cooke, clerk of the Board of Public Works, and Miss Hattie M. [sic] Griswold, at one time connected with the City Hospital, were married today at 1 o'clock, at the home of the bride in Dansville, N. Y. Before returning to Oswego, Mr. and Mrs. Cooke will visit friends in the East. Both the bride and groom have many friends in this city, where, upon returning from their wedding trip, they will make their future home."[115] Hattie, born in Michigan in 1861, had been employed as a nurse in Oswego Hospital in 1887 and 1888. How they became acquainted is unknown.

Cooke's long tenure as a city employee was periodically celebrated in the press and he literally worked until he dropped.[116] On the Saturday before he died, he became sick at City Hall. Although his illness was described as a cold, he continued to fail, finally succumbing on Tuesday morning, March 3, 1921.[117] He was eighty-seven years old.

His death evoked several expressions of appreciation:

> Colonel Cooke was essentially a soldier in all that he did. Methodical and painstaking, he regarded his duty to the public as the principal aim of a long and useful life, working oft-times with a certain knowledge that a municipality is an ungrateful employer. His books and accounts were kept up to the minute. Colonel Cooke was of the fine old school. He was an official who gave his all to his duty, and he lived an honorable and upright life that is a fine example of public devotion and strict attention to trust . . . He died as he lived, and there will be universal regret at the passing of a good friend, a tried and true soldier and veteran, and a man who always kept his word and his self made pledge of service.[118]

Mayor John Fitzgibbons equally laudatory: "He was a faithful employe [sic] and a good citizen."[119] The Common Council voted the following Resolutions:

> Whereas, Colonel Edward A. Cooke, for practically fifty years a faithful employe [sic] of the city of Oswego, passed away on March 3d, 1921, after a brief illness, and Whereas Colonel

Cooke served the city as a civil employe [sic] with the same spirit of loyalty and devotion as he displayed in the service of his country during the dark days of the Civil War . . . and Whereas, As Deputy City Clerk of the city of Oswego, clerk in the Department of Works and Registrar of Vital Statistics, was reliable, trustworthy and thoroughly competent, discharging every duty punctually and carefully, showing tact and courtesy in his dealings with all who came in contact with him, and Whereas, In his death, the city of Oswego loses a faithful and efficient public servant and worthy citizen, therefore, be it Resolved, That this Common Council while deploring the death of Colonel Cooke, hereby records its appreciation of his high qualities.[120]

Harriet died in Oswego on July 1, 1941. How she spent her twenty-plus years of widowhood is unknown. Her passing was only briefly noted in the local newspaper.[121] She had no near surviving relatives.

Edward A. Cooke, Catherine "Kittie" Cooke, and Harriet Griswold Cooke are buried in Riverside Cemetery in Scriba, New York, section D.

Figure 2.18. Harriet Griswold Cooke lived quietly in Oswego for many years following her husband's death. Author's collection.

Dr. Samuel James Crockett

Samuel James Crockett's entire life was dedicated to making the world around him a better place. In the short sixty-eight years of his life, he committed himself to his nation, his community, and his patients.

Crockett was born in Baltimore, Maryland, on January 12, 1837, the son of immigrants, Hugh G. Crockett (1806–1887) and Margaret Boyd (1806–May 24, 1847). Ardent abolitionists, Hugh and Margaret moved their family to Sterling, Cayuga, New York, in order to escape the tense atmosphere regarding slavery in Maryland. Samuel attended local schools and Fairfield College, intending to become a teacher. He developed an interest in medicine and began his medical training in 1858 at the same time he was teaching in Kentucky.

He also joined the Clark County, Kentucky, home guards. According to one version of the story, Crockett resigned his teaching position when the Civil War began and left Kentucky to join the army in Illinois. Another, more credible version is that Crockett was teaching in Sterling, Whiteside, Illinois.[122] He first enlisted in Co. B, 127th IL on September 5, 1862, but was discharged, reason unknown, about a month later at Camp Douglas, Chicago. He mustered into Co. A, 1st US Cavalry on November 6, 1862, in Chicago.

By the time Crockett joined the 1st US Cavalry, it had already seen considerable action as part of the Army of the Potomac. Crockett himself participated in thirty-four battles, including Fredericksburg, Kelly's Ford, Brandy Station, Gettysburg, Wilderness, and Cold Harbor.[123] The 1st Cavalry was detailed from August 16 to 20, 1864, to destroy grain and forage and seize cattle as part of General Sheridan's Shenandoah Campaign. On August 17 the Confederates captured Crockett near Winchester, Virginia.

A letter written to his father from the prisoner-of-war (POW) camp in Danville, Virginia, on December 14, 1864, attempted to allay the family's fears about him while simultaneously expressing frustration at the government's lack of assistance to the prisoners:

> Prison life and fare have made their mark on me but I bear them better than you would suppose from one of my disposition. I have written home a number of times since I was captured, To Lib from Winchester and Staunton and to you from Lynchburg. I did not send you any address as I was always expecting to be sent further south . . . We have been looking

anxiously for something to be done for us by our Government, either in the way of exchange or by sending clothing, but so far we have looked in vain . . . I had hoped to visit you this winter but that hope is almost gone. But please God the hour of deliverance will come some day in his own good time and these days seem like a troubled dream . . . You must all do as I do, "hope and trust."[124]

Deliverance did not come until February 21, 1865, when he was paroled from Pemberton Prison in Richmond, Virginia.[125] When he was discharged on November 6, 1865, his health was shattered by poor treatment during his confinement.

Samuel resumed his studies, graduating from Jefferson Medical College in Philadelphia, Pennsylvania, in 1867, after which he settled in Oswego City and began his practice. He remained there until 1872 when he moved to Sandy Creek, his home for the rest of his life.

Figure 2.19. Dr. Samuel J. Crockett devoted his life to his patients and his community. Courtesy of the Half-Shire Historical Society.

Crockett quickly developed a thriving practice. The local newspapers regularly reported that he had set a broken arm, treated someone for diphtheria, or bandaged a head kicked by a horse. Yet he found time for pleasurable activities as well.

While he resided in Oswego, Dr. Crockett joined Rensselaer Bailey Post No. 19 GAR, so it is not surprising that he was heavily involved in organizing a GAR post in Sandy Creek.[126] Early in 1881 area veterans began to recruit members for a new post, and on May 16, 1881, Andrew Jackson Barney No. 217 received its charter. Crockett was unanimously elected the first commander, a position he would hold many times. Upon his election, Crockett reportedly remarked, "In accepting the office of commander, in the course of a very neat and happy speech, Dr. Crockett said there was no reason why Post 217 should not become one of the largest posts in the county, and he had no doubt all the comrades would assist."[127] His prediction would become fact, as Post Barney enjoyed one of the biggest memberships in Oswego County.

He also dabbled in local politics, serving as a member and president of the village board. It is interesting to note the reason he resigned from that position in 1891: "Dr. Crockett has placed in the hands of the clerk of the village board his resignation as president of the village board. The doctor is so busy that he finds it impossible to do justice to his patients and the village at the same time."[128]

He maintained memberships in various medical organizations, such as the Oswego County Medical Society and the Central New York Medical Society. At various times the local press reported that he had delivered scholarly papers at medical conferences. He served as a pension examiner for many years.

On June 12, 1872, Samuel married Frances Doolittle, born in 1845, daughter of Chauncey Butler Doolittle (March 23, 1803–December 25, 1863) and Delight Adeline Dean (February 2, 1820–July 5, 1897). They were the parents of three sons, only one of whom reached adulthood. The boys were Robert L. (1873–April 27, 1874), Hugh C. (March 1881–October 1881), and Robert Lewis (February 23, 1876–May 27, 1946). Robert also became a doctor and a surgeon. He practiced with his father in Sandy Creek for several years before moving to Oneida, Madison, New York, where he was elected village mayor. He was a pioneer in the use of x-ray machines in Central New York. Robert married Mabel Eloise Smith (August 6, 1878–September 14, 1965) on January 18, 1900, and was the father of two daughters and a son.

Like her husband, Frances participated in Sandy Creek's civic life. She was a member of the Ladies' Aid Society of the Congregational Church and was elected president in 1889.[129] She was a charter member of the Ladies' Wednesday Club organized in 1894 and a charter member of the Woman's Relief Post chartered in 1896.[130] She and Samuel, a member of the Board of Education, annually hosted a reception for the high school graduating class. They also belonged to the Hawthorne Club, a social and literary group which met weekly at members' homes to discuss authors such as Dickens, Shakespeare, Pope, Emerson, and Percy Shelley.

Dr. Crockett succumbed to heart disease on April 23, 1906, in Sandy Creek. An obituary described him as

> a man of more than ordinary ability and strength of character. He had inherited from his Scotch ancestry those traits of character that make men noble, high minded and true. Strong in will power, yet kind and sympathetic. A man of decided convictions, yet tolerant toward those who differed from him. He loved the true, the beautiful and the good as was exemplified in his love of flowers and children . . . Faithful to his friends, kind in disposition, self-sacrificing in spirit, and ever responsive to the call of duty. Like the Divine Physician "he went about doing good." He served his generation faithfully and well, and rendered to his fellow citizens valuable service, through his wise judgment and timely counsel.[131]

After her husband's death Frances moved to Oneida to live with Robert's family. She died there on August 27, 1926. A touching obituary noted her death: "Mrs. Frances C. Crockett . . . was a woman of refined sensibilities and of rare Christian character. To know her was to love her. Her whole life was identified with all that was pure, noble and uplifting in the community where she lived. Her Christian faith expressed itself in Christian work and in service for others. Her death was in keeping with her life, peaceful, glorious and triumphant."[132]

Dr. Samuel Crockett, Frances Doolittle Crockett, and their infant children are buried in Woodlawn Cemetery, Sandy Creek, plot O 19. Dr. Robert Lewis Crockett and Mabel Smith Crockett are buried in Oakwood Cemetery, Oneida, New York.

Figure 2.20. The Crockett family plot occupies a large space near the back of Woodlawn Cemetery, Sandy Creek, New York. Author's collection.

Freeman Henry Cross

Although a talented musician, Freeman Henry Cross built his reputation in the community through devices which literally "made the lame to walk." For this achievement he is recognized as a notable Oswego County veteran.

Freeman, son of Henry Cross (February 28, 1807–November 28, 1884) and Elizabeth "Eliza" A. Winters (April 10, 1808–February 4, 1895), was born in the town of Richland on July 14, 1848. He learned to play the drum and in 1862, at the age of fourteen, he enrolled as a musician in Co. C, 147th Regiment. He was one of the youngest men in Oswego County to serve in the Civil War. He was undoubtedly exposed to all the battlefield horrors endured by the 147th, particularly at Gettysburg, Wilderness, and the siege of Petersburg, since young musicians were also employed as litter carriers, messengers, and nurses.[133]

Upon returning to Oswego County at the war's end, Cross trained as a machinist in the shop of Fisher and Ling.[134] As a consequence he undertook a career constructing surgical appliances for people afflicted with paralysis. One of his clients was Dr. William Henry Cox, a veteran of the 110th Regiment. Dr. Cox suffered a series of paralytic strokes, which forced him to abandon his medical career. Because of Cross's braces, however, Cox was able to stand and walk.[135]

On November 25, 1870, Freeman Cross married Delia Gates (June 1848–May 28, 1927). They were the parents of Mary (August 19, 1873–November 2, 1873) and Willard (April 1872–October 20, 1936). Willard, a traveling salesman for his father's business, was married several times and more than once found himself in difficulty as an alleged bigamist. His wives were (1) Mina E. Carpenter (July 24, 1869–October 5, 1953) whom he married September 21, 1892; (2) Josephine Sara Longtin (July 10, 1880–January 12, 1964) whom he married on February 7, 1902; (3) Letta Ina Yeaton David (July 1875–September 30, 1943) whom he married on July 16, 1906; and (4) Dora Cross White (October 14, 1877–March 4, 1970) whom he married on June 18, 1929.

Figure 2.21. Freeman Cross's talents and skill permitted the physically impaired to walk. Courtesy of *Grip's Historical Souvenir of Pulaski*.

Despite the demands of a thriving business, Cross found time for outside interests. He became involved in the 147th Reunion Association and served as president in 1904 and 1905.[136] In 1904 he was appointed to a committee exploring the possibility of erecting a monument dedicated to all Oswego County Civil War soldiers and sailors.[137]

Cross was a charter member of Joseph Bradley Butler Post No. 111 GAR, organized on August 27, 1879, in Pulaski, New York. He was elected commander from 1907 to 1911 and died in office. Newspaper accounts testified to his commitment to the post, which included speaking at banquets and conventions, organizing Decoration Day activities, and visiting area schools to talk about his wartime experiences.

Additionally, he organized and directed the Freeman H. Cross Drum and Bugle Corps, which annually participated in Decoration Day services in Pulaski.[138] While not active in local politics, he was twice appointed to the Pulaski Village Board of Health, serving as president during his first term.[139]

Figure 2.22. Freeman Cross enlisted in the Union army as a musician. Courtesy of the Library of Congress.

Notable Civil War Veterans of Oswego County | 55

Cross's death "after an illness of a few weeks" was front-page news in Pulaski. An obituary paid tribute to his accomplishments as a soldier, citizen, and man:

> He was a mere lad, only fourteen years of age, when he was accepted as a drummer boy in the 147th Regiment, N. Y. V. and served three years. After the war he returned to Pulaski and learned the trade of machinist and later took up the profession of correcting deformities by use of appliances which has made the lame to walk in hundreds of cases. He was so skilled that no deformity of limb seemed too severe for him to help the patient. His work was not confined to this locality alone but was called for in the remotest parts of the country . . . He was the youngest member of the Post and on him the older members relied for much of the work

Figure 2.23. Freeman and Delia Cross are buried in Pulaski Village Cemetery. Author's collection.

which keeps the organization moving . . . The passing of Mr. Cross takes from our community a man who will be greatly missed. He was a good citizen, a good husband and father, a willing supporter of all that pertains to the workings of the community, the church and the school.[140]

By 1913 Delia was living in Rochester, where Willard resided. After her death on May 28, 1927, her body was returned to Pulaski for burial.[141]

Freeman Henry Cross, Delia Gates Cross, Mary and Willard G. Cross, and Dora White Cross are buried in Pulaski Village Cemetery, section B.

Reverend Horace Melvin Danforth

Horace Melvin Danforth was born on November 8, 1826, a child of Luther Danforth (October 23, 1781–April 4, 1857) and Henrietta Ellsworth (May 1, 1786–April 2, 1841). He was a direct descendant of Nicholas Danforth (1588–1637) and Elizabeth Symmes (?–1629). Fleeing religious persecution in England, Nicholas and six surviving children allegedly sailed for the New World in 1634.[142] He and Henrietta moved to Fort Covington, Franklin, New York, where Horace and many of his siblings were born.

Horace became a Methodist minister. Details about his training are sketchy but it is known that he became associated with the Black River Conference, later renamed the Northern New York Conference.[143] His first assignment was in Waddington, New York.[144]

Horace and Caroline "Carrie" Winters (March 12, 1828–November 3, 1885) were married in 1849. They were the parents of one child, Jennie (1850–1914).

The couple was in Evans Mills, Jefferson, New York, when the Civil War began. Horace enrolled and mustered into Co. I, 14th NY HA on December 21, 1863, with the rank of second lieutenant. His tenure with that outfit was brief. On January 19, 1864, he enrolled in the 6th NY HA, mustering in on February 24 as a first lieutenant. When he mustered out on July 27, 1865, he was a captain. An interesting letter to the editor by 1st Sgt. F. B. Ainsworth, Co. M, 6th NY HA, demonstrates with what respect Danforth was held by his men. This letter was written in support of Danforth's promotion to captain:

Capt. D., before entering the service, was engaged in the ministry, and belonged to the Black River Conference, of which he is still a member. When the President issued a proclamation for men in October 1863, he feeling it his duty to respond to the call, resigned his avocation in the ministry, and came forth to fight the battle of his country. He was commissioned 1st Lieut. in this regiment, but did not join it till February 1st. The regiment soon became acquainted with his moral worth, and he was known only to be honored and respected. Capt. D. cannot be too highly spoken of as an officer. He is endowed with far more than ordinary military genius, and possesses every qualification requisite to constitute a good soldier and to do honor to his position. His kind disposition to please and render happy all who are placed under his command, has had the effect of winning their entire confidence and esteem. But few men have a brighter future before them than Capt. D. May success attend him.[145]

Figure 2.24. Reverend Horace M. Danforth was a dedicated Methodist minister. Courtesy of *Grip's Historical Souvenir of Camden*.

Kindness and dedication of purpose, as described here, were evident in Reverend Danforth's long tenure as a Methodist minister.

Methodist ministers were habitually moved from one area to another approximately every two years. Thus the Danforths found themselves in many places across northern New York. They were in Oswego City in the late 1860s and in the 1880s, where Horace was in charge of Trinity Methodist Church. It was during this tenure that he joined John D. O'Brian Post No. 65 GAR.

By 1885 he and Caroline were ministering in Herkimer. In September Caroline contracted pneumonia and her recovery was "considered doubtful."[146] She died in Herkimer on November 3, 1885, and her body was taken to Oswego for burial:

> In our obituary column we note the death of Caroline W., wife of Rev. H. M. Danforth of Herkimer, N. Y. The intelligence will be received with sorrow by all her friends and they were many in this city and vicinity. Rev. Mr. Danforth came to this

Figure 2.25. Caroline Danforth died in Herkimer County and was buried in Riverside Cemetery, Scriba, New York. Author's collection.

city in 1867 and remained two years in charge of Trinity M. E. church. He was in charge of the church at Scriba for one year before he came to Oswego. Mrs. Danforth had been a great sufferer and was confined to her bed for eight months before her death.[147]

Four years later Horace married Sarah P. Jersey (1833–February 20, 1910): "Rev. Horace M. Danforth of Oswego, Presiding Elder of the Oswego Conference district, was united in marriage to Miss F. [sic] Jersey, on Wednesday, June 19, 1889, at Beekmantown, N. Y. The cards announce that Mr. and Mrs. Danforth will be 'at home' at 110 E. Third street, Oswego, after July 1st."[148]

Rev. Danforth's dedication to his ministry was described by a reporter:

> The Rev. H. M. Danforth has rightly been termed a "Prince of Workers"—He performed last Saturday and Sunday, inside of thirty hours, work that two should have done. He preached four Sermons, conducted Love Feast, led the prayer meeting and attended the funeral service of Mr. Steele. And in this connection we might properly add, that the working Pastor has during the year preached four sermons on an average a week, and has been absent from his desk by vacation but one Sabbath, while at the same time he has given his attention to the other duties devolving upon him as a Pastor.[149]

Those "other duties" included "marrying and burying" his congregants. Local newspapers were full of announcements of marriages and funerals at which Danforth officiated.

In addition to his professional obligations, however, Horace found time for personal pleasure. He Joined Philanthropic Lodge No. 164 F&AM and J. Parson Stone Post No. 482 GAR, both in Camden, New York. At one point he also belonged to Ross Post No. 31 GAR in New Hartford, Oneida, New York.

Reverend Danforth's last assignment was in Clayville, Oneida County.[150] When he decided to retire, he and Sarah returned to Camden: "He became strongly attached to the people and the place, and when poor health compelled him to leave the field, he made Camden his home to enjoy its beauty and the pleasant association of the people."[151]

Upon his death on April 13, 1905, an obituary listed the many places he had served the Methodist Church: Waddington, Russell, Depuyster, Evans Mills, Scriba, Oswego, Camden, Fulton, Adams, Herkimer, New York Mills, Alexandria, and Clayville.[152]

Danforth's death was widely noted. The obituary published in an Oswego newspaper paid tribute to his service and to his character:

> The deceased was well known in this city, having served here as pastor of the East Methodist Church [Trinity] from 1867 to 1869 and was the Presiding Elder of the Oswego district from 1887 to 1891, with his residence here. He was a forceful speaker and a man of much ability and influence in the pulpit. The deceased had been in the ministry from 1854, when he was licensed to exhort, to 1899, when he retired and took up his home at Camden. He was a man whose kind acts and deeds stand forth as a monument to his life's work in a manner beyond the description of any pen.[153]

The funeral was held from his daughter's home:

> Veiled by his country's flag, his remains were borne by his comrades of the Grand Army of the Republic to the railway station; thence to Oswego, N. Y. At the home of his daughter, Mrs. F. S. Thrall, concluding services were held . . . and the body was conveyed to Riverside Cemetery, where the committal was held. A soldier of the cross and a soldier of the flag, and a hero always, was the brave, manly, and true Horace Melvin Danforth.[154]

All the bearers were members of Post O'Brian No. 65 GAR.[155]

Shortly after her husband's death, Sarah, who had no children, moved to Holyoke, Hampton, Massachusetts, to live with a niece.[156] Upon her death on February 20, 1920, her body was returned to Oswego for funeral and burial.[157]

Reverend Melvin Danforth, Caroline Winters Danforth, Sarah P. Jersey Danforth, and Jennie Danforth Thrall are buried in Riverside Cemetery in Scriba, New York, section T.

Figure 2.26. A flag-draped coffin carried Rev. Danforth to his final resting place in Riverside Cemetery, Scriba, New York. Author's collection.

Figure 2.27. Sarah Danforth, who died in Massachusetts, was buried in Riverside Cemetery with her husband, Horace. Author's collection.

Thomas DeWitt Deans

The names of notable Civil War veterans of the town of Constantia must include that of Thomas DeWitt Deans, soldier, citizen, entrepreneur. Throughout his long life he displayed a dedication and devotion to civic responsibility which deserves particular notice.

T. D. Deans, as he was frequently called in newspaper articles, was born on October 17, 1847, in the town of Constantia, New York. He was a son of John Deans (June 1819–January 10, 1894) and Clarissa Lane (1822–October 23, 1898). Much too young to enter the war in its early years, he finally persuaded his father to allow him to enlist in Co. F, 189th Regiment on September 5, 1864. His company left the state on October 23.

The 189th saw considerable action in the short year it was mustered. Attached to the Army of the Potomac, it participated in the siege of Petersburg and was engaged in such battles as Hatcher's Run, Boydton Plank Road, and the Appomattox Courthouse Campaign, at the end of which General Robert E. Lee surrendered.

Deans, who was present when the surrender occurred, secured a memento of the historic moment by cutting out a piece of the root of the apple tree where General Ulysses S. Grant and General Lee allegedly held their first meeting. After the war he had the wood fashioned into a watch fob resembling a miniature Bible, to one side of which was pinned in gold the GAR logo.

Figure 2.28. One side of Deans's prized watch fob carried the GAR logo. Courtesy of the Cleveland, New York, Historical Society.

On the other was the Masonic square and compass. As Deans told a reporter, "This doesn't look very valuable . . . but, as badly as I need money, I wouldn't take $1,000 for it."[158]

Discharged from the service on May 30, 1865, Deans returned to Oswego County. He was an undertaker in Cleveland with his father for many years.[159] Following his father's death, he ran the business alone until 1917.[160] That he was interested in improving local business opportunities is evidenced by the fact that he was elected to a two-year term on the board of directors for the newly formed Chamber of Commerce.[161]

Deans is not, however, notable for his business pursuits. He is noteworthy because of his many and varied avocations.

An ardent Republican, Deans was heavily involved in local politics. Over the years he held such offices as assessor, town clerk, and notary. He was a longtime justice of the peace[162] and made news when he held court.[163] In 1902 he was elected Cleveland Village president. When the idea for a soldiers' monument for Cleveland was broached, Deans chaired the committee. He was elected a director of the Cleveland Water Supply in 1916.[164]

He was active in the Methodist Episcopal Church, superintending the Sunday school and serving on the board of trustees. In 1923 he was the president of the North Shore Sunday School Association.[165]

Figure 2.29. The other side of Deans's watch fob is decorated with the Masonic square and compass. Courtesy of the Cleveland, New York, Historical Society.

Deans was a member of Cleveland Lodge No. 613 F&AM, and it was alleged that he had held every office except that of secretary.[166]

He was very involved with the Homer Lester Farmer Post No. 16 GAR. The exact date of the post's organization is unknown, although Deans claimed it had been formed in 1880 with forty-three charter members.[167] At some point its number was changed to 569, although the exact date and reason are unknown. As with all GAR posts, the enrollment dwindled until by 1932 Deans was the sole survivor. He held many positions within the organization and at the end was commander by virtue of being the only living member.[168] In the final years of his life he was honored by local organizations for his military service.[169]

Deans was married three times. He and Isabel Smith (1848–July 26, 1897) were married on May 3, 1866. She succumbed to Bright's disease.[170]

Ada M. Congdon (December 1871–December 20, 1920) was first married to Charles E. Kime (1868–February 1898) who died of tuberculosis in North Carolina.[171] She and Thomas Deans were married September 27, 1899. They had no children but adopted a daughter, Margaret (1904–*post* 1957). With Deans, Ada was active in Cleveland Chapter No. 269 Order of the Eastern Star.[172] Ada's cause of death was pneumonia.[173]

Figure 2.30. Isabel Deans is buried in Cleveland Village Cemetery. Author's collection.

Figure 2.31. Ada Deans is also buried in the Deans family plot. Author's collection.

Deans married Claribel Houck Somers (November 28, 1871–December 19, 1957) on July 14, 1924, in New Jersey. She had previously been married to Wesley J. Somers (June 1870–January 1918) with whom she had one son. Born in Albany, New York, Claribel died in the city of Oneida "after a brief illness." She had been active in the Order of the Eastern Star and the Rebekahs.[174]

In late April 1935 Thomas Deans was taken to Canastota Hospital suffering from a strangulated hernia.[175] He died there on May 8.

The local newspapers carried obituaries emphasizing that he had been the last member of H. L. Farmer Post No. 16 GAR.[176] He was accorded a full military funeral: "The last rites were conducted with military honor, the flag covered casket being borne to the cemetery by a caisson and firing squad from Fort Ontario, Oswego, who were accompanied by Raymond-Faulkner-Cook Post of the American Legion as an escort . . . The last bugle call was sounded, and volley fired over the flower strewn grave of one whose memory will live long in the hearts of his friends."[177]

Thomas DeWitt Deans, Isabel Smith Deans, and Ada Congdon Kime Deans are buried in Cleveland Village Cemetery. Claribel Houck Somers Deans is buried with Wesley J. Somers in Slate Hill Cemetery in Sharon, Schoharie, New York.

Figure 2.32. Thomas Deans was the last Civil War veteran in Cleveland, New York. Author's collection.

James Doyle

Irish immigrant, boot maker, coal seller, soldier, citizen, and politician, James Doyle devoted his entire adult life to serving his adopted country. And he did it with only one arm.

Doyle's exact birth date and parentage are murky. His gravestone records a birth date of 1826, but the *Town Clerks' Registers* provides an exact date of November 1, 1824. His father's name is unknown but his mother Margaret (1802–December 3, 1877) was living with her son and family in Oswego in 1875.[178]

According to available information, James Doyle settled in Oswego City in 1837 soon after arriving in the United States. He worked for Millis and Leverich boot and shoe sellers, and after that firm ceased operations he opened his own company, as advertisements in local newspapers demonstrated.

He became associated with the Old Oswego Guards, the 48th Militia, of which he ultimately was colonel.[179] It was as a member of this unit that he lost his arm. He and Benjamin Brainard were injured on Saturday, July 13, 1850, while "firing minute guns in honor of the memory of President Taylor. They were acting as gunners, and were in the act of ramming down the cartridge, when the gun went off. The piece, a small six pounder, had become considerably heated, which was doubtless the cause of the explosion. Mr. Doyle was very badly hurt. His right hand was completely shattered, requiring immediate amputation above the wrist, and one of his eyes was nearly blown out of his head."[180]

At about the same time James married Margaret McCanna (1834–November 2, 1917), a native of Oswego County. They became the parents of nine children, seven of whom reached adulthood. John L. (October 1850–August 28, 1931) married Margaret "Maggie" A. Ferris (April 2, 1857–October 19, 1942) on September 26, 1880; James H. (1853–d.y.). Catherine "Kittie" (1856–October 9, 1944) married John H. Kelly (1848–June 21, 1916) on April 29, 1908; Elizabeth "Eliza" (1858–d.y.); Mary Rowe (1860–*post* 1949) married James C. Hinchcliffe Sr. (December 24, 1859–October 5, 1941) on September 20, 1905; Caroline "Carrie" C. (1863–November 3, 1941) married Charles Stephen Barrett (1865–December 11, 1934) on October 22, 1896; James Peter (1866–May 21, 1928) married Mary Frances Lyons (1870–August 7, 1933) on August 15, 1912; William Stewart (1868–December 9, 1948) married Kathleen Burns (1874–April 19, 1927) on August 28, 1907; Charles Montcalm (September 15, 1875–December 3, 1930) married Frances Lowell Richards (1885–January 21, 1962) on September 30, 1925.

In the summer of 1862, Doyle recruited Co. I, 110th Regiment and became its captain. Shortly before the regiment left Oswego, the men of the 48th, many of whom would go with him, presented him with a sword as a token of their regard: "We are sure that you will wear this sword without disgrace to the givers, in defence of the Union we love, and in upholding the Constitution as we received it from our forefathers."[181]

The 110th was part of General Nathaniel Banks's Nineteenth Corps, which besieged Port Hudson, Louisiana, from March to July 1863. On June 14, while leading his company in a reckless attempt to take the heavily fortified citadel, Doyle was severely wounded in the side. He rejoined the regiment after it had been detailed to Fort Jefferson, Dry Tortugas, in February 1864. He was assigned to Co. G but later was chosen to organize the 2nd Florida Cavalry "composed of refugees, rebel deserters, etc. and given a commission as lieutenant-colonel."[182]

On February 20, 1864, Colonel Doyle was involved in what has been described as the southernmost battle of the Civil War, a little known skirmish fought at Fort Myers, Florida. The area was cattle country and the Union army had recently confiscated about 4,500 animals meant for the Confederate army. Angry civilian farmers, subsequently dubbed the "Cow Cavalry," set out to wrest control of Fort Myers from Colonel Doyle, his 2nd FL Cavalry, and a few men from Co. K, 110th Regiment. When a demand was made to surrender, Doyle replied: "Sir—Your demand for an unconditional surrender has been received. I respectfully decline; I have forces enough to maintain my position and will *fight you* to the last."[183] The attack lasted several hours:

> By the arrival of the Tortugas from Key West this morning, we learn that a fight occurred at Fort Myers. The rebel force was supposed to be about 1500 strong. They sent in a demand for the surrender of the Fort within twenty minutes. Col. Doyle sent a reply that he would be ready to fight them in twenty minutes, and proceeded to do so. They had a right smart fight for a short time, when the Johny [sic] Rebs finding they were getting the worst of it, withdrew and skedaddled.[184]

After the war James Doyle returned to his family and business. In 1868 a grateful nation awarded him the rank of brevet lieutenant-colonel.[185] A Democrat, he became involved in politics, representing the party at state conventions for several years. He was elected Oswego city clerk in 1866. He lost that post when the Republicans took over City Hall.[186] In 1869 he ran for sheriff and won, a feat much commented upon because of his party affiliation. A local newspaper offered grudging compliments on the achievement:

> We [hear] that our Democratic friend, Col. James Doyle has been elected Sheriff of Oswego County by a large majority. The county is Republican, but complications have arisen [which] worked for the interest of Col. Doyle who carried the county. With the exception of his objectionable politics, Col. Doyle is one of the most worthy gentlemen in that or any other county, and if the office must go to a Democrat, we

know of none that [will offer] greater satisfaction than Col. Doyle or perform his duties more faithfully.[187]

That Doyle was appreciated in spite of his "objectionable" political affiliation was illustrated the night he and General William T. Sherman shared a railroad seat: "On taking his seat in the car at Richland, he invited Col. Doyle to his side, and conversed very freely upon general matters. Mr. Benedict came along and introduced Col. Doyle in a facetious way as a 'Copperhead sheriff in a Republican county.' The general replied that 'any man who was in the Union Army of the rebellion is right, whatever name you give him.'"[188]

When Doyle's term ended in 1872, the following appeared: "Many of our citizens know and respect and admire Colonel James Doyle, the retiring Sheriff of Oswego county. His administration has been a very successful one and he goes out of office, if possible, more popular than [when] he came in."[189] Sheriff Frank Low later appointed Doyle an undersheriff. He was elected city tax collector in 1879.

Besides politics, the colonel participated in local veterans' affairs. He was a member of the Veterans' Reunion Association and served as its president in 1879. He was also a guiding light in the formation of Rensselaer Bailey Post No. 19 GAR, serving as commander. When that post failed, he transferred his membership to John D. O'Brian Post No. 65.

James Doyle died in Oswego on November 30, 1882:

> Shortly after three o'clock yesterday afternoon, the soul of Col. James Doyle was given up to his Maker. His many friends, both in this city and abroad, will be pained to learn this, but the event seemed inevitable for a number of weeks, yet while life lingered, they hoped for the best. About four months ago he was attacked with that fatal disease known as cirrhosis of the liver, and although he knew he must die, he bravely bore up against the disease during his long period of sickness.[190]

Friends from the Veterans' Association, Post Doyle, and the 48th Regiment gathered to remember him. One of the outcomes of the meeting was Resolutions stating,

> Whereas, Our beloved comrade, Col. James Doyle, after a long and painful illness, which was borne with heroic fortitude,

has crossed the stream of time and pitched his tent on the eternal field from which no soldier has returned; and, Whereas, He has for forty-five years dwelt in our midst, and has been an important factor in the common weal of our town, and having filled to the entire satisfaction of his fellow citizens and great credit to himself various civic and military positions, therefore, be it Resolved, that it seems eminently proper that we who have been his comrades in the Old Oswego Guards, the Oswego County Veteran Association and the Grand Army of the Republic should perpetuate and keep his memory fresh and green by these eulogistic resolutions; Resolved, That in the death of Colonel Doyle, Oswego has lost in the meridian of life, one of her best known men, who was a true, generous and faithful friend, an enlightened and public spirited citizen.[191]

Figure 2.33. Colonel James Doyle's untimely death saddened the entire Oswego community. Author's collection.

Figure 2.34. Margaret McCanna Doyle was well regarded in Oswego City. Author's collection.

Margaret outlived her husband by many years. She died after a short illness and was described in an obituary as "one of Oswego's most honored and respected women . . . Mrs. Doyle was beloved by a large circle of friends, all of whom had the greatest respect for her sterling qualities."[192]

Colonel James Doyle, Margaret McCanna Doyle, Charles Montcalm Doyle, and William Stewart Doyle are buried in St. Paul's Cemetery, Oswego, section K.

Gilbert C. Dutcher

Frequently overshadowed by his flamboyant brother Himan P. Dutcher (August 29, 1846–May 21, 1928), Gilbert C. Dutcher, born in 1844, nevertheless deserves to be included among the notables featured in this book. His tortured life provides a prime example of the suffering endured by those who survived the horrors of the Civil War even when their tour of duty was of short duration.

The sons of Peter C. Dutcher (*ca.* 1815–*post* 1845) and Laura Bennett (1831–July 5, 1867), Gilbert and Himan Dutcher spent much of their childhood in the household of Laurens Horton, their stepfather.[193] In August 1864 the brothers enlisted in the 184th Regiment. This outfit saw little action, its only real battle occurring at Cedar Creek, Virginia, on October 19, 1864, made famous by the story of General Sheridan's ride to repel the Rebels. Himan Dutcher participated in this clash and years later his reminiscences were published in a local newspaper.[194]

Gilbert Dutcher, however, did not participate in this battle. According to a deposition he provided in support of his pension claim, dated October 17, 1885, on or about September 25, 1864, he contracted rheumatism as the result of "exposure in stormy weather being without shelter or protection and without sufficient clothing." Testimony in another deposition dated February 25, 1888, elaborated on his illness: "I felt pains in my legs arms shoulders and back. I was stiff[;] I did not know what was the matter with me." He was sent to a field hospital near Middletown, Virginia, where he remained for several weeks. He arrived at his regimental camp on the evening of October 19 after the battle had ended. In the deposition quoted above, Dutcher noted that after returning to his regiment, "I done duty right along although I was affected with [rheumatism] right along[.] My limbs did not swell any and never have swelled any to speak of but I suffer a great deal of pain. In damp and wet weather I always get worse than I am in dry weather."

He completed his tour of duty, returning to Oswego on July 4, 1865. He did not, however, go home as Himan did because, in the words of his aunt, Ellen Bennett Fairtile, "His stepfather was cross to him." Ellen described in graphic detail what she saw when Gilbert appeared at her boarding house. He was "lame and crippled and could hardly get around." He was so sick that he was unable to work for several months.[195]

Dutcher had apprenticed at R. J. Oliphant's printing office and book bindery in Oswego. Oliphant promised his workers who went into the service that their jobs would be waiting for them if they were fortunate enough to return home.[196] When he had regained a semblance of health Gilbert returned to work. Oliphant remembered "that he looked emaciated and in a feeble state of health." Several employees echoed Oliphant's assessment, remarking that Gilbert could only manage light work and adding that there were many days he could not work at all. According to John M. Schuler, "Mr. Oliphant favors him [and] he is kept here more on account of a favor than the amount of work he does."[197] John H. Tibbits echoed the sentiment: "Mr. Oliphant did not know whether to give him work because he was not a healthy man but said he took pity on him and set him to work[;] it was more from sympathy that he was put to work there than anything else."[198]

Dutcher's pension claim was initially rejected because he was not deemed too ill to do "manual labor" which was the standard for obtaining a pension.[199] He persisted, however, and the result was a file containing over two hundred pages of witness testimony, doctors' reports, and requests for increases once the pension had been granted.

Throughout the many pages of testimony, Dutcher revealed that he had sought medical advice and medications from numerous doctors, all to no avail. In 1871 he met Miss Helen V. Forsyth (November 1855–January 21, 1929), daughter of Dr. William B. Forsyth. Dr. Forsyth testified that Dutcher appealed to him for medical treatment:

> I am his father in law and I knew him in 1871 when he was courting my daughter but did not know anything special about him except that he was an honorable young man. In 1872 I was called upon to treat him for Rheumatism. I found him suffering from it[.] He was stopping at my house at this time [and] he spent several weeks there. I treated him during the time he remained at my house . . . The Rheumatism affects him all over[;] it now does and has done for a long time.[200]

Gilbert Dutcher and Helen were married August 1, 1872, and became the parents of four children. Laura Alcestis "Allie" (July 1873–May 24, 1941) married Delancey Vosburgh (1870–1939) on January 15, 1894. Caroline Elizabeth (September 1875–July 12, 1949) m1 Herbert Munroe (1867–February 4, 1917) on November 20, 1900, and m2 Eric L. Lindquist (1875–October 1, 1949) on November 12, 1937. George Signet (1879–1963) married Constance Mary Hamilton (1884–1945) on January 1, 1913. Helen Louise (November 1, 1891–February 15, 1955) married John A. Stone (1892–May 2, 1936) on September 30, 1919.

They had only been married a short time when Gilbert decided to go to Chicago. Himan was living there and perhaps Gilbert thought the change of climate and scenery might improve his health. He found work in a book bindery, but in 1878 he returned to Oswego where he and Helen lived until their deaths.

Despite ill health, Gilbert Dutcher was an active member of John D. O'Brian Post No. 65 GAR. He was installed as junior vice commander in 1885.[201] He apparently never served as commander but in 1898 he was installed as officer of the day.[202] His name appeared frequently in local newspapers as a member of various committees charged with planning the post's Memorial Day activities.[203]

He also participated in reunions of the 184th Regiment. In 1889 he was named to the executive committee responsible for planning the next gathering.[204]

Dutcher's health declined steadily over the years. He died on July 25, 1898. The official cause of death was pneumonia, complicated by heart disease: "At five o'clock this morning as the result of a week's illness with pneumonia, occurred the death of Gilbert C. Dutcher, one of Oswego's most highly respected citizens . . . Mr. Dutcher was born in Oswego fifty-four years ago and has always made this city his home. While a young man he entered the employ of R. J. Oliphant, where he

Figure 2.35. Gilbert Dutcher's regiment saw little battlefield action but he suffered from the effects of exposure and disease for the rest of his life. Author's collection.

Figure 2.36. Helen Forsyth Dutcher outlived her husband by many years. Author's collection.

learned the trade of bookbinder, and where he has been employed in that capacity for nearly forty years."[205] A funeral announcement revealed that Oliphant closed his business so employees might attend the service.[206]

Helen never remarried. Upon her death on January 21, 1929, she was buried next to Gilbert.[207]

Gilbert C. Dutcher, Helen Forsyth Gilbert, and their children and spouses are buried in Riverside Cemetery, Scriba, New York, section O.

William Dewey Ferguson

Although he spent the majority of his long life as a civilian, William Dewey Ferguson's personality was defined by the time he spent in the Union army. Lauded for bravery and efficiency, he served as a model for other officers to emulate.

Ferguson, the son of Hiram Ferguson (January 26, 1809–July 14, 1863) and Ethelinda Dewey (December 2, 1808–June 27, 1860), was born in the town of Orwell on August 11, 1831. Three more sons and a daughter would be born to this couple.[208] William, like his father, became a millwright. In 1855 the family resided in Williamstown, New York, but by 1860, with the exception of William, all had migrated to Story County, Iowa.

On July 14, 1856, William married Helen A. Monroe (1835–May 13, 1887), daughter of Barnabas Monroe II (October 6, 1809–May 29, 1875) and Avis Mallory (March 30, 1815–February 18, 1892), residents of Sandy Creek. Shortly after their marriage the couple moved to North Carolina where Ferguson "was the builder of the first trussed wooden bridges in the land of the Confederacy, using slave labor contracted for yearly . . . It was just before the war broke out that the major and his wife, seeing the thickening clouds of rebellion gathering in ominous pall, fled from North Carolina to his old home county in New York State."[209]

The couple was living in Sandy Creek in 1860. Shortly after war was declared in April 1861, Oswego County raised the 24th Regiment. Ferguson enlisted and became captain of Co. G which had been recruited in Sandy Creek. In January 1863, upon the resignation of Colonel Timothy Sullivan, several of Ferguson's fellow officers made an unsolicited appeal to Governor Horatio Seymour to select Ferguson as his replacement:

> Captain Ferguson has been connected with the regiment since the date of its organization . . . during which time he has under all circumstances by his gentlemanly deportment commanded the respect of all with whom he has been associated . . . We regard Captain Ferguson as an excellent disciplinarian, and fully believe that he possesses all those peculiar and essential qualities requisite for an efficient officer, necessary to redeem our regiment from the great demoralization into which it has fallen by a neglect of its interests and a lack of discipline.[210]

Ferguson did not obtain the requested rank and mustered out a captain on May 29, 1863. He returned Sandy Creek, probably having no idea he would soon be back in uniform.

As the war dragged on, more replacement troops were needed, and in the summer of 1864 Oswego County furnished the 184th Regiment, which was under the command of Colonel Wardwell Green Robinson.

Figure 2.37. William Dewey Ferguson had the distinction of serving in two Oswego County regiments. Courtesy of the New York State Military Museum.

So great was the need for troops that several companies were sent ahead of the rest. Ferguson, who had reenlisted and mustered in with the rank of major, was in charge of this detachment.

The 184th Regiment became part of General Sheridan's Shenandoah Campaign but its only real battle occurred at Cedar Creek on October 19, 1864. Many years later Ferguson recalled his participation in that engagement:

> When the firing commenced on our front Lieutenant Philips asked me if I heard it. I said yes and that it sounded bad. Just then an orderly from General Wright's headquarters rode up and gave orders to get my men in line as quickly as possible . . . We were ordered to form line of battle and did so and immediately went into action, advancing to the top of the hill . . . As all know of that battle, we were driven some four miles and then we drove the rebels back over the same ground and camped on the same ground we left in the morning, and started in squads to find the men of our command who we knew were left killed or wounded in the morning.[211]

The 184th Regiment mustered out on June 30, 1865, at City Point, Virginia, but the journey home was delayed, a situation with which the usually gentleman-like Ferguson became increasingly frustrated:

> A characteristic story is told of the major that at the close of the war when the boys from this section were expected in Fulton for a Fourth of July celebration the returning soldiers were held up in Binghamton when the railroad officers said that they had no train in commission to take the men to Fulton and that there would be some delay. Promise after promise was made but not fulfilled until the major's patience was exhausted, whereupon he marched into the offices of the railroad company and threw down the gauntlet with: "If there is not a train ready within an hour to take my men to Fulton I'll have my men requisition a train and I have a half dozen men who can run the engine without trouble." The train was ready within the hour.[212]

A return to civilian life did not mean the end of his military involvement. In 1866 he was commissioned brevet lieutenant colonel "for meritorious conduct in the war."[213]

As a veteran of two regiments, Ferguson participated in veterans' organizations for both the 24th and the 184th. Annually, his name appeared among those who had attended reunions, generally named an honorary president or asked to make remarks.[214] He joined Daniel Schenck Post No. 271 GAR in Fulton and served as commander in 1906. He was often selected a delegate to state and national encampments.

Veterans frequently received priority when certain public appointive offices were available, and Ferguson was selected in 1870 to be inspector of lumber for Oswego City.[215] Later he was chosen commissioner of charities in Fulton, a position he held until 1912. His job was to aid the poor, especially families of poor veterans, in times of need. According to published reports he was the oldest man ever to hold the position. When he retired at age eighty, he bragged that "not a cent of the city's money has been spent except in cases of proved destitution."[216]

Additionally, the major belonged to the United American Mechanics, at whose events he might be called upon for an impromptu speech. For example, it was reported that at a recent banquet Ferguson "toasted 'the Red, White and Blue,' giving a graphic account of Civil War experiences while commanding under the stars and stripes."[217] He also belonged to the Borrowed Time Club, so named because only those over seventy years of age were permitted to join. In 1913 Ferguson was the treasurer of the two-year-old organization.[218] He was a charter member of Sandy Creek Lodge No. 564 F&AM and a member of Hiram Lodge No. 145 F&AM in Fulton.[219]

William and Helen Ferguson were the parents of two children, Sidney Monroe (1858–October 24, 1920) born in North Carolina, and Hattie Lunette (February 19, 1864–July 4, 1948), both of whom must have caused their father considerable anguish. Sidney married Alice M. Sheffield (1860–?) on November 9, 1884, in Story County, Iowa. Declared insane in 1911, Sidney was confined to an asylum. According to his death certificate, he died in the Indiana Hospital for the Insane.[220] Hattie's life was also unhappy. She married William R. Shayes (1866–1935) in 1886

Figure 2.38. William and Helen Monroe Ferguson were prominent residents of Sandy Creek, New York. Author's collection.

and became the mother of four children. At some point before 1900 Shayes abandoned the family.

After Helen died in 1887, Ferguson lived with a woman only known as Nettie P. (November 1853–*post* 1915). In 1900 she claimed to be his wife and to have been married for ten years. How much they actually lived together is a matter of conjecture. In 1905, for example, Ferguson was enumerated living alone in an apartment building. His daughter was with him when he died. Nettie applied for a widow's pension on June 9, 1915, but did not succeed in obtaining it. Several reasons are possible: (1) she remarried; (2) she died before the process could be completed; (3) she and Ferguson were never legally married. No marriage record has been located, and such was Ferguson's status in the community that a new marriage would have been noted in the press. In fact, with only one possible exception, no further mention of Nettie has been found, suggesting that she reverted to her unknown maiden name.[221]

Major William Dewey Ferguson died on May 18, 1915. Local newspapers covered his death and funeral extensively over the next few days, and he was eulogized in all the obituaries. The following is an exemplar: "His courage was never questioned, his leadership of men was powerful and the men of his command testify that with the major leading them was none who would not follow."[222]

Major William Dewey Ferguson and Helen A. Monroe Ferguson are buried in Woodlawn Cemetery, Sandy Creek, New York, plot F 244. Her parents are also buried in that plot.

Delos Gary

A man of numerous talents, Delos Gary was prominent in Oswego City's affairs for many years. His death at the age of 39 cut short a career which promised to be even more illustrious.

Delos Gary (September 10, 1831–July 27, 1870) was the son of George Gary (1793–1855), a Methodist minister, and Elizabeth Armitage (1798–1838). At the time of Delos's birth, Reverend Gary was ministering in Oneida County. After attending the local schools, Delos entered Wesleyan University in Middletown, Connecticut. He moved to Oswego County after graduation to become principal of Mexico Academy. When a high school was formed in Oswego City in 1853, he was its first principal.[223]

Not content with his current occupation, Gary decided to become a lawyer, studying with Albertus Perry. It is unknown when he was admitted to the Bar, but by 1860 he was practicing with his brother-in-law, Charles Richardson, Esq.

When the 147th Regiment was raised in the summer of 1862, Gary singlehandedly recruited Co. G and became its captain. Shortly before the regiment left for war his colleagues in the legal profession presented him with a sword and sash as an expression of their esteem. He responded: "Should death meet me in the field, I ask that the grave that closes over my body may cover my many faults and defects, and that I may have a kindly place in your memories."[224]

The 147th Regiment was organized shortly after the 110th. Because of the local War Committee's efforts, coupled with substantial bounties,

Figure 2.39. Delos Gary recruited an entire company for the 147th Regiment and became its captain. Courtesy of the New York State Military Museum.

more men were recruited than were necessary for the 110th. As a result, another regiment was approved with over eight hundred men on the muster roll. Unlike the 110th, however, the 147th saw extensive action in the Army of the Potomac. Most notable was its participation in the Battle of Gettysburg on July 1–3, 1863, during which Captain Gary suffered a serious head wound. He reported for duty in November only to discover that he had been discharged for "disability," although he was now healthy enough to rejoin his company. By January 1864 he had returned to Oswego, where he resumed his legal practice.

In the late 1850s Gary had served as undersheriff for two different sheriffs. The war suspended his political aspirations, but by 1864 he was again on the campaign trail, this time as a supporter of General George McClellan, the Democratic challenger to President Lincoln. He received vigorous criticism for abandoning the Republican Party, evidenced by a letter to the editor signed by "A Union Man." The anonymous writer described a rally held by the Democrats in Williamstown at which Gary spoke: "The little Mackerals and the Villain-Dames exhausted all the copper and depopulated four towns to fill a small room of 16 by 24 to hear a proselyte from the Lincoln faith, a Captain, it is said to his shame, Capt. Gary, whose only eloquence consisted in the broad assertion that 'four years ago he voted for Abraham Lincoln but hereafter should vote the Democratic ticket.' "[225]

Gary ran for district attorney on the Democratic ticket in 1866 but lost to his Republican rival William H. Baker, 8,287 to 5,558 votes.[226] Undaunted, he ran for city recorder, today known as city judge, against Wardwell Green Robinson, a brilliant attorney and former colonel of the 184th Regiment. This time he was victorious and held the office until his untimely death in 1870.[227]

In 1859 Delos Gary married Catherine "Kate" Martin (1840–October 14, 1864), the daughter of local prominent attorney Robert Martin and his wife, Lucy. The couple had no children and Kate's life ended unexpectedly:

> We are pained to announce that our fellow townsman Delos Gary, Esq., who has been for some days traveling in the eastern part of the county, was yesterday recalled by a telegram announcing the sudden and dangerous illness of his wife, and arrived in town just in time to witness her death. Mrs. Gary was a most estimable woman. She was born and had always

lived in this city and had endeared herself to a large circle of friends by her gentle, kindly disposition, her many natural and acquired advantages, and a pure Christian character. Her sudden death has cast a gloom over many hearts. To the fond indulgent husband, the loving parents and sister who have thus been heart-stricken, we would offer our earnest sympathy. Theirs is indeed a bitter cup.[228]

From 1868 until early 1870 Recorder Gary carried out his duties faithfully as reported in numerous newspaper articles. He was plagued with ill health, probably tuberculosis acquired during the war, and was required periodically to take a few days to rest. On April 27, 1870, he took what he thought would be a short leave of absence but from which he would never return. In June he traveled to Binghamton, Broome, New York, to stay with his sister, Maryette Gary Clark (April 2, 1821– November 15, 1887). He contracted pleurisy and died on July 27, 1870.

The news of his passing elicited much grief and consternation in Oswego. Both the Common Council and the Grand Jury issued Resolutions in remembrance of his service. A lengthy obituary paid tribute to his life and career:

Figure 2.40. Catherine "Kate" Martin Gary was the daughter of one attorney and the wife of another. Author's collection.

As a lawyer he was one of the most careful and successful members of the Oswego County bar. His talents were conspicuous among his legal brethren, and by force of them he was rising rapidly. As a judge, he was ready to decide and conscientious in his ideas of exact and equal justice, which was the basis of his action in all cases. No man ever brought better legal abilities to the Recorder's bench, and none ever more intelligently and faithfully executed the functions of his office for the protection of the public interests and still for the reformation of criminals in the purification of society. As a companion and friend he was genial and open-hearted as well as open-handed, and in this connection there are hundreds who will mourn his death.[229]

Figure 2.41. Due to a clerical error, Captain Gary's gravesite was unidentified for almost 150 years. Author's collection.

Following a funeral held at Christ Church in Oswego, Delos's body was taken to Riverside Cemetery where it was laid beside Kate's in the family plot. For the next 150 years, however, his gravesite was unidentified. It would not be located until 2019 when an amateur genealogist made it her mission to find him.[230]

Captain Delos Gary, Catherine Martin Gary, her parents, and Charles and Cornelia Martin Richardson are buried in Riverside Cemetery, Scriba, New York, section V.

Joseph M. Gould

Joseph M. Gould's life was cut short by the horrors of the Civil War. He earned his place among the notables of Oswego County because he fought and died for his country.

Born *ca.* 1841 to John Dyer Gould (1795–October 22, 1878) and his second wife, Phoebe Holden (*ca.* 1809–July 22, 1883), Joseph lived his entire life in Phoenix, New York. Information on his muster card reveals he was nineteen years old, stood six feet tall, and had gray eyes and dark hair. Some researchers have assigned him a birth date of March 11, 1840, but he was seven in 1850 and thirteen in 1855, suggesting a birth date of 1843. According to his gravestone he was twenty-two years, five months, and twenty-seven days of age when he died. If the inscription on the stone is correct, he would have been born in April 1841.

Gould enlisted in the 81st Regiment on September 23, 1861, at Volney, New York, and mustered into service the same day as a member of Co. C. On February 6, 1862, he transferred to Co. G. The 81st Regiment was reconstituted as a veteran volunteer organization in 1864 and Gould reenlisted on February 24, 1864.

The veteran regiment became part of the Army of the Potomac and was present at the battle of Cold Harbor on June 3, 1864. It also participated in the siege of Petersburg, which began later that month. Dr. William H. Rice, surgeon assigned to the 81st Regiment, reported that Gould "was wounded while in the line of his duty at Division Head Quarters, 1st Div., 18th A. C. near Petersburgh, Va. by one of the enemy's sharp shooters on the 6th day of August last, and in consequence of said wound I amputated his left leg above the knee."[231]

Dr. E. M. Allen's letter finished the story. Allen stated that Gould was admitted to General Hospital, Fortress Monroe, Virginia, on August

9, 1864 "suffering from amputation of left thigh, result of Gun Shot Fracture of left Femur received near Petersburg Va. August 6th 1864 and died Sept. 3rd 1864 of Pyaemia following amputation of Left Thigh."[232]

Gould's cause of death was noted in a lengthy obituary:

> Another of our brave and patriotic sons has given up his life in the cause of his country. Sergeant Joseph M. Gould, Co. G, 81st regiment, died at the U. S. General Hospital at Fortress Monroe, on the 3d inst. He had been detailed to do provost duty at General Headquarters, 18th corps, and was singled out by a rebel sharpshooter and struck in the leg, shattering it so that amputation became necessary. He was shortly after removed to Fortress Monroe, where he was attacked with chill fever, and this, in the absence of the kindest care, proved to be more than his constitution would endure. His young and faithful wife was with him in his last hours, and through her tireless perseverance she succeeded in having his body embalmed and brought home for interment. The deceased was son of John Gould of Volney, in this county. He has shared in all the trials and dangers of the 81st, and leaves a large circle of friends and acquaintances, none of whom will more deeply mourn his loss than his comrades in arms.[233]

The "young and faithful wife" mentioned in the obituary was Sarah L. Fuller Gould (1841–*post* 1900). One of the benefits of reenlisting was a thirty-day furlough. When Sarah applied for a widow's pension, she was required to prove she had indeed been legally married. The couple, she testified, had been married on April 10, 1864, in Baldwinsville, and the officiating minister provided a record. Their short-lived marriage ended when Gould died at Fortress Monroe. Possessing the wherewithal to have a body embalmed and returned to the family was unusual, and it is possible that John and Phoebe assisted financially. Gould's body was shipped home and was buried in Phoenix Rural Cemetery. He was the first Civil War veteran to be interred there.

In 1880 when James Barnes and fifteen others formed a GAR post in Phoenix, they chose to name it after young Gould for that very reason.

Sarah obtained a widow's pension after the necessary corroborating testimony had been filed. Her allotment, eight dollars per month, began in May 1865, retroactive to September 3, 1864. The money, however,

Figure 2.42. Sergeant Joseph Gould was the first Civil War veteran buried in Phoenix Rural Cemetery. Author's collection.

was paid quarterly and she needed some way to earn a living in the meantime. Like every other widow of the era, Sarah had few choices. Perhaps she could teach (if she was literate), hire out as a housekeeper or nurse, or take in laundry. Sarah opted for the most obvious solution: she remarried. A short newspaper announcement revealed that Alonzo Collins of Clay, Onondaga, New York, had married Mrs. Sarah L. Gould of Baldwinsville in Syracuse, New York, on March 11, 1866.[234]

The couple lived on a farm in Cicero, Onondaga County, in 1870. What happened to them for the next thirty years is unknown. They reappeared in the 1900 federal census living in Wayne, Minnehaha, South Dakota. Alonzo was sixty-eight and Sarah was sixty. She had no children. No further record has been located.

Joseph M. Gould and his parents are buried in Phoenix Rural Cemetery, section 14.

Andrew J. Hirschbolz

Although born in Germany, Andrew J. "Andy" Hirschbolz risked his life not once but twice in defense of his adopted country by serving in different regiments in different states. His compassion for former foes, although their names were unknown to him, marks him as a notable Civil War veteran of Oswego County.

The son of Andrew Jakob Hirschbolz (1800–October 12, 1886) and Maria Anna Brunner (1820–February 19, 1903), Andrew was born on May 2, 1844, in Dillingen, Bavaria, Germany. The family immigrated to the United States in 1856 and settled in Oswego City. The elder Hirschbolz was a shoemaker and later operated a hotel, in both of which businesses his son assisted.

In 1860 Andrew Hirschbolz, an apprentice barber, lived in Oswego City with his parents. At an unknown date he moved to Chicago, Cook,

Figure 2.43. Andrew J. Hirschbolz was a colorful character in Oswego who won widespread recognition for his annual pilgrimage to Riverside Cemetery, Scriba, New York, to decorate the graves of Confederate soldiers buried there. Author's collection.

Illinois, where he worked as a barber in a hotel operated by Francis Trowbridge Sherman, the original colonel of the 88th Illinois Regiment. On May 5, 1862, Andrew enlisted and was mustered into Co. E as a drummer. The 88th, known as the 2nd Chicago Board of Trade Regiment, saw action in Tennessee. His time with the outfit was short because he was injured and captured at the battle of Stone River, Tennessee, on December 31, 1862. Later in life, Hirschbolz would tell the story of the woman and her daughter who came upon him as he lay in an old public building, unable to speak because of severe dehydration. According to the tale, the woman nursed him back to health, although she had a son in the Confederate army. When Hirschbolz was exchanged he vowed to do something to repay her kindness.[235] He would find a way shortly after the war ended.

Details of Hirschbolz's military career are somewhat muddled. He allegedly served in an Iowa regiment before enlisting in the 88th IL. There is no mention of such service on his pension card, which merely indicates he was discharged from that regiment on February 2, 1863. His muster information, however, states that he was dishonorably discharged on March 12, 1863. In all likelihood that was a clerical error based on a lack of information. Otherwise he would not have been able to claim a pension or join the GAR. That Hirschbolz returned to Oswego on furlough is known because of an incident which made the news many years later.

As told to a reporter, Philip Onett

> said that while the war was being waged in the South it was rumored that everything was in readiness for an invasion of the northern States. Ordinance [sic] Sergeant Ambroch, a soldier of the Regular army, was in charge of Fort Ontario and who was also captain of the German militia company, received sealed order from the War Department to have the Post garrisoned. About the time of the scare Major Hirschbolz was home on a furlough and he joined the company. None of the residents of the city knew that the Fort was to be garrisoned and Company C, then doing provost duty for the city, was marched into the Fort at midnight by Major Hirschbolz with a muffled drum. In the morning Oswegonians were surprised to see that the post was occupied and an American flag flying from the ramparts. Major Hirschbolz said this morning

that the Germans had twenty kegs of beer and several large cases of switzer cheese as large as carts . . . They remained in the old Fort until the scare wore off, or rather until the beer ran out.[236]

Although the men could laugh in 1914 at their wartime antics, the war was no laughing matter. In 1864 another call came from the Lincoln administration for an infusion of new regiments. While Oswego County busied itself with recruiting the 184th Regiment, Onondaga County worked on enrolling men for the 185th, also known as the 6th Onondaga. Andrew enlisted in Syracuse on September 8, 1864, and mustered into Co. D as a musician. He was reportedly wounded in action at Quaker Road, Virginia, on March 29, 1865, although his admission form to Bath National Soldiers' Home dated November 16, 1885, reveals he contracted chronic bronchitis at Quaker Farm, Virginia. He had also lost his left eye, but the circumstances are unknown. He apparently remained with his unit because he consistently claimed that he was present when General Lee surrendered at Appomattox on April 9.[237] He was discharged from Campbell Hospital, Washington, DC, on June 2.

Hirschbolz returned to Oswego and resumed barbering. He was one of the first letter carriers hired in Oswego City in 1879: "Shortly after that he was appointed one of the six letter carriers by the late John A. Place, postmaster. In those days the carriers worked ten or twelve hours a day and had long routes, and as a result of arduous duties his health broke down and he had to retire from the postal service."[238]

On December 31, 1865, he married Aletha/Althea Mary Kingsley (July 19, 1846–October 22, 1908) by whom he was the father of four sons. Andrew Brewster (September 9, 1866–April 20, 1914) married Hortense M. Fox (December 29, 1869–November 6, 1956) on June 14, 1892. Charles J. (December 20, 1867–December 30, 1893) never married. Joseph (March 1870–April 19, 1920) married Elizabeth "Lizzie" Doty (1874–*post* 1905) on January 16, 1891. Ferdinand John (January 22, 1872–June 9, 1915) never married.

Like many others, Andrew became interested in local Republican politics. His ambition to hold public office, however, went unfulfilled due to the local political climate. An angry member of Oswego's German population criticized the Republicans' sleazy behavior toward one of their own: "The action of the Republicans has shown us Germans that the Republicans have no use for us. They had no use for Andy Hirschbolz and they had no use for Frank Schilling . . . Oh, yes how they love us Germans!"[239] Nevertheless "Andy" participated in ward caucuses and city meetings, at one of which he was called to preside. The reporter gave a delightful description of his command of English: "The meeting was unanimously and enthusiastically in favor of Mr. Hirschbolz and that gentleman came forward and took up the gavel. Mr. Hirschbolz's English is not perfect and his rich German accent was truly amusing but not very intelligible. We did understand him, however, to say that the present incumbent of the office of Recorder had done nobly for four years and why should he not do nobly for four years to come?"[240]

Hirschbolz was also a member of DeWolf Hose Co. No. 1, Oswego City Volunteer Fire Department. In 1900 he was the retiring president of the Oswego County Volunteer Firemen's Association. He was a charter member of the St. Boniface Society, whose mission was to raise funds for building St. Peter's Church in Oswego.[241] He was also a charter member of the German Benevolent Association founded in 1858 to care for "their own members, in sickness, and the widows and orphans left in their care."[242] His most prominent membership, however, was in John D. O'Brian Post No. 65 GAR. It was in conjunction with the post's annual pilgrimages to local cemeteries that Hirschbolz became widely known.

Since the organization of the GAR in 1866, each post had been obligated annually to decorate the graves of veterans in nearby cemeteries. Every year the local newspapers reported on the committees established by the posts to place flowers and flags on the graves. Hirschbolz, as a member of O'Brian Post No. 65, was naturally involved with this yearly responsibility, but remembering that kind woman who nursed him back to health encouraged him to engage in an activity which some of his comrades considered inappropriate, to say the least: "When Mr. Hirschbolz returned here after the war in 1865 his first thought was of the lonely and unhonored graves up the river. On the day before Memorial Day of 1866 he took flowers and flags to the cemetery and decorated nine graves. At that time the feeling ran high and he was roundly criticized for his kindly act."[243]

During the Civil War, Confederate prisoners were detained at Fort Ontario in Oswego City. Nine of them died, and when the fort's commandant refused to bury them in the post cemetery, they were taken to Riverside. Their names apparently were never recorded, but nonetheless each year Hirschbolz decorated their graves with flowers.[244] Despite initial criticism, he performed this ritual until shortly before his death.

At first, the backlash from the post was so severe that he was threatened with court-martial. According to reports, General Henry Alanson Barnum, commander of the Department of New York, intervened and put a stop to the threatened action. If true, this must have happened in 1871 or 1872. Hirschbolz is said to have responded to his critics with these words: "If it is treason to the flag to show this little respect to our former fallen foes I am ready to answer for it. When General Grant received Lee's sword at Appomattox did he not return it to him signifying the return of peace? I was there and saw it, you were not there." In time his compassion for former foes made him a local celebrity, and even toward the end of his life his yearly act was mentioned in the press.[245]

Aletha Hirschbolz died in 1908. An obituary called attention to her sudden death: "Mrs. Hirschbolz was in excellent health until four o'clock this morning when she was stricken with apoplexy . . . At 11:20 o'clock this forenoon, surrounded by her sorrowing family she passed from earth's scenes forever . . . She was a woman of many admirable

Figure 2.44. Aletha Kingsley Hirschbolz was the mother of four sons. Author's collection.

Notable Civil War Veterans of Oswego County | 93

traits of character and intense devotion to her family endeared her to all who knew her."[246]

Over the years Andrew Hirschbolz suffered several setbacks. He was severely injured after falling on a city street; his barber shop was destroyed in a disastrous fire; his political accomplishments fell short of his aspirations. In 1910 he decided to return to Germany to reunite with relatives and childhood friends. Through letters to his sons he kept the community apprised of his activities.[247]

There was one piece of news which Hirschbolz neglected to report to the folks back home. While he was in Europe he married Louise Eckl (1876–October 26, 1923). The local press reported the unexpected event: "The friends of Major Andrew Hirschbolz, who returned recently from Germany, are congratulating him on his marriage while abroad.

Figure 2.45. Andrew J. Hirschbolz served his adopted country in two different regiments and states. Courtesy of the *Oswego Daily Palladium*.

His friends were taken by surprise when he introduced his wife to them. Mrs. Hirschbolz was formerly Elizabeth Eckel [sic] and she kept a fashionable dress-making establishment in Vienna."[248] Four years later, Louise presented Hirschbolz with his only daughter, Louise (August 24, 1914–March 3, 1990).

Andrew J. Hirschbolz died on December 16, 1915, after an illness of four weeks. According to his obituary, he succumbed to a "complication of diseases." His lengthy death notice detailed his military career and subsequent activities, particularly his annual pilgrimages to Riverside Cemetery: "Mr. Hirschbolz . . . never forgot his old war days and had a warm spot in his heart for his old Confederate rivals-in-arms."[249]

Mrs. Hirschbolz applied for pensions for herself and little Louise. When she died eight years later, Hortense Hirschbolz, Andrew Brewster's widow, became the girl's guardian.[250]

Major Andrew J. Hirschbolz, Aletha Kingsley Hirschbolz, Louise Eckl Hirschbolz, and several other members of the family are buried in St. Peter's Cemetery, Oswego, priest section. Louise's grave is unmarked.

Edwin Lester Huntington

Edwin Lester Huntington was a direct descendant of Samuel Huntington, a signer of the Declaration of Independence.[251] While notable for his military service and his political activity, he especially deserves credit for helping to bring electricity to the town of Mexico.

Edwin was born on July 8, 1839, in Mexico, New York, to Edwin Huntington (June 1, 1805–May 20, 1870) and Lucy Ann Gregory (1809–January 1, 1851). He spent most of his life in the town where he was born.[252]

Edwin, aged twenty-one, enlisted in the 24th Regiment on May 1, 1861, and mustered into Co. B on May 17. He served two years, participating in battles such as First Bull Run, South Mountain, Fredericksburg, and Chancellorsville. He mustered out on May 29, 1863. Not content to remain at home while the war still raged, he enlisted on December 23, 1863, in the 9th NY HA, mustering into Co. L. He transferred to Co. L, 2nd NY HA on June 27, 1865, mustering out on September 29, 1865, as a second lieutenant.

After the war ended, Huntington continued his military associations. He organized Co. I, 48th NYSNG, nicknamed "Huntington's

Guards," and was the company's captain. They were a familiar sight to those attending Decoration Day ceremonies in Mexico for many years.

In civilian life, Huntington operated a drug and dry goods store in Mexico. Every week his advertisements were prominently displayed in the *Mexico Independent*. Among the remedies he sold were West's Liver Pills, Dr. Carter's Kidney and Backache Tea, and Hill's Piles Pomade, advertised specifically for the ladies. He also sold paints, perfumes, jewelry, books, stationery, clocks, and silverware.[253] He gave up the store in 1893, concentrating on other business endeavors.[254]

Edwin married Florence Adelle Allen (May 19, 1848–April 20, 1888) on September 1, 1868. They were the parents of Edith Louise (July 30, 1871–January 30, 1928) who married Clinton Avery (March 30, 1872–March 14, 1917) on March 5, 1890, and Lucy Adelle (March 22, 1875–April 19, 1954) who married Dr. Louis De Laittre Pulsifer (October 12, 1872–October 26, 1948) on June 18, 1902.

Several years after Florence's death, Edwin Huntington married Mary A. Tourdot (April 1862–October 8, 1943) on December 23, 1891, in Syracuse, Onondaga, New York. They had no children.

Huntington was interested in local veterans' organizations. He was a charter member of Melzar Richards Post No. 367 GAR in Mexico. He served as commander numerous times, overseeing the annual Decoration Day celebration. His comrades presented him with a rocking chair as a token of their esteem after he completed eight consecutive terms: "Mr. Huntington responded in a very happy, feeling manner, saying that words were inadequate to express himself, but if they could open the windows of his heart they would then know how well he appreciated their kindness."[255]

The night Frank M. Earle, village president, gave the post a memorial book in which to record soldiers' war stories, Huntington responded eloquently:

> In behalf of the Post I thank you for your kind expressions in this presentation and to the donor, Mr. Earle, I will say that these comrades who marched shoulder to shoulder, slept side by side, bore one another's burdens and administered to each other's wants when wounded or in sickness during the trying days of the rebellion, will now hold before me the broad mantle of loyal, fraternal charity if I am unable, as their representative, to group into sentences words adequate to

express our gratitude for this book. I can hardly imagine that when he placed his name on the subscription for this volume he fully realized the magnitude of the gift; its value cannot be measured in money; the histories that are to be recorded in on its pages are priceless. As has been intimated, we find here pages to record this presentation, our individual soldier records, also what we know must surely come, our death and place of burial, and when there are no more recruits to muster into our ranks, and we have been mustered out, one by one, until the last meeting has been held, we also find a page to record the final work of the Post . . . And when the drum has beaten and the bugle sounded 'lights out' over the grave of the last comrade, then this book will be closed . . . The true veteran does not desire public praise, but only asks for the esteem of his fellow men as a good citizen, and to be

Figure 2.46. Edwin Huntington lived his entire life in Mexico, New York, and was instrumental in bringing electricity to the village. Courtesy of *Grip's Historical Souvenir of Mexico, NY.*

recorded as one who was true to his country in its time of need . . . But in his mature years, with his deeds of valor still fresh in his mind, and have it made known to him that his history as a veteran soldier is to be placed in this book and to be preserved as his individual record of the part he bore in the defense of his country, it is then that the veteran finds that he cannot express in words that deep sense of gratitude swelling up from his heart toward his friend, who has made it possible for every comrade, no matter how humble, to have his name and the service he rendered to his country handed down to generations yet unborn. You have builded better than you thought. You have given more than you supposed. Comrades, we are receiving greater than we expected. We appreciate it with hearts overflowing with gratitude.[256]

As a GAR leader, Huntington advocated and worked for a monument to be placed in Mexico Village Cemetery.

Figure 2.47. Edwin Huntington was an important supporter of the campaign to raise a GAR monument in Mexico, New York. Author's collection.

Determined to include the name of every soldier and sailor who called Mexico home, he published lists in the local newspaper and encouraged his fellow citizens to add to that list to ensure that all men from the town would be included.[257] When the monument was dedicated on July 4, 1889, Huntington, post commander, presided.[258]

Edwin Huntington was active in the 24th Regiment's Reunion Association, of which he served as president in 1899 and 1900.[259] He was a member of Mexico Lodge No. 136 F&AM and Mexico Chapter No. 135 RAM, holding offices in both groups.[260]

Over the years Huntington held a variety of local positions. He was a notary public, cemetery commissioner, and trustee of Mexico Academy. He was a member and longtime president of the Thief Detective Society, a prototype of today's Neighborhood Watch.[261]

Huntington's political career began in 1881 when he was unanimously nominated for sheriff by the local Republican caucus and elected by an overwhelming majority.[262] He attempted another run for sheriff in 1899, but when the Republicans expressed support for another candidate, he withdrew and organized instead a winning campaign for town supervisor, an office he held for several years.[263]

In 1887 the Village Improvement Society was organized in Mexico, and one of its goals was the electrification of the village, particularly the street lamps. A few were installed on a trial basis for a month. Certain prominent citizens, such as Huntington, had their businesses wired for electric lights.[264] Installing electricity within the village was big news and many opinions were voiced on the matter. While some complained that taxes would rise and common laborers would derive no benefits, others pointed out that electrifying the village would draw new business to the area, thus creating more jobs. It was rumored that the trustees had a financial interest in bringing electric lights to the village, a charge vehemently denied.[265] In the end, the voters approved the plan and by 1891, the company, under the direction of E. L. Huntington, Linus B. Cobb, and Charles E. Hocknel, provided electricity for the entire village.[266] Huntington became the superintendent and manager of the Mexico Electric Light Company, holding the job for several years.

When Edwin Huntington died on April 13, 1915, he was a respected and admired community member. E. L. Huntington Post of Sons of Union Veterans No. 75, in which he took a great interest, was named after him as a sign of esteem.[267] He never lost his interest in politics and veterans' organizations. He was frequently a delegate for

Figure 2.48. The Huntington monument stands in the middle of the large family plot in Mexico Village Cemetery. Author's collection.

Figure 2.49. Mary Turdot was Edwin Huntington's second wife. Author's collection.

local Republican caucuses. He often attended state and national GAR encampments. Concluded one obituary: "Mr. Huntington was a familiar figure at all Republican gatherings. He was a wise political counselor and an ardent, active worker."[268]

Little is known about Florence Adelle, but Mary became actively involved in the Woman's Relief Corps, holding the office of treasurer for several terms and attending GAR encampments with her husband. She died in Mexico and was buried in the family plot.[269]

Edwin Lester Huntington, Florence Adelle Allen, Mary A. Tourdot, and Edith and Lucy Huntington and their husbands are buried in Mexico Village Cemetery, section G north.

Albert Lindley Lee

Perched on the highest point of the cemetery, Albert Lindley Lee's gleaming white monument marks a remarkable man's final resting place. His career encompassed both civilian and military service to his nation but he never forgot that he began life in Fulton, New York.

Figure 2.50. General Albert Lindley Lee's monument stands on the highest point of Mt. Adnah Cemetery, Fulton, New York. Author's collection.

Notable Civil War Veterans of Oswego County | 101

Albert Lindley Lee was born on January 16, 1834, the son of Moses Lindley Lee (May 29, 1795–May 19, 1876) and Ann Case (January 13, 1815–November 24, 1883). Moses was a well-to-do physician and politician, holding office in both chambers of the New York State Legislature as well as the United States House of Representatives.

Albert Lee graduated from Union College in Schenectady, New York, in 1853 at the age of nineteen. After graduation from Yale Law School he practiced in Fulton from 1855 to 1857. He then moved to the Kansas Territory where he helped found the *Elwood Free Press*. He was elected a district judge in 1859, a position he held in 1861 when the Civil War broke out.[270]

He mustered into the 7th Kansas Cavalry, also known as Jennison's Jayhawkers, in the fall of 1861 as a major. On May 17, 1862, he was promoted to colonel. The unit saw action in Tennessee and Mississippi under his command. In January 1863 he was promoted to brigadier-general and had charge of cavalry brigades in the Army of Tennessee until attached to Major-General John A. McClernand's 13th Corps as chief-of-staff. When Theophilus Garrad was sent home on sick leave, Lee assumed command of the 1st Brigade, 9th Division, 13th Corps.

Figure 2.51. Albert Lindley Lee began his military career in Kansas. Library of Congress.

During the assault on Vicksburg, Mississippi, on May 19, 1863, he was seriously wounded in the face.

Lee returned to duty in late summer. In August 1863 he was placed in command of the cavalry division of General Nathaniel Banks's 19th Corps in the Department of the Gulf and was involved in the ill-fated Red River Campaign (March 10, 1864–May 22, 1864).[271] He mustered out on May 4, 1865.

He did not, however, return to New York State. Instead, he settled in New Orleans, Louisiana, where he edited the *New Orleans Republican*. He was an eye witness to the New Orleans massacre, which occurred on July 30, 1866, as the Republican-led Louisiana Constitutional Convention met to enact measures to guarantee civil and political rights for African Americans. Former Confederate soldiers, aided by the local police, attacked both whites and blacks and killed several hundred people.[272]

It was in Louisiana that Lee met his future wife, Louisiana native Victorine Lind Foley (1830–December 29, 1918), reportedly the widow of a Confederate officer. She and Lee were married in Hoboken, New Jersey, on June 10, 1869.

Victorine was the mother of two children. In 1870 she and Albert lived in New Orleans with Albert II, aged two years, and Jacob, twelve days. Although Albert II was always identified as Lee's son, his birth date of May 11, 1868, makes that claim dubious. It is more likely that he was Foley's child.[273] Jacob, later known as Victor, died in Liverpool, England, at the age of twelve.

In 1880 the family resided in New York City but soon after moved to Europe, where they traveled widely. Lee was offered a position in the American Consulate in Paris but refused because he "didn't want to be tied down."[274] Not until 1890 did he and Victorine return to the United States permanently. He became an associate with Robert Goodbody and Company, bankers and stockbrokers, with which organization he was loosely affiliated until his death.[275]

Lee never actively participated in politics in later life, although in 1864 he was a nominee for the House of Representatives from Kansas and for the United States Senate from Louisiana in 1868.[276] He was, however, a staunch Republican. He was a member of the Loyal Legion, an organization for former Union officers. He also belonged to the Union League Club, a private social group in New York City, and Garfield Post No. 25 GAR in Wichita, Kansas. He and his brother, Horace Gaylord (November 4, 1837–March 24, 1904), a veteran of the 147th Regiment

NYSV, were enrolled the same date in late 1885, when Albert was visiting in the United States. The post's descriptive book does not provide an exact mustering in date.

In December 1907 Lee contracted a fatal case of pleurisy, dying on December 31 in New York City. His death was widely reported, but an interesting piece appeared in an unlikely source, the *Wall Street Journal*:

> By the death of Albert L. Lee, Wall Street loses one of its best representatives. He had retired from active participation in its work for some years, without, however, relinquishing all interest in its affairs. He had a wide and unobtrusive influence on the best minds of the city. He was modest, able, unprejudiced, and unaffected. His modesty can be gathered from the fact that men who had enjoyed his acquaintance for many years did not know that the unassuming, white-haired, courteous gentleman had been seriously wounded when leading his brigade at the assault on Vicksburg. Gen. Lee was not advertised on the front pages of the yellow press nor exploited by muck rake magazines, but he was a truer type of the Wall Street man than many who were better known.[277]

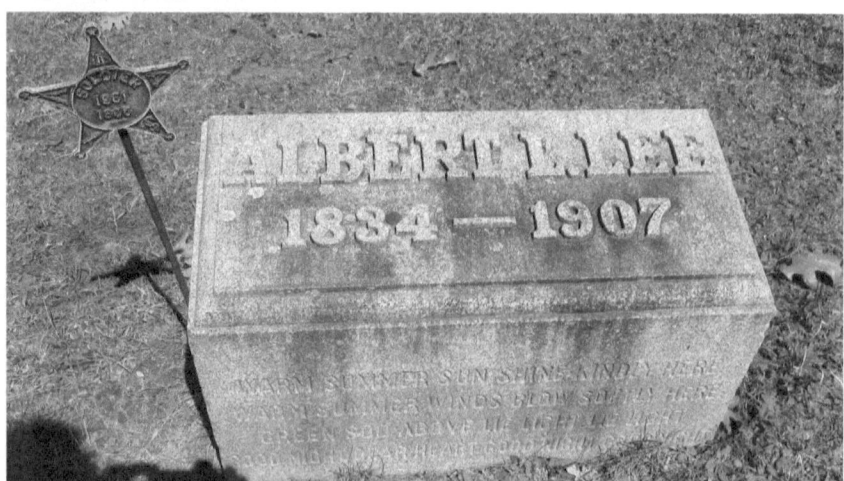

Figure 2.52. The inscription on General Lee's gravestone reads: "Warm summer sun shine kindly here, / Warm summer winds blow softly here, / Green sod above lie light, lie light, / Good night dear heart good night, good night." Author's collection.

Locally, however, little attention was paid to Lee's passing. A brief notice reported that his body had been sent to Fulton for spring burial.[278] Later in the month, Thomas H. Lake, a friend and fellow soldier, wrote a lengthy tribute to the man: "I have just been made aware of the death of . . . my former school mate, friend and Commander, Brigadier-General Albert L. Lee, than whom no braver man ever drew saber. He was kind and generous and born to command. He was, I believe, the only Brigadier-General of Oswego County. As chief of cavalry on Gen. N. P. Banks' staff, he was prominent in saving the army under General Banks from annihilation. The citizens of Fulton should well be proud of General Lee and his record."[279]

The apparent neglect of a native son would soon be remedied. Shortly before his death, Lee expressed a desire to construct some sort of public building in Fulton in memory of his father, Dr. Moses Lee, but died before he could make a final decision. When Victorine came to the city to superintend the placement of his monument, she announced that she was donating $30,000 to build a hospital for the citizens of Fulton.[280]

When the hospital was dedicated in 1910, a large celebration took place, complete with speeches lauding General Albert Lindley Lee, whose name was going to be attached to the building. One of the speakers that day was Daniel F. Kellogg, who spoke at length on the man's character:

> Like everyone and everything he will be forgotten. The story of his wit and grace and charm will be less and less told and will finally be heard no more. But in the hearts of those who knew him there will live while life lasts the thought of the rare and generous soul that dwelt in the frame so stately and urbane; and they will confess to themselves and to each other that if they could wring from the gods a gift dearer than any other for those who bear their name or in whose veins their blood shall run in years to come, it would be that upon them might rest something of the strong power of friendship, so winning and so true; the fine sensitiveness of perception and sympathy; of the hand of help stretched out with the giver veiling his face; the high resolves of honor; the fearless courage; the abiding common sense; the lambent humor; the fascination of manner that bound friends and passing acquaintances alike to enchantment; and the pure and sustained possession of an ideal American manhood that were true of Albert Lindley Lee.[281]

Figure 2.53. A. L. Lee Memorial Hospital served the greater Fulton community for over a century. Courtesy of the Friends of Fulton History.

Periodically, Victorine donated money and equipment to the hospital, promising that she would remember the facility in her will with a bequest of $50,000. When she died, and the will was publicized, however, it was disclosed that her grandchildren, Norman and Barbara, would inherit

Figure 2.54. Victorine Lee is buried beside her husband in Mt. Adnah Cemetery, Fulton, New York. Author's collection.

the entire estate, valued at $192,000. Neither her son, Albert II, nor the hospital received anything. The will was contested on the grounds that she had signed it fifty-six hours before her death and was probably incompetent to do so.[282] The grandchildren nevertheless prevailed.

Victorine died in New York City at the age of eighty-seven.[283] Her body was transported to Fulton and buried near the magnificent monument atop the hill in Mt. Adnah Cemetery.

Brigadier-General Albert Lindley Lee and Victorine Lind Foley Lee are buried in Mt. Adnah Cemetery, Fulton, New York, section 23.

James H. Lee

"Some are born great, some achieve greatness, and some have greatness thrust upon them." Thus says Malvolio, a character in William Shakespeare's comedy *Twelfth Night*. If anyone had greatness thrust upon him, it was James H. Lee, a recipient of the Congressional Medal of Honor.

James Lee was reportedly born in 1840 but his early life is cloaked in mystery. Depending on the year and the circumstance, he was born in Queens County, Suffolk County, Genesee County, or Onondaga County. It is generally agreed that his parents moved to Buffalo, Erie, New York, sometime between 1840 and 1850 and that by the time Lee was ten, he was an orphan. Thereafter, a family named Clark living in Baldwinsville allegedly adopted him. In 1855, the first year he appeared in the census records, he resided with Napoleon B. and Alpha A. Clark in Lysander, not Baldwinsville. He was not listed as a child but as a laborer, and his age was erroneously given as seventeen.

In 1859 James Lee embarked on a three-year journey in a whaling ship, and if the received information is correct, he was nearly killed in a fight on an unnamed island when he attempted to aid several shipmates. He was stabbed seven times and left for dead on the shore. Men sent to the island to retrieve his body discovered that he was still alive.[284]

The Civil War was in progress when he returned to the United States. In November 1861 he joined the crew of the *Robin Hood* at New London, Connecticut. The ship was being sent to Charleston, South Carolina, with a cargo of stones to be dumped into the harbor as part of a blockade. On January 10, 1862, he enlisted in the US Navy and was temporarily assigned to the *Ohio*. He transferred to the USS *Kearsarge* on January 23, 1862, serving on that ship until his discharge.

Lee was to have greatness thrust upon him on the morning of June 19, 1864. After months of chasing the CSS *Alabama*, responsible for sinking many Union ships, the *Kearsarge* destroyed the much larger vessel off the coast of Cherbourg, France.[285]

Lee, stationed at one of the guns below decks, described the battle in his diary:

> A steamer was now seen coming off Cherbourg harbor and she was soon made out to be the famous cruiser Alabama. We gave chase and at five minutes to eleven the battle began. Semmes opened the ball by firing seven shots at us before we replied. The firing was then kept up without intermission for one hour and five minutes, when we ceased firing for she had hauled down flag and fired a gun to windward as a token of defeat. They lowered a boat and put for us. We could then see she was sinking and in fifteen minutes the celebrated

Figure 2.55. The USS *Kearsarge* chased the CSS *Alabama* for months before sinking her off the coast of France. Courtesy of the Library of Congress.

rebel steamer was no more. It was just one hour and twenty minutes from the time the first shot was fired till the Alabama sank to rise no more . . . The greatest naval fight on record is ended and victory has perched on our banners. The Kearsarge will be a name that will be remembered for time immemorial . . . The first broadside from his starboard battery went over us. After that I had no time to watch the battle. I looked out for no one and dodged the shot and shells. I worked at my gun with far more coolness than I supposed I should have in a time like that, but after the first round I cared nothing about it.[286]

Later, he would be praised for that coolness under fire when recommended for the Medal of Honor.

The commendation, awarded under General Orders No. 45, stated: "[James H. Lee] served as seaman on board the U. S. S. Kearsarge when

Figure 2.56. James H. Lee never received his Medal of Honor. Courtesy of the American Numismatic Society Museum.

Notable Civil War Veterans of Oswego County | 109

Figure 2.57. The citation on the reverse of Lee's medal reads: "Personal Valor / James H. Lee / Seaman / USS Kearsarge / Destruction of the Alabama / June 19, 1864." Courtesy of the American Numismatic Society Museum.

she destroyed the Alabama off Cherbourg, 19 June 1864. Acting as sponger of the No. 1 gun, during this bitter engagement, Lee exhibited marked coolness and good conduct and was highly recommended for his gallantry under fire by the divisional officer." Lee, however, never received the Medal of Honor, which is located in the collection of the American Numismatic Society Museum in New York City.[287]

The artillery explosions that day ruptured Lee's right eardrum and he was discharged at Boston on November 30, 1864. Although this injury was serious, another more sinister health issue incurred while on active duty would ultimately claim his life.

By summer 1865 Lee had returned to New York State and was living in Sterling, Cayuga County.

James Lee married Julia Elizabeth Place (June 4, 1844–May 20, 1895), daughter of Oswego town residents Lyman Tripp Place (February 11, 1822–February 3, 1882) and Harriet E. Horton (June 9, 1812–February

Figure 2.58. James H. Lee succumbed to tuberculosis acquired while serving in the US Navy. Courtesy of the H. Lee White Maritime Museum.

7, 1861), on June 9, 1866. Until 1874 the couple resided in Sterling. They had no children.

In January 1872 Lee used his influence with Republican state legislators to secure a position as assistant Assembly door keeper.[288]

The couple became involved in the Grange movement which was organized on November 6, 1873. The first Grange established in Oswego County, Hope No. 14, was located in the town of Oswego, and James Lee was its first master.[289] He and Julia were the first state assistant stewards.[290] Lee was named Oswego County's first deputy state grange master and was responsible for organizing ten more chapters, including Sandy Creek and Volney, which were still active in 1990.[291]

When Lee's health no longer permitted him to be an active farmer, he and Julia moved to Oswego City, where he managed the Merchants' Hotel, located on the corner of West Second and Bridge Streets.[292]

At some point he joined Oswego Lodge No. 127 F&AM, but how active he was able to be is unknown. According to his obituary, he had ceased managing the hotel "when failing health caused him to give up any kind of active business."[293]

James H. Lee died on August 9, 1877.

Although his obituary claimed he had died of "brain fever," his friends were well aware that he had suffered from tuberculosis since his

Figure 2.59. Julia Place Lee took an active interest in the budding Grange movement. Courtesy of the H. Lee White Maritime Museum.

Figure 2.60. James H. Lee's government grave marker memorializes his MOH. Author's collection.

navy days. Julia applied for a widow's pension in 1889 and the extensive file proves categorically what had caused her husband's death. The pension, granted in 1890, was retroactive to August 9, 1877. She received eight dollars per month until March 19, 1886, when the monthly allotment rose to twelve dollars.

Lee's own application was denied because no records could be located to prove that he had contracted the disease in the line of duty. He clarified why he had not consulted a doctor: "On his papers he explained as the reason why he did not go into hospital, a note stating that it was regarded as shirking duty and therefore he would not go, but preferred to use such medicines as he had with him." Julia contacted her husband's old shipmates to obtain evidence for her claim. John Bickford gave an exact description of the disease's inception: "he caught a very heavy cold on a rainy night sitting in the boat waiting for the officers. Cold settled on his lungs and affected his bronical [sic] tubes which he had not got well of when he left the Kearsarge about November 1864."[294]

Figure 2.61. James and Julia Lee are buried in the Place family plot in Rural Cemetery, Oswego Town, New York. Author's collection.

Philo Wheeler, an Oswego town resident, added: "for the last five years of his life said Lee was unable to [do] any work & that affiant was present when Lee died & that he died of consumption."²⁹⁵

John A. Place testified that Lee had consulted several doctors about his condition. One of them, Dr. J. A. Milne, "gave him no hope of final recovery. Dr. Balcom with myself were with him when he died."²⁹⁶

Julia succumbed to peritonitis in Oswego City on May 20, 1895. An obituary cited her dedication to the Grange movement: "Mr. and Mrs. Lee were especially active and efficient in establishing the order of the Knights of Husbandry, or Grangers, and were charter members of Hope Grange of Southwest Oswego, in which they took a deep interest in the earlier days, and which has become one of the most flourishing organizations in this section of the state."²⁹⁷

James H. Lee was considered "a man of integrity and intelligence, and one of his distinguishing traits of character, when in health, was his untiring activity. He was resolute, earnest, and untiring in the discharge of every duty." When he learned that he had been recommended for the Medal of Honor, he "always modestly said that he did not know what he did during the battle to entitle him to it. But it was an honor of which any American citizen might feel very proud, to be singled out in a crew of over one hundred and sixty men, all told, and designated by the commander as one of the number entitled to special praise, where every man was a hero, where all fought with a coolness which won the admiration of the world."²⁹⁸

James H. Lee, Julia Elizabeth Place Lee, and her parents are buried in Rural Cemetery, town of Oswego, section Acre.

Lucius V. S. Mattison

Born to pioneer settlers in the town of Scriba, Lucius "Luke" Mattison lived a long and productive life as a citizen, soldier, and politician. Although a controversial figure, he was admired and esteemed as a leading member of the greater Oswego community.

L. V. S. came into this world on November 21, 1842, a son of Truman Mattison (September 14, 1812–February 11, 1893) and Amelia Sterns (1813–1882).²⁹⁹ He grew up on the family farm but his career aspirations were evident in 1860 when he applied to Secretary of War J. B. Floyd for an appointment to West Point Military Academy. After listing his educational qualifications, he wrote: "I was brought up to labor and feel myself constitutionally prepared to withstand all the privations of the strictest military discipline."[300] It is unknown what, if any, response the young man received, but he did not have to wait long for the opportunity to join the military.

In August 1861 Oswego County raised the 81st Regiment. L. V. S. was mustered in as a private on September 14 and assigned to Co. D. He reenlisted when the unit was reorganized as a veteran regiment.[301] Over four years of service, he progressed through the ranks until he was promoted to lieutenant colonel on March 1, 1865.

The 81st Regiment participated in battles such as Malvern Hill, Fair Oaks, Cold Harbor, and the long siege of Petersburg. The regiment lost many men, and every year the surviving veterans remembered the bloody battle of Cold Harbor, fought on June 3, 1864: "The histories of the war show that in the battle of Cold Harbor the Eighty-first New York lost more men per capita than any regiment in the [18th] corps which participated in the engagement."[302] When Richmond fell on

Figure 2.62. Lucius V. S. Mattison's fondest desire as a young man was to enter the military. Courtesy of the Scriba Historical Society.

April 3, 1865, the 81st was the first regiment to enter the city. Mattison personally tore down the Confederate flag and replaced it with the stars and stripes. He also liberated about four hundred Union soldiers from Thunder Castle and Libby Prison, taking with him the keys to those places when he left.[303]

The 81st was present at Appomattox on April 9, 1865, when General Robert E. Lee surrendered.

After the war, Mattison returned to Oswego County. He wanted to enter the Regular Army and sent a letter to Secretary of War Edward Stanton on December 12, 1865, requesting a commission as a captain. To bolster his application, he prevailed upon his congressman, DeWitt

Figure 2.63. These keys are reputedly those taken by Colonel Mattison after the 81st Regiment liberated the Union prisoners in Castle Thunder and Libby Prison. Courtesy of Walnutts Antiques.

Clinton Littlejohn, and his state senator, Cheney Ames, to write recommendation letters.[304] Apparently nothing came of this request.

Mattison studied civil engineering and in 1870 was a foreman on the railroad. He later became a construction supervisor for the New York State Capitol Building. He was also named assistant supervisor for the construction of an industrial school for the Elmira Reformatory.[305]

He originally was a member of Rensselaer Bailey Post No. 19 GAR. Later he joined John D. O'Brian Post No. 65 in Oswego, chartered on August 5, 1878. In 1879, he was appointed to a committee to find all the graves of Union soldiers in Oswego County so those without family gravestones might be furnished a government marker.[306] At an unspecified date in 1887, he transferred his membership to Lewis B. Porter Post No. 573 in Scriba, New York, and served as its commander for twenty-five consecutive years.[307]

His GAR membership led to state offices. In 1903 he withdrew from the race for senior vice-commander in the New York Department. He was instead appointed chair of the Council of Administration and elected a delegate to the national encampment.[308] He was selected for the National Council of Administration in 1906.[309] This appointment was significant because, as pointed out in the article, this body "has legislative power from encampment to encampment."

Mattison also took an interest in politics. A short article appearing in an Oswego newspaper reported: "L. V. S. Mattison of Oswego is a member of the 'Independent Citizens' Association' a new political party formed in New York yesterday."[310] In the main, however, he was a staunch Republican who regularly supported his party's candidates on all levels. In 1878 and in 1889, for example, he was chosen as a delegate from Scriba to the Republican State Convention.[311] For twelve years he held a political appointment as assistant librarian in the New York State Senate Chamber.[312]

Other civic activities included memberships in Frontier City Lodge No. 422 F&AM and in the Old Settlers' Association of Oswego County. (See Francis C. Squires's section later in this chapter.) He was president of the 81st Regiment's Veterans' Volunteer Association for several terms and regularly attended annual reunions.[313]

While Mattison's standing in the community was on the rise, his domestic situation was on the decline. At an unknown date after the 1865 New York census was taken, he married Caroline "Carrie" A. Gillmore (1847–August 31, 1891). In 1875 he and Carrie lived in her parents' home in Oswego. The couple subsequently separated. Mattison claimed he obtained a divorce from Carrie in March 1877 in Illinois, later learning that it might not be valid in New York State. He had gone to Illinois, he alleged, "in accordance with the wishes of his wife who desired to avoid publicity here where she and her family are known." Later that year he came into possession of a letter addressed to Mrs. L. V. S. Mattison and "paying no particular attention to the addressee, he tore the envelope open and found that the letter was not for him but for her." After making a copy of what he deemed evidence of an "improper intimacy" between Carrie and the unnamed correspondent, he returned the letter to the carrier with directions to take it to "Mrs. Carrie A. Gillmore." Carrie, angered that her husband had not only received but had opened her mail, had him arrested. The affair made news all over the country, and the hearing officer initially ruled that opening a spouse's mail was illegal.[314] The case was heard in Syracuse, and on December

Figure 2.64. Caroline Gillmore Mattison Search is buried with her parents in Riverside Cemetery, Scriba, New York. Author's collection.

23, 1878, all charges were dismissed "on the ground that the evidence showed the defendant opened the letter by mistake."³¹⁵

Carrie herself attempted to obtain a divorce, but the suit was dismissed because the referee "finds no cause of action."³¹⁶ Ultimately, however, the couple obtained what both had so fervently desired: "At a special term of the supreme court for the third judicial district, Justice T. R. Westbrook, presiding, held in Kingston, Ulster county, on the 20th of July [1881], a decree of absolute divorce was granted Col. L. V. S. Mattison, of Scriba, against his wife, Carrie Gilmore [sic] Mattison."³¹⁷ At the time, Carrie and her parents, Abner K. Gillmore (1817–February 7, 1896) and Augusta M. Reed (1828–March 3, 1901), were living in Cleveland, Cuyahoga, Ohio. It is difficult not to speculate that they were in Ohio for a reason. According to the marriage laws of New York State, the only two grounds for divorce at that time were adultery and desertion. It may be argued that Carrie and her parents had moved to Ohio so that Mattison might argue that she had abandoned him.

Figure 2.65. Colonel Mattison and his second wife, Mary Sinclair Oliver, died within a short time of each other. Author's collection.

On August 30, 1884, Carrie married Edward Search, about whom nothing is known, in Cleveland. She died in Oswego on August 31, 1891.[318]

Mary Sinclair Oliver, born in 1849, and Lucius Mattison were married on January 17, 1882. They were the parents of Elizabeth "Bessie" M. (1884–1971). Mary died in Oswego on March 4, 1909.[319] Her husband followed her a little more than a year later, on June 17, 1910.

Mattison's death was widely noted.[320] A local obituary paid glowing tribute to the man and reviewed his life and career:

> Few men in the county were better known or had a larger number of acquaintances than Colonel Mattison. For twenty-five years in succession he had been commander of Post Porter, No. 573, G. A. R., of Scriba, and every encampment

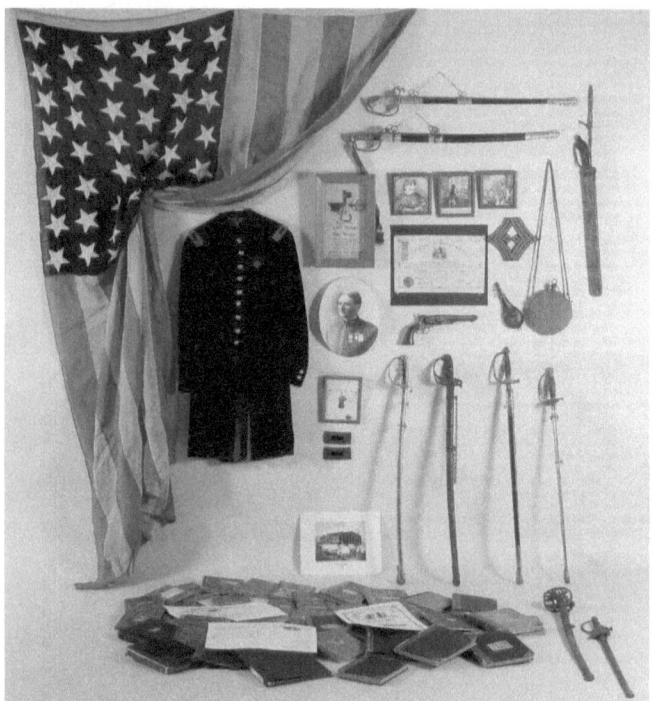

Figure 2.66. This collection of Mattison memorabilia once belonged to his only child, Elizabeth M. Scoville. Courtesy of www.Invaluable.com.

and reunion of prominence found Colonel Mattison one of the conspicuous figures. He . . . was deeply interested in the preserving of historic records relating to the county and its affairs . . . The only surviving relative is a daughter, Mrs. Charles Scoville of this city. The funeral will be held Monday with military honors.[321]

Colonel Mattison, Mary S. Oliver Mattison, and Elizabeth Mattison Scoville are buried in Riverside Cemetery, section G. Caroline Gillmore Mattison Search, her parents, and several siblings are buried in section T.

James A. McKinley

Born in Canada of Irish stock, James A. McKinley repaid his adopted country's opportunities with over fifty years of hard work, civic responsibility, and military service, defending an ideal dear to the hearts of all Irish people: freedom.

McKinley was born in August 1837 in Kingston, Ontario, Canada, a son of John McKinley (1801–June 22, 1877) and Sarah Caffrey (1811–1847). He immigrated to the United States in 1850 with a brother, William Patrick (September 11, 1831–September 21, 1889).[322] James McKinley became a blacksmith. In 1862 he married Jane Reid (September 1836–March 19, 1917), a native of Ireland who had immigrated to the United States as a young girl. They were the parents of seven known children: Catherine "Kate" A. (*ca.* 1865–December 11, 1934), unmarried; Sarah F. (1867–December 25, 1943), unmarried; William A. (1868–October 29, 1944), unmarried; Mary E. (1871–July 29, 1920), unmarried; Robert Emmett (1873–November 10, 1944) married Eva B. Elmhurst (October 1883–September 26, 1922) on July 24, 1907; Louise (1877–March 27, 1965) married Colonel Alfred Ballin (June 30, 1874–January 30, 1946) on June 15, 1909; and Edward James (November 1, 1886–May 13, 1949), unmarried.

Recruiting for the 147th Regiment was in full force in the late summer of 1862. A compulsory draft loomed on the horizon, and potential volunteers were promised substantial bounties, a perquisite unavailable to draftees. The local newspapers supported the recruitment efforts with stories about rallies and the benefits of enlisting:

Gov. Morgan announces by proclamation that the State bounty of fifty dollars will be continued to those who volunteer in the new regiment until Saturday, the 6th day of September, and that after that day it will be paid only to those who enlist for three years to fill up the old regiments. All, therefore, who desire to secure the State, County, and city Bounty, amounting to one hundred and thirty dollars, besides the one hundred dollars Government bounty at the end of the war, *should enlist in our new regiment immediately.* Let the word go forth; let it be rung in every neighborhood, on every street corner, at every household shrine: *the fourth Oswego Regiment must be completed this week!* . . . Unless our quota is raised *drafting will take place in this county.* Let no man say after he is drafted, that he did not have fair warning. Volunteering must be hurried forward with more briskness and enthusiasm now than ever. Every man to the work. Let it be the great business of the week. Hurry up the enlistments. The wounded and dying soldiers on the field cry for help. A bleeding country demands instant and tremendous efforts and sacrifices for its salvation. To the work, then; to the work! Work with your money, work with your brains,—work up our new volunteer force to a full regiment and running over, before Monday morning next.[323]

James A. McKinley answered that call, enlisting and mustering into Co. I on September 11, 1862, as a first lieutenant. He was promoted to captain on July 22, 1863, shortly after the battle of Gettysburg, holding that rank when he mustered out on June 7, 1865.

At the war's end, McKinley returned to Oswego City, his wife, and his blacksmithing business. In 1885 he circulated a petition for an appointment as a special treasury agent, from which nothing apparently happened.[324] His interest in law enforcement bore fruit in 1887 when he passed the Civil Service examination and was appointed a guard at Auburn State Prison.[325] For some unexplained reason he did not actually begin his employment until February 1888.[326] In May he had the misfortune to be the guard on duty when Harry W. Phillips, sentenced to three years for larceny, escaped. Published reports revealed that Phillips enjoyed a freedom not accorded most prisoners because he was the warden's cook. (The warden was not at the prison when the escape occurred, arriving from a vacation shortly thereafter.) Phillips availed himself of a set of the warden's clothing and, when McKinley was distracted by a call from the prison hospital, climbed over the wall. Several days later he was captured, having injured himself severely when he fell, and returned to the prison.[327]

McKinley was suspended from duty pending an investigation into the escape.[328] How long his suspension lasted is unknown, but since a death notice published in many newspapers across the state revealed he had once been assistant warden at the facility, it was probably of short duration.[329]

Other postwar occupations were described in his obituaries:

> With the close of the war Captain McKinley returned to this city and became interested in canal boats. For several years he conducted these boats successfully and retired to take a position, superintending the construction of bridges and culverts on the old Midland railroad at Norwich, where for several years he made his home. Returning to this city he entered the employ of the R. W. & O. road and was in the company's black-smith shop, where he remained until a few years ago, when he resigned, owing to failing health and has since lived quietly at home.[330]

Early on, McKinley became involved with politics, although as a Democrat his hopes of holding public office in Oswego County were slight. He ran for county treasurer and ward supervisor, losing both contests. He was frequently chosen as a delegate for his party's local conventions. In 1880 he was associated with a group of Democrats who supported Winfield Scott Hancock for president.[331]

His involvement as a volunteer fireman began soon after he arrived in Oswego, evidenced by an advertisement for a fundraiser in 1853 for which McKinley was a member of the arrangements committee.[332] In 1862, shortly before entering the military, he was elected second assistant engineer without opposition.[333] In 1885 the Oswego Common Council appointed him to the city's fire council.[334]

McKinley was a member of John D. O'Brian Post No. 65 GAR but his real love was the 147th Veterans' Association in which he was very active. In 1879 he served on the group's executive committee, and in 1896 he was president.[335] It was in connection with the 147th Veterans'

Association that he participated in a momentous occasion. On June 25, 1886, the organization appointed a committee to attend a reunion in Gettysburg "with instructions to locate and mark the several positions held by the regiment during the battle and to obtain so far as possible information of members of the several companies who were buried on the field in the National Cemetery there and to report to the organization upon their return."[336]

Two years later McKinley was a member of the delegation which traveled to Gettysburg for the dedication of the regimental monument.

The ceremony, originally planned for July 1, was delayed until July 3 due to transportation problems.[337]

Figure 2.67. Veterans of the 147th Regiment raised the money to have this monument built and erected near the spot on the Gettysburg battlefield where they held the line against advancing Confederate forces on July 1, 1863. Courtesy of Darlene Woolson.

McKinley returned to Gettysburg in 1893 as part of a large delegation of veterans invited to attend the unveiling and dedication of the New York State monument. The event drew participants from all over the country. An article published in the local press listed the names of veterans from the 147th who were planning to attend.[338]

James McKinley suffered no injuries during the war, and although he had applied for and obtained a pension in 1880, he claimed no disability in 1890. Nevertheless he was a sick man, suffering from what was called long-term "stomach trouble." He died on October 25, 1905, at his home in Oswego City. An anonymous correspondent composed a heartfelt eulogy:

> By the death of Captain James A. McKinley Oswego loses one of her most distinguished veterans. Probably no soldier of our country had a more creditable record. As a member of the famous 147th New York Volunteers, he did his full share in make the fighting record. He was a typical volunteer soldier. Brave, kind hearted, cool when coolness was required, fiery as Sheridan when dash and daring were called for, quick to take offense, but quicker still to apologize if he was in the wrong. A loveable man and a good citizen . . . Hail and farewell to you, Captain James.[339]

Figure 2.68. James McKinley led an interesting and varied life in Oswego. Author's collection.

Figure 2.69. Jane Reid McKinley lies next to her husband and is surrounded by several of their children in St. Peter's Cemetery, Oswego. Author's collection.

Jane McKinley outlived her husband by many years:

Jane McKinley, widow of Captain James A. McKinley, died late last night at her home . . . after an illness of about three months. Mrs. McKinley was born near the city of Limerick, Ireland, coming to Oswego with her parents seventy years ago . . . She was a member of St. Mary's Church and the League of Prayer. While the announcement of her death has been expected at almost any time for the past week or two, it nevertheless came as a shock to many friends.[340]

Captain James A. McKinley and Jane Reid McKinley, as well as their children, Catherine A., Edward J., Mary E., Robert Emmett, Sarah F., and William A., are buried in St. Peter's Cemetery, Oswego, New York, section WV. Louise and Colonel Alfred Ballin are buried in Arlington National Cemetery.

Daniel McSweeney

Daniel McSweeney's long life began in Ireland and ended in Pittsburgh, Pennsylvania. Along the way he would have enough adventures for several lifetimes. The son of Daniel McSweeney (1807–July 2, 1862) and Mary A. Brennan (1815–January 19, 1904), he immigrated with his parents to the United States *ca.* 1850 and became a naturalized citizen in 1862.

McSweeney, who enlisted in the 21st "Barnes" Battery, NY LA, on September 11, 1862, was captured by the Confederates near Port Hudson, Louisiana, on February 28, 1864, and sent to Andersonville. He suffered the horrors of that prison until it was evacuated later that year. Where he was sent subsequently is unknown, but according to his muster card he was exchanged in January 1865. After recovering, he returned to his unit and was discharged from the service on September 8, 1865.

For the next fifteen years, Daniel lived with his mother and brothers in Oswego City where he ran a grocery store. He was active in John D. O'Brian Post No. 65 GAR and in St. Patrick's Society, of which he was president in 1874.[341]

His life would change dramatically in late summer of 1879 when a gang of counterfeiters began circulating fake coins and bills throughout the county. Known as the Ingersoll Gang, the forgers soon attracted the attention of the United States Secret Service. McSweeney became involved because one of his workers, Frank Gibson, confessed to him that he had attempted to pass off forged coins as change.

Figure 2.70. Daniel McSweeney spent many months in Andersonville POW camp. Courtesy of the New York State Military Museum.

His role in uncovering the ring was as an "amateur detective" but because of his help, the culprits were arrested in late January 1880 and put on trial. For weeks the trial and its colorful characters dominated the news.[342]

McSweeney was praised for his role in breaking up the gang, and shortly thereafter a brief newspaper article revealed he was changing his occupation: "Daniel McSweeney, the special United States detective who was largely instrumental in ferreting out the Ingersoll counterfeiters, will retire from the grocery business next week. It is understood that he will enter the United States secret service."[343]

Another change in the newly minted Secret Service agent's life took place soon thereafter. On February 15, 1882, he and Mary H. Sheridan were married in St. Mary's Church in Oswego. Mary, daughter of Michael Sheridan (1810–November 13, 1888) and Ann _____ (1815–ca. 1880), was born in Oswego City on March 29, 1849. In 1900 she reported that she had borne six children, four of whom survived: Kathleen (May 21, 1883–February 10, 1960), Daniel Sheridan (July 18, 1886–January 2, 1965), Claire Alma (December 10, 1890–*post* 1965), and Mary H. (December 16, 1891–July 6, 1948). The daughters all became school teachers in Pittsburgh, Pennsylvania. Daniel Sheridan went into advertising. He apparently was married when he registered for the draft in 1917, but his wife's name is unknown. She never appeared in any census records with him, although his death certificate described him as a widower.

It was not long before McSweeney's name appeared again, this time as a bona fide Secret Service agent. As reported by Secret Service Chief A. L. Drummond,

> On Thanksgiving day, 1880, I went down to Brockway's hiding place in the woods, near Jamaica, L. I. I was accompanied by officers James J. Scanlon and Daniel McSweeney. We dug up twenty-two steel and copper plates, about $50,000 in counterfeit $100 national bank notes and several hundred sheets of fiber paper. Among the plates were those used in printing the 6 per cent bonds found on Doyle, and also the plate for a $1,000 5-20 coupon bond, none of which had yet been printed.[344]

In the ensuing years McSweeney's name was frequently associated with the federal government's attempts to smash counterfeiting rings. In

1881 he was instrumental in closing down a ring in New York City: "A dispatch from Daniel McSweeney to undersheriff McElroy today, says: 'We have met the enemy, and they are ours.' This is understood to refer to the capture of a large gang of counterfeiters by secret service officers in New York, which was concluded this morning. The operation and result were similar to those in the case of the Oswego gang of counterfeiters."[345] "Boston Buck," described as an "expert old counterfeiter," was brought down through the efforts of Agent McSweeney and his assistants in 1885.[346] McSweeney participated in the arrest of Chauncey Marble and Elizabeth Grant for passing counterfeit coins in 1891.[347] In 1893 he represented the US Treasury Department during the prosecution of William Mulcahy, an Oswego County resident, also charged with passing counterfeit coins.[348]

Agent McSweeney left the United States Secret Service during the mid-1890s and established a private detective firm known as Barring and McSweeney. Strikes by coal miners were then a common occurrence, and one of the firm's best known cases involved solving the mystery of the explosion of a "Hungarian shanty" in which a man was severely injured and a boy was killed.[349] In 1896 Barring and McSweeney agents infiltrated an illegal gambling establishment.[350]

Daniel and Mary McSweeney lived in different places throughout their marriage. Kathleen was born in New York City. The family resided in Oswego in 1892 and in Baldwin, Allegheny, Pennsylvania, in 1900 and 1910. By 1918 when Mary died, the family had settled in Pittsburgh. The three daughters were teachers and Daniel Sheridan was a clerk in a newspaper office.

Mary died unexpectedly of pneumonia on February 6, 1918. An obituary published in an Oswego newspaper detailed her life:

> Mrs. McSweeney was born in this city, the daughter of the late Mr. and Mrs. Michael Sheridan. She was a devoted attendant of St. Mary's church and her early education was obtained at St. Mary's school after which she attended a school at Savannah, Ga., where she completed her education . . . During her life time, Mrs. McSweeney kept up her interest in Oswego and the friends of her girlhood still here [were] looking forward with pleasure to an extended visit which she contemplated making here the coming summer . . . Because of unsettled weather conditions the funeral will be held in Pittsburgh.

Later in the season the remains will be brought to this city and laid at rest in St. Paul's Cemetery.[351]

Mary's body was put in the vault of Calvary Cemetery, Pittsburgh. Despite what was reported in her obituary, her body was not delivered to Oswego until 1919, apparently because "under the law there a year had to elapse before the removal of the body was allowed."[352]

Daniel McSweeney was still working when his wife died. According to the 1920 census he was a clerk for a coal company. An obituary claimed he was a weigh master for the Pittsburgh Coal Company. On July 29, 1920, at the age of seventy-five, he fell down a mine shaft at Montour, Pennsylvania. He died on August 7, 1920. His death certificate revealed he had suffered a broken femur but the cause of death was pneumonia.[353] An interesting obituary reviewed his life:

Daniel J. McSweeney, formerly of this city, died in a Pittsburgh, Pa. hospital on Saturday night from injuries sustained

Figure 2.71. Although Mary Sheridan McSweeney died in Pittsburg, Pennsylvania, she was buried in her hometown, Oswego City. Author's collection.

Figure 2.72. After Daniel McSweeney was fatally injured when he fell down an elevator shaft, his body was returned to Oswego for burial. Author's collection.

from falling from a case in a mine shaft . . . Years ago, Mr. McSweeney was in the grocery business at East Second and Bridge streets. Later he was in the United States Secret Service and made a wide reputation as a detective. He broke up many counterfeiting gangs. After retiring from the United States service he was an inspector for several large coal companies in the Pittsburgh district . . . His remains will arrive here on Wednesday and the funeral will be held that day"[354]

Daniel McSweeney, Mary H. Sheridan McSweeney, and their daughter, Mary H. McSweeney, are buried in St. Paul's Cemetery, Oswego City, section K.

Oliver Burrill Mowry

Not quite seventeen years old when he enlisted in the Union army, Oliver Burrill Mowry lived long enough to bury all his friends and comrades in arms. He was the last surviving Civil War veteran in Oswego County.

Oliver Mowry was born on November 8, 1847, in the town of Richland, New York, to Ephraim D. Mowry (July 23, 1827–April 17, 1912) and Helen Hannah Peckham (1821–August 19, 1883). He and his siblings grew up on the family farm. In 1865 he was a cheese box maker.

Shortly before he died, he dictated to his granddaughter, Ella Mowry, his memories of time spent in the service of the United States. He enlisted on August 28, 1864, claiming to be seventeen, and mustered into Co. G, 184th Regiment. He freely admitted that the $1,000 bounty heightened his patriotic fervor. Much of the memoir deals with travel and camp life. Mowry's company saw no actual combat, spending its time on picket duty in the waning months of the war. One incident, however, illustrates the pluck and intelligence he and a "chum," Delano Moody, possessed:

> One day I was talking with one of the cavalrymen and he showed me a book of army regulations and all of the drill tactics in it. I asked him if I could take it and he said that I could have it as they had no use for it. My chum and I looked through it and became very interested in the flag drill. We thought that we could learn it for our own amusement, so we made some little flags to signal across the tent and soon became experts at it . . . We were acting as a guard between the Northern and Southern Armies. Some time in February the flag sergeant came down from the Fort to Colonel Robinson and said that one of his men was sick; he had flagged City Point for a man but there was none available. Someone said that there were one or two men in the regiment who had "played" at flagging but did not know how good they were. The sergeant said he wanted to take one of the men back with him and if he was good he would keep him . . . I told my chum to go . . . Two weeks after his visit the Sergeant came down again; another man was "laid-up" with eye strain and he wanted me to go up there. I said I would be glad to go if the Colonel would let me; the Colonel did let me go so my "buddy" and I were together again. So you can see what we commenced in fun turned out well for us.[355]

LAST LIVING VETERAN

OLIVER B. MOWRY

Figure 2.73. Oliver Mowry was the last Civil War veteran in Oswego County. Courtesy of the *Mexico Independent*.

Oliver Mowry mustered out in June 1865. He finished school and for a time was a teacher himself. One of his students was Ella Albertine Calkins (July 14, 1854–March 25, 1940). On July 22, 1871, they were married in a double wedding with two friends, Cordelia "Delia" LeRoy and John Mattison.[356] In time they produced eight children, seven of whom survived to adulthood. Maude M. (June 25, 1874–January 27, 1927) married William Lyman Whitney (September 21, 1873–August 20, 1961) on November 24, 1897. Dr. Earl Albert (February 14, 1876–October 12, 1942) married Margaret S. Brennan (May 20, 1877–December 19, 1956) on September 27, 1905. Julia Belle (April 3, 1880–September 22, 1935) married Grant George Edick (April 30, 1881–April 22, 1939) on December 18, 1902. Ethelyn F. (February 14, 1888–June 17, 1970) and Bessie E. (December 3, 1889–May 16, 1976) were unmarried. Charles Erwin (September 26, 1893–April 26, 1969) married Rena Mae Halsey (January 12, 1897–March 27, 1996) on March 17, 1917. Courtland "Court" McKinley (December 10, 1896–October 26, 1965) married Leila Margaret White (October 12, 1899–February 13, 1988) on July 26, 1927. The eighth child is unidentified and probably died soon after birth.

A farmer for much of his life, Oliver Mowry owned a herd of prize Holstein cows and was noted for his raspberries and apples. He was a longtime member of the Oswego County Holstein Club and was honored in 1934 for being the group's oldest member.[357]

Also active in Mexico Grange No. 218, of which he was a charter member, Mowry was appointed in 1894 to be deputy and inspector of all Granges in Oswego County. He sang in the choir for the North Mexico Methodist Church and was a member of the Mexico Cornet Band.

He belonged to a men's bridge club, which met regularly.

His favorite organization, however, was the GAR. He originally was a member of J. B. Butler Post No. 111 in Pulaski, New York, but in 1918 transferred to Melzar Richards Post No. 367, of which he was the last commander and the last surviving member.[358]

Mowry's attendance at the Gettysburg reunion in 1938 was memorable:

Figure 2.74. Oliver Mowry's interests included membership in the Mexico Cornet Band. Courtesy of *Grip's Historical Souvenir of Mexico*.

The biggest thrill that 91-year-old Civil War veteran Oliver B. Mowry experienced in attending the 75th anniversary of the Battle of Gettysburg was a ride in a police car. Mowry said the bus in which he was riding to the Oak Hill peace memorial dedication became bogged down in traffic. So he and five other union army veterans "commandeered" a passing police car. "The ride in that Black Maria was one of the fastest I ever had." Mowry added, "It was one of the highlights of an eventful trip. We sure rode in style."[359]

His excitement at the adventure was noted in another article: "'That spree,' said Mrs. Mowry, 'has made him 10 years younger.'"[360]

In addition to the GAR, Mowry was active in the Oswego County Civil War Veterans' Association and was president when he died in 1940. In previous years, he had held the office of vice president and had been called upon to preside at sessions when the current leader was too ill to attend. When the group assembled in 1937, thirteen members were living but only six were healthy enough to travel to the meeting.[361]

For years he and the dwindling number of veterans were honored guests at Memorial Day celebrations and Fourth of July parades. He was frequently called upon for remarks or recitations.

As early as 1928 Mowry was the only man left of nineteen who had served from Holmesville (Fernwood).[362] More comrades answered "the last roll call" until, with the passing of William H. Belchamber (January 23, 1847–July 21, 1940), Mowry became the county's last Civil War veteran.

Ella Mowry also had an interesting life. As previously stated, Oliver Mowry had been her teacher. When the couple celebrated their sixty-seventh wedding anniversary, Ella "with a twinkle in her eye" quipped, "I met him when I was going to school to him. He tried to boss me then and he's still trying to do the same thing." She taught in local schools for twenty years: "Her first school was in Albion where she obtained a position after receiving her teaching certificate when only 15 years of age. She was teaching in the Manwarren district when she married Mr. Mowry at the age of 17."[363] Ella died "after a long illness" on March 25, 1940.[364]

Seven months later, Oliver Mowry suffered a series of strokes which ultimately proved fatal. Because he was the last Oswego County Civil War veteran his death was especially meaningful and his funeral was largely attended by local military orders, including several American

Figure 2.75. Ella Calkins Mowry taught school for many years in addition to rearing a large family. Author's collection.

Legion posts and the Daughters of Union Veterans of the Civil War, of which he was an honorary member:

> A soldier's burial was given the last member of the once great group of Oswego County men who fought in the Civil War, Sunday afternoon when the soft notes of the bugle sounded Taps over the last resting place of Oliver Burrill Mowry . . . the last Boy of Blue in the county . . . Mr. Mowry died Friday afternoon from the effects of a third stroke suffered a week ago Tuesday. He had survived two earlier strokes in the summer and was looking forward to voting in the fall election. He had not missed casting his vote for president since 1865 when he voted for Lincoln by soldier's franchise because he was below the age of 21 . . . Active until struck down by the summer's illness, Mr. Mowry continued to take an active participation in community and home affairs, taking particular interest and work in his garden which became his hobby in recent years . . . His erect figure and snow white head will be missed in future Memorial Day parades which were some of the highlights of his life recently. For the past

Figure 2.76. Oliver Mowry is buried next to Ella in Daysville Cemetery. Author's collection.

years, his position as the village's last Civil War veteran earned him the position of honor in the annual parade and observance at the village soldier's monument . . . Mr. Mowry was an active member of patriotic and civic organizations . . . In a touching ceremony, the American flag which draped the casket was removed by members of the firing squad, folded horizontally and given to the chaplain, Rev. Barnard, who presented it to Dr. Mowry, oldest son of Mr. Mowry.[365]

Oliver Burrill Mowry, Ella Albertine Calkins Mowry, and several of their children are buried in Daysville Cemetery, town of Richland, New York, section 4.

Lawson Read Muzzy

In the annals of Oswego County newspaper publishing, Lawson Read Muzzy must be counted among the foremost editors. A long tenure with the *Pulaski Democrat* earned him the respect and admiration of all his peers in the business.

He began life in Deep River, Middlesex, Connecticut, when his father, Reverend Lawson Muzzy (January 12, 1812–June 29, 1877), a Baptist minister, was the preacher there. His mother, Orilla Read (1817–October 4, 1876), gave birth to him on March 3, 1846.

The Muzzy family resided in Adams, Jefferson County, New York, during the Civil War. Young Lawson, sometimes known as Read, was enrolled and mustered into Co. C, 186th Regiment at Adams on September 7, 1864. At the time he worked in a grocery store. He received a bounty of $1,000 for enlisting.[366] Although only active for a year, the 186th engaged in the siege of Petersburg; participated in the battle before Petersburg on April 2, 1865; and occupied the city on April 3. The regiment was involved in the Appomattox Campaign which culminated with General Lee's surrender. The soldiers mustered out on June 6, 1865, at Alexandria, Virginia.

By 1867 Lawson Muzzy had settled in Mexico, New York, and was learning the printing business from Henry Humphries, owner/editor of the *Mexico Independent*. When the proprietor of the *Pulaski Democrat* died in 1869, Muzzy bought that newspaper and embarked on a publishing career which would extend until October 1895.

Lawson Muzzy married Alma "Allie" P. Witt in Northville, Cayuga, New York, on June 23, 1869. He received some good-natured teasing from his colleagues concerning this happy event:

> Yesterday afternoon a young man named Lawson R. Muzzy, an employe [sic] in the office, left home somewhat suddenly, carpet bag in hand, wending his way towards the Depot. It appears that he took the 3:22 train for Oswego, but we have seen nor heard nothing of him since, and what has become of him is a mystery . . . Mr. M. has always borne the best of character. We have ever found him prompt and faithful in the discharge of all his duties, never absenting himself from business without the best of reasons for so doing; it is no wonder, therefore, that his sudden and unlooked-for disappearance creates much surprise . . . We have, for some time past, observed that he was a little absent-minded, but didn't think it anything very strange, as most young men of his age and temperament are prone to be so at times. We have thought the matter over a good deal, and talked with the

office hands about it, and have come to the conclusion that he is about to do some rash thing. For quite a while past he has been heard to mumble to himself "Northville," "silk hat," "patent leather boots," "superfine black cloth coat," "white satin vest," "diamond ring," "O speed the time, the *blessed* time when . . ." and other singular phrases . . . It would not, therefore, much surprise us to learn that he is on his way to Northville for his "Dear Mary Jane," and that he is about to desert the ranks of bachelors and go over to the benedicts. If so important and sensible a step be taken by him, many will be the wishes for a long, useful and joyous life to him and his fair young bride.[367]

The merriment continued in the next issue, wherein the marriage was announced and the couple wished "a long life and as much happiness as is good for them."[368]

Lawson and Alma Muzzy became community stalwarts in Pulaski. Both were devout Baptists and took an active role in their church life. Of Alma it was said,

> She was an ardent worker in her church and no little credit is her due for the success of the enterprise which brought into existence the beautiful church edifice which is the house of worship for the Baptist society of this village. Her hand was ever extended to aid every interest of the church and her devotion to her friends and family was a marked characteristic of her great heart for others, and so long as her health would permit she was generous in her gifts of time and means to every worthy cause.[369]

Lawson Muzzy, in addition to his professional obligations, was active in J. B. Butler Post No. 111 GAR, Pulaski Lodge No. 415 F&AM, and Pulaski Chapter No. 279 RAM. He was a staunch Republican, serving two terms as town of Richland supervisor. In 1889 President Benjamin Harrison appointed him Pulaski village postmaster, a position he held for four years.

A tale about the disuse of the stove pipe hat provided a humorous description of the man:

LAWSON R. MUZZY

Figure 2.77. Lawson Read Muzzy was the long-time editor of the *Pulaski Democrat*. Courtesy of the *Pulaski Democrat*.

There was a time when the editor of the Democrat, the late Lawson R. Muzzy, never left the sanctum under any other cover than a tall hat. He wore that style of hat even after the bicycle craze struck this town and a farmer tells us he will never forget seeing Mr. Muzzy lose his pedals going down a hill. He was dressed in Prince Albert and high hat and when he came down that hill, feet extended to each side and gripping his handlebars like mad, his eyes set and his heart in his mouth, he made a good picture for Life.[370]

The Muzzys were the parents of five children, only one of whom survived infancy. Beulah (June 10, 1870–May 25, 1932) married Dr. George Francis Adams (1863–October 10, 1937). She died "after a lingering illness." George was fatally injured in a hotel fire in Kenosha, Wisconsin. The other children were Richard B. (1874–1874), Lawson J. (July 1, 1876–August 1882), Richard W. (1878–1878), and Edna (June 1883–October 1883).

In 1895 ill health forced Muzzy to sell the newspaper to Byron Seamans. His last editorial read in part:

> Words of farewell are always sad and especially so when they precede the separation of intimate friends and acquaintances of long standing. Warned by failing health we have arranged for retirement from all business cares. For twenty-six years our best endeavor has been given, and more of our physical and nervous force expended than has proven advisable. With a trembling hand and tears of regret we cannot suppress, we lay down what has been our life-work, and say to the thousands who read The Democrat, Good-bye.[371]

In the ensuing years, the Muzzys lived in several places. When the 1900 census was taken, they resided in Olean, Cattaraugus County. They spent winters in Washington, DC, and Muzzy wrote periodically about political topics. They were living in Kenosha, Wisconsin, in 1908 when Alma died of cancer in the Pennoyer Sanatorium where her son in law practiced. Her body was returned to Pulaski for burial.[372]

Lawson enjoyed traveling and in 1908 undertook a trip around the world. He was in London when King George V was crowned.[373] He and his granddaughter, Dorothy Adams, were on another tour in 1912 when he became ill and decided to return to the United States. According to reports, they left Wisconsin in June and had visited London, Paris, and Berlin. Due to his ill health, they began their journey home on November 7.[374] Muzzy died early in the morning of November 17 when the ship on which he and Dorothy were sailing, the *Princess Irene*, was four days out of New York City.[375]

Muzzy's funeral in Pulaski was attended by a large segment of the population. The front page of the *Pulaski Democrat* was devoted to a description of the ceremonies:

> At an early hour friends assembled at the church, so eager were they to pay tribute to the memory of an honored citizen. A large delegation of Masons and Grand Army men came in bodies. The service was conducted by Rev. E. A. Rogers. The choir rail of the church, where Mr. Muzzy was always found when in active relations with the church, was draped in mourning. Beautiful flowers rested upon the casket . . . The Masons marched in a body to the cemetery and the burial

Figure 2.78. Although Lawson and Alma Muzzy died elsewhere, their bodies were returned to Pulaski, New York, their home for many years. Author's collection.

services of the fraternity were recited. The Grand Army was also present in a body to do honor to their departed comrade.

Before his death, Muzzy asked Byron Seamans to deliver the eulogy which was also quoted in the extensive coverage.[376] The sentiment felt by all was summarized in an out-of-town newspaper: "A good man has gone to his reward . . . Mr. Muzzy was one of the most lovable of men, energetic and a most interesting person to meet."[377]

Lawson Muzzy, Alma P. Witt Muzzy, their infant children, and his parents are buried in Pulaski Village Cemetery, section 4. Beulah Muzzy Adams and Dr. George F. Adams are buried in Green Ridge Cemetery, Kenosha, Wisconsin.

Samuel Merwin Olmstead

Warfare affects more lives than those of the combatants on the battlefield. It also touches every member of each soldier's family and at times leads to unintended outcomes. This statement has no truer confirmation than the story of Samuel Merwin Olmstead.

Samuel, son of Orimel B. Olmstead (February 14, 1806–October 12, 1884) and his second wife, Elizabeth Crocker (1815–November 17, 1862), was born on February 14, 1844, in Orwell, New York. He was Elizabeth's third child of seven and was often called Merwin. He was described on his muster card at standing five feet, eight inches tall, with dark hair and blue eyes.

According to the *Adjutant-General's Report*, Samuel first enlisted in the 24th Regiment on May 7, 1861, mustering into Co. G. He mustered out on July 1, 1861, after serving three months. He reenlisted on December 28, 1861, and was reassigned to Co. G.

By early summer 1862 everyone, including the Lincoln administration, knew the war would not end soon. President Lincoln worried constantly about the vulnerable position of the District of Columbia, fearing it would be overrun by the Confederates in an effort to force a peace treaty which would result in the establishment of separate country in the South. In July he formed the Army of North Virginia and placed General John Pope in charge, hoping that this action would lessen the Confederates' strength in the eastern part of the country and thwart their ambitions to invade the District of Columbia. Pope's opportunity

Figure 2.79. Samuel Merwin Olmstead lay on the battlefield for three days before he was rescued. Courtesy of the New York State Military Museum.

to repay Lincoln for his confidence came in late August 1862 at the second battle of Bull Run. Pope's forces repelled General John "Stonewall" Jackson's soldiers on August 28 but were unable to finish the job the next day. In the evening of August 29, General Lee arrived with reinforcements. On August 30, battle was rejoined. Around 4 p.m. General Lee's forces initiated an advance which finally drove the Union army, including the 24th Regiment NYSV, out of the area. It was during this time that Olmstead was wounded, as recorded by his father: "Samuel M. Olmstead was wounded in the last Bullrun [sic] on the 30th day of Aug. 1862 between 4 & 5 o'clock PM."[378]

On Olmstead's muster card a clerk mistakenly noted that he had been killed in battle on August 30, 1862, but the reality was much harsher. He lay on the battlefield for three days: "[He] remained on the battle field untill [sic] Tuesday afternoon 2nd day of September when Mr. J. L. Shram a nurse was sent out [and] came in sight of him[.] he was past Speaking to him but Motioned to him[.] he gave him some nourishment but he died that afternoon[.] Mr. J. L. Shram buried him."[379]

Orimel Olmstead, Samuel's father, was a prominent businessman in Orwell. Despite the fact that he was fifty-six years old, he raised Co. C, 110th Regiment in late summer 1862 and became its captain. The 110th arrived in Baltimore, Maryland, on September 1, 1862, and went into camp at Patterson Park. Captain Olmstead had no idea what had happened to his son until Elizabeth contacted him, saying she had been informed that Samuel was dead and had been buried on the battlefield:

> A nurse exploring the battle field found and administered to his necessities until his death, and in the absence of his friends, buried him, conveying the dreadful news to the mother at home. She immediately informed his father at Baltimore; obtaining a furlough he hastened to Washington where he found the nurse and taking an ambulance and a lead coffin, proceeded to find the lonely grave . . . The remains of the son, accompanied by the stricken father were brought back to their home in Orwell. This sad duty performed, the night after the funeral he started back to his regiment.[380]

The story, unfortunately, does not end there.

When returning to his regiment, Captain Olmstead was taken severely ill with "fever" and after arriving in Baltimore was taken to a private home to recover. Elizabeth traveled to Baltimore to care for

Figure 2.80. A brokenhearted Captain Orimel B. Olmstead escorted his son's body to Orwell for burial. Author's collection.

him, in spite of the fact that she was in mourning for her son and had several young children at home: "His devoted wife hastened to his bedside and administered to him day and night till his death seemed inevitable. In sorrow, deprived of sleep and broken down with anxiety and care, insomnia seized upon the wife. Opiates being administered she fell into a sleep from which she never awoke. Her death occurred Nov. 17, 1862 . . . Dear ones came and bore her remains to the family home."[381]

Shortly after Elizabeth's death, Prudence (October 3, 1828–November 11, 1866), Captain Olmstead's eldest child by his first wife, Permilia Jane Palmer (October 11, 1811–June 9, 1830), went to Baltimore to care for him until his discharge on December 1, 1862, on account of "disability."

The board of supervisors met on December 9, 1862, and unanimously approved Resolutions for Captain Olmstead in his double bereavement. The statement read, in part:

Figure 2.81. Elizabeth Olmstead died after traveling to Baltimore to care for her sick husband. Her body was returned to Orwell, New York, for burial. Author's collection.

Whereas, he has sacrificed upon the altar of his country a promising and much beloved son, who fell while nobly fighting her battles, and Whereas, the partner of his bosom, has suddenly fallen a victim to a total disease after following her husband to the tented fields of the south to administer to his necessities when prostrated by sickness, therefore, Resolved, That while we commend and admire the lofty patriotism that prompted our friend and former associate to make so great a sacrifice, we extend to him and the surviving members of his family our heartfelt sympathy in this, their deep affliction.[382]

Captain Orimel Olmstead married Julia A. Gilbert (April 7, 1823–May 12, 1906), his third wife, on August 30, 1864. They had no children but she held the family together until the captain's death of heart disease on October 12, 1884.

Samuel Merwin Olmstead was among the lucky soldiers whose families had sufficient connections and financial wherewithal to have their sons' bodies brought home for burial. Nevertheless, his death brought pain and suffering to the entire family. His mother's death was a loss for both husband and surviving children, and his father's illness forced him to resign his commission.

When the GAR monument in Evergreen Cemetery, Orwell, was dedicated in 1894, Henry H. Lyman, a veteran of the 147th Regiment, paid tribute to Captain Olmstead:

> Among [the 110th's] first captains was one of Orwell's most highly respected citizens, the late O. B. Olmstead—a frank, outspoken man whose whole life was in sympathy with everything honorable and right; a man in years, far past the military age, but whose patriotism lead [sic] him to undertake the hardships

Figure 2.82. Orimel B. Olmstead was married three times. His last wife was Julia A. Gilbert. Author's collection.

of field service way beyond his strength beside the boys of his friends and neighbors. His health soon failed and greatly to his sorrow and mortification he was mustered out. I can see him now as I saw him 32 years ago . . . stretched upon a cot, pale and weak, enfeebled by exposure and disease, having no anxiety for himself but grieved and crushed in spirit because he could no longer be with the boys who had volunteered with him.[383]

Foremost among the "boys" for whom he grieved was his own lost son, Samuel.

Samuel Merwin Olmstead, Orimel B. Olmstead, Elizabeth Crocker Olmstead, and Julia A. Gilbert Olmstead are buried in Evergreen Cemetery, Orwell, New York, section 5. Permilia Jane Palmer Olmstead's grave has not been located.

Smith Parke

Sometimes the horrors of war are better reflected in the stories of ordinary men than in impersonal battlefield statistics. Such is the sad tale of Smith Parke, an ordinary man.

Parke was born on May 5, 1818, in Camden, Oneida, New York, the son of Sage Parke (June 7, 1783–September 8, 1848), a War of 1812 veteran, and Almira Preston (October 11, 1789–November 28, 1840). They were pioneer settlers and farmers in Amboy, New York.[348]

Smith Parke married Harriet J. Stewart (December 29, 1820–July 12, 1862), a Massachusetts native, on October 24, 1839. They were the parents of six children: Mary Almira (July 14, 1841–1911) married Edwin Perry (September 1836–1914) on August 11, 1869; Clark Stewart (1845–November 12, 1862), unmarried; Harriet Esther (August 26, 1849–April 2, 1878) married Asahel Charles Wallace (1843–April 13, 1879) in 1870; Martha Janette (September 8, 1853–*post* 1880?); DeWitt Clinton (November 8, 1856–March 15, 1921) married Addie Elizabeth Houghton (September 17, 1859–December 12, 1929) on May 10, 1876; Fanny Isabella (September 9, 1859–August 3, 1879), unmarried.

When the Civil War began, the citizens of Oswego County enthusiastically recruited its first regiment, the 24th. Despite the fact that Smith Parke was forty-three years old and married with six children, he nevertheless enlisted on May 4, 1861, at Parish, New York, for a period of two years, mustering into Co. D on May 17.

Parke had a medical problem the examining doctors should have discovered but either did not find or chose to overlook. He was suffering from tuberculosis and how he managed to pass the physical examination is unknown. That he was indeed ill is confirmed by his son's pension file, according to which Parke had not been able to support his family since 1858.

There might have been a couple reasons for his eagerness to enlist. Perhaps he sincerely believed that the Union must be preserved. He might also have considered the financial incentives. Privates earned sixteen dollars per month (although not always paid on time, due to circumstances). At the time all thought the war would be of short duration. Military service, therefore, was considered a good way to earn extra money for the family.

The 24th Regiment was sent to Elmira, New York, for training, where living conditions were primitive at best and the food, according to a writer identified only as S., was terrible: "Would that I could obtain the aid of Wisdom's Goddess to supply opprobrious epithets to be used in connection with the food and contractors. We have literally 'nothing to eat and plenty of it.' Beef and potatoes of the cheapest kind, with once in a while pork and beans and very weak coffee comprise volunteer's fare. This is the dark side of our life."[385] The regiment departed Elmira on July 2 and traveled to Washington, DC. Although the men were held in reserve when the first battle of Bull Run was contested, they did picket duty for nineteen days without any protective cover. Observed S. H. Brown, "Our men are enjoying themselves, as far as camp life is concerned, better than they did during the nineteen days we were on picket duty, sleeping on the 'cold, cold ground.'"[386]

Conditions did not improve. As the hot Virginia summer gave way to a cold and damp autumn, the soldiers in the 24th Regiment were ordered to Upton's Hill where they built fortifications and settled in for the winter. The environment worsened Parke's already disease-ridden lungs. His muster card gives no indication that he was admitted to any hospital but he was discharged at Upton's Hill on January 2, 1862, for "disability." Discrepancies exist concerning his discharge. His muster card says he was discharged on June 2, 1862, which cannot be correct. This error was repeated in the *Adjutant-General's Report* which used the original forms as a guide. According to the *Town Clerks' Registers*, Parke arrived home on January 6, 1862. It may have been possible for him to travel from Virginia to Oswego County in four days if railroad connections were perfect, but that is pure conjecture. In all likelihood, the clerk had to rely on someone's imperfect memory for an arrival date.

By this time, Parke was very sick. Dr. Joseph Pero reported "that I attended said Smith Park [sic] during his last illness at the aforesaid Place and that the said Smith Park died at Amboy, Oswego County, on the 17th day of February, AD 1862 of consumption of long standing."[387]

Harriet, left with six children, four of them younger than sixteen, did not apply for a widow's pension. Everyone agreed that Parke had suffered from consumption before entering the service. In other words, he had not contracted the disease "in the line of his duty" and therefore was ineligible for a pension. Additionally, Harriet was ill herself and had been for years. She died on July 12, 1862, probably of the same disease which carried off her husband.

Figure 2.83. Smith Parke was discharged from the army for "disability" and died shortly after returning to Amboy, New York. Author's collection.

Figure 2.84. Harriet Parke's death made her six children orphans. Author's collection.

Clark Stewart, barely seventeen years of age, suddenly found himself the head of the household. He and his siblings were destitute because, as William H. Butler and Harry Turner testified, "the poor master of the town sold their property to pay for funeral expenses of their parents and the money was all used up for that."[388]

About this time, recruiting was taking place across Oswego County for the 147th Regiment. Although underage, Clark, commonly called Stewart, enlisted on August 27, 1862. According to Dr. Frank Low, "the said Stewart enlisted into the service of the U. S. that he might the better support his brother & sisters, that he so enlisted after the death of his father and that he left all his bounty for his sisters that he got at the time of enlisting."[389]

The 147th Regiment left Oswego City on September 27, 1862, and traveled to the District of Columbia where instead of training for combat the soldiers were put to work digging ditches. Letters sent home were filled with complaints over dismal conditions and lack of food. Treatment of sick men was also criticized.

We have a number of sick on hand and it's only through the mercies of God that they are cared for. They will not take them in the hospital, or give them any stove or bedding. We are trying to have a little better place to put the sick in; we are putting up a new tent for them. We have to drive down crooked stakes and lay poles on them; and in this way make the beds. It keeps the sick off the ground. They have lain on the ground heretofore, and if they have care, it comes from one of their kin or friends in the same company; and that is all they have to rely on, and if the friend's money is gone, the sick soldier must suffer from want of care.[390]

Figure 2.85. Clark Stewart Parke, who enlisted in the 147th Regiment to support his siblings, succumbed to typhoid fever a few months later. Courtesy of Gulfport Bob—Find a Grave.

Stewart was luckier than most. When he became ill he was taken to Presbyterian Hospital in Georgetown, where he succumbed to typhoid fever on November 12, 1862. In the space of ten months the Parke children had lost their father, mother, and older brother.

The rest of the story is quickly told. John Howard of Mexico, New York, was appointed legal guardian of the orphaned Parke children. He secured pensions for them, based on Stewart's service, which were paid until each child reached the age of sixteen. Mary and her husband died in Dudley, Worcester, Massachusetts. Harriet and her husband died in Sandy Creek, New York. Martha and Fanny, both teachers, lived in Putnam, Windham, Connecticut, with DeWitt. Fanny is buried in DeWitt's plot in Grove Street Cemetery. Martha disappeared after the 1880 census and may have married. DeWitt was a longtime deputy sheriff in Putnam as well as the superintendent of the local children's home.

Smith Parke, Harriet J. Stewart Parke, and his parents are buried in Amboy Center Cemetery. Clark Stewart Parke is buried in Soldiers' and Airmen's Home National Cemetery in Washington, DC.

Francis M. Pease

Among the notable Civil War veterans of Oswego County must be included Francis M. Pease, who had the dubious distinction of being captured by the Confederate army not once but twice. His experiences as a POW in southern prisons provided graphic confirmation of the tales other survivors told.

Francis "Frank" Pease was born in the town of Scriba on February 28, 1844, a son of Albert Pease (1816–December 21, 1891) and Christiana G. Worden (1812–December 30, 1886). Like his father, he was a cooper. Little is known about his childhood, but he apparently attended school because he kept a now-lost Civil War diary and wrote letters to his parents, at least one of which ultimately found its way into a local newspaper. His enlistment paper describes him as five feet, eight inches tall. He had brown hair, blue eyes, and a light complexion.

On August 30, 1862, Francis Pease and his father went to New Haven, New York, where he enlisted in the 147th Regiment, and was later mustered into Co. F. Albert signed a consent form giving permission for his son to enlist, although Francis was eighteen years old.

Young Pease's first date with destiny occurred at Gettysburg, Pennsylvania, on July 1, 1863. It is an oft-told tale how the 147th Regiment, beleaguered by two Confederate regiments, held the line when other regiments were in retreat; how their leader, Colonel Francis Miller, wounded and carried off the field by his panicked horse, was unable to convey to his men the order to retreat; how Major George Harney took over command and led the few survivors off the field; how many of them were trapped in the infamous railroad cut and forced to surrender. Francis Pease was one of those men:

> For fifteen or twenty minutes we fought hard, when the rebels flanked us on the right and began advancing upon us in large numbers. The firing from both sides was very rapid. Finally we got the order to retreat and we lost no time in obeying, leaving an awful sight of dead and wounded upon the field. As we retreated we got into a railroad cut or ravine. We were moving as fast as we could, which was not very fast, because the ravine was crowded and there were a good many wounded men that had to be helped along. After we got into the cut the rebel bullets whistled over our heads. Soon the Johnnies were upon both sides of us, standing upon the banks in large numbers, and we were compelled to throw down our arms and surrender.[391]

Pease was sent to the rear and several days later paroled, after which he traveled to a camp in Carlisle, Pennsylvania, to await an exchange of prisoners. By October he had returned to the 147th.

The war effort, suspended during the winter, was renewed in the spring of 1864 when General Ulysses S. Grant became the commander of the Army of the Potomac. His mission: be wherever General Lee was to end the war as swiftly as possible. The 147th saw hard fighting in the months ahead. Between May 5 and June 12 the regiment participated in eight important conflicts, the first of which was the infamous battle of the Wilderness, fought on May 5 and 6. Grove Dutton, a member of Co. D, later described his experiences during the two days:

> Early the next morning [May 5] we fell in line and marched along a road leading from the river. In a short time the First Brigade moved in line of battle to our left and struck the enemy

and musketry commenced immediately. We had been resting, but "fall in" was the order and we were immediately advanced in line of battle through the thick woods and underbrush to form on the right side of the First Brigade . . . The bushes were so thick we could not see a rod ahead, but the rebels were lying down and could see us better. A number were killed and wounded before they had a chance to fire . . . Most of us bore to the left in our retreat but some kept straight to our rear and ran right into the enemy and were made prisoners. I never was so turned around in my life, and I think most of us were confused as regards points of the company . . . The woods, meanwhile, had caught fire and the smoke was dense.[392]

One of those captured soldiers Dutton mentioned was Francis Pease, now a POW for the second time in less than a year. His fate this time was much different from what he experienced in 1863, thanks to events and policies beyond his control.

In 1863 President Lincoln approved recruiting African Americans for the Union army, a move which enraged the Confederates. Lincoln's government demanded that both white and black captured soldiers be paroled and exchanged. When black soldiers were taken, however, they were oftentimes killed or returned to slavery. Moreover, General Grant disliked the policy of parole and exchange, arguing that exchanged soldiers quickly returned to their units to fight again. (This was also true of the Union army, as shown in the case of Francis Pease.) The combination of the two problems led to the creation of prison camps in both the North and the South, the most notorious being Camp Sumter in Georgia, better known as Andersonville, where forty-five thousand Union soldiers were imprisoned and approximately thirteen thousand died from starvation and disease.

It is unknown when Francis Pease arrived in Andersonville. According to Reverend Isaac M. Foster, Co. H, 46th NYSV, who was also captured at the battle of the Wilderness, Foster first went to Danville, Virginia, where he remained a short time before being transferred to Andersonville.[393] Danville Prison, located near the Virginia–North Carolina border, was composed of six buildings which became so overcrowded that it was said each man had only four square feet in which to maneuver. Poor food and disease took its toll on the prisoners.

Figure 2.86. Danville Prison was a notorious Confederate POW camp. Courtesy of the Library of Congress.

It is possible that Pease, who alleged he had spent time in Danville, arrived there at approximately the same time. In later years Charles Dashner recalled seeing him when he arrived at Camp Sumter: "I was taken prisoner October 19, 1863 and taken to Belle Island Prison and in March 1864 I was taken to the Rebel Prison at Andersonville Ga. and was there when said Pease came."[394] While in this prison, continued Dashner, Pease suffered from scurvy. A yet more serious condition was later termed chronic gastritis. Oscar M. Coon, a childhood friend and fellow POW, related that Pease "suffered with disease of his stomach while he was confined in said Rebel Prison and complained a great deal of suffering from said disease."[395]

Pease's ailment, common among prisoners, was caused by the "cob meal" they were fed:

> The cornmeal fed to the prisoners was "unbolted," meaning that the bran and the kernel were not separated. Simply put, the cob was ground up with the corn. The unbolted cornmeal was largely indigestible, and it produced all types of intestinal disorders, the most common of which was diarrhea. To men

already weak from hunger, the rough cornmeal acted like tiny razor blades in their lower intestines. Many Andersonville survivors claimed that they still suffered from intestinal distress decades after being released from prison.[396]

The arrival of General Sherman's army in Georgia in June 1864 and the fall of Atlanta on September 2 forced Andersonville officials to evacuate most of the prisoners to other locations. The prison was located on Sherman's route and Confederates feared that his soldiers would wreak terrible revenge on them should they discover the prisoners' horrible living conditions. Some thirty thousand men had to be moved and Florence, South Carolina, was selected as their destination. Florence, home to three railroads, was considered a secure place to construct a new camp. When the first men arrived in September 1864, however, building was incomplete. In short order, twelve thousand men were delivered to a prison where they had very little protection from the elements.

Conditions at Florence were worse than at Andersonville, as Samuel Eliot, a soldier in Co. A, 7th PA, described: "While at Andersonville, I did not suppose the rebels had a worse prison in the South, but I have

Figure 2.87. Camp Sumter, located in Andersonville, Georgia, was the most reviled prison of the Civil War. Courtesy of the Library of Congress.

Figure 2.88. Union prisoners complained that conditions at Florence, South Carolina, were worse than at Camp Sumter. Courtesy of the Library of Congress.

now found out that they have. This den is ten times worse than that at Andersonville. Our rations are smaller and of poorer quality, wood more scarce, lice plentier, shelters worn out, and cold weather coming on."[397]

Pease was released from this prison at North East Ferry, North Carolina, on February 27, 1865, and taken to Camp Parole, Maryland, arriving on March 12. A thirty-day furlough granted on March 17 was intended to help restore his health, but when he returned to the 147th he was too feeble for active duty. He mustered out with the regiment on June 7.

Pease's return to civilian life was difficult. He suffered from gastritis for the remainder of his life, sometimes so severely that he was unable to work. When he finally applied for a pension in 1880, he testified to his poor health:

> That I was not treated at my Regt. it being at the close of the war of the Rebellion and returned home sick having returned a short time before from the Rebel Prisons Danville, Va.

Andersonville Ga. & Florence SC. I was treated for several months soon after I returned home . . . for Stomach Ailment that the different doctors called Chronic Gastritis of the stomach . . . Have suffered very much with my stomach ever since the War and paid out a good deal doctoring. Have very small means to live upon & have a family to support. Have not done a day's work since last Jan. Have been confined to the house most of the time. How long I may survive God only knows.[398]

The depositions of friends and neighbors confirmed his allegations of ill health. Byron C. Earl, for example, testified: "[Pease] came home in June 1865. He was soon taken sick and was sick for months with difficulty of the stomach and has been afflicted ever since . . . [He] is unfitted for performing hard labor, suffers very much with pain in his stomach, lasting at times for weeks incessantly."[399] In a later deposition, Earl added: "I remember . . . hearing the family tell how Frank like to a died. They sent for the Dr. & he finally got better . . . I remember of laughing at him or Joking him about his Stomach & belly being all sunk in[;] he was rather more than what was the generality of People."[400] Lucian Hammond concurred with Earl:

> That I saw said Pease immediately after his discharge from the army and that he came home ailing with a disease of his stomach and came down sick with said disease and was sick for a long time and that said Pease continued very poorly and unable to do but very little work for years . . . that said disease has destroyed his stomach and has undermined his whole system so that he is totally disabled for the performance of any kind of manual labor.[401]

After years of trying, Frank was finally granted a pension on September 25, 1885. He would enjoy its benefits only briefly.

Why he did not apply for a pension before 1880 is unknown, but by that time he was a married man. He married Catherine "Kittie" B. Lord (June 23, 1851–January 22, 1904) on February 13, 1877. The date also marked the tenth anniversary of the marriage of her sister, Abby, to Otis Miner, a veteran of the 81st Regiment.[402] Their only child, Mable A. (November 15, 1881–July 7, 1965), married Arthur Hart (1879–1964), a longtime postal worker in Oswego City.

Despite his afflictions, Pease attempted to involve himself in the community. In 1871 he was enrolled as a charter member of the short-lived Amos N. Kibbe Post No. 81 GAR. He was a member of Beacon Light Lodge No. 464 IOOF.[403] He participated in local Republican politics and was elected Scriba tax collector in 1880, inspector of elections in 1882, and assessor in 1884.[404] He attended Oswego Business School briefly, tried his hand at raising fruit, and attempted to raise subscriptions for a projected, but never written, book on his Civil War experiences.[405]

It is possible that Pease's quest for a pension took so long was because he developed a cancerous tumor on his jaw. Since the tumor was not acquired in the military, the pension board had to ensure he was not applying on that account. The growth was surgically removed but reappeared and was described by one doctor as being "as large as a two-quart pail."[406] The pension was finally granted on September 25, 1885, but Pease, who refused all further treatment for his jaw, died on March 11, 1886, at the age of forty-two years and eleven days.

Figure 2.89. Francis Pease's imprisonment during the Civil War resulted in years of physical suffering. Author's collection.

That Francis Pease had survived his ordeal in southern prison camps was testimony to his grit and determination when so many comrades-in-arms of the 147th succumbed, including Francis Devendorf (1832–July 13, 1864), David Wheeler (1833–August 23, 1864), Charles H. Jennings (1842–October 12, 1864), and Peter Douglas (1833–October 5, 1864), all of whom are buried in Andersonville National Cemetery. John Wetherby (1844–December 1, 1864), whose actual capture date is unknown, died in the POW camp at Salisbury, North Carolina, and was buried among the "unknowns" there. Pease's life and death bear graphic witness to the sufferings of soldiers on both sides of the war.

Figure 2.90. Catherine Lord Pease survived her husband by many years, subsequently marrying Himan P. Dutcher, another Civil War veteran. Author's collection.

Francis Pease had the forethought to write a will in which he named his brother-in-law, Otis Miner, guardian to his daughter Mable. She obtained a minor's pension which remained in effect until she turned sixteen. Kittie also obtained a pension which she forfeited when on March 11, 1891, she married Himan P. Dutcher (1846–1928). She died on January 22, 1904: "For three years she had been an invalid, and despite the fact that she suffered much, she bore her trials with true Christian fortitude."[407]

Francis M. Pease, Catherine Lord Pease Dutcher, and his parents are buried in North Scriba Union Cemetery, lot 180. Mable A. Pease Hart and Arthur Hart are buried in Riverside Cemetery, Scriba, New York, section O.

Peter Pitcher

Peter Pitcher was the son of Gottlieb Pitcher (September 12, 1757–July 5, 1838) and Mary Pedick (May 12, 1770–February 6, 1861). Gottlieb, a native of Saxony, was a veteran of the Revolutionary War. He and Mary, born in Holland, were married in Johnstown, Fulton, New York, on December 1, 1787. They settled in Sullivan, Madison, New York, where Peter was born on July 29, 1801. He enjoyed the distinction of being one of the oldest men from Oswego County to serve in the Civil War.

Gottlieb Pitcher and his family moved to Oswego County in 1814 and became residents of the town of Palermo. In 1828 Peter married Margaret Blair (November 17, 1808–February 17, 1909). Many years later, Evaline Griswold, an attendee at that wedding, recalled "going to a wedding when five years old in a sleigh drawn by oxen. The contracting parties were Peter Pitcher and Margaret Miller [sic]."[408]

Peter and Margaret Pitcher were the parents of eight known children, all of whom survived to adulthood: Frances (August 16, 1832–February 18, 1888) married William G. Rector (1825–December 23, 1893) *post* 1850; Otis E. (January 21, 1835–January 12, 1926) married Margaret J. Grant (March 3, 1843–March 2, 1915) in 1865; William Egbert (June 16, 1837–March 25, 1903) married Alzina Olmstead (June 1837–August 12, 1911) in 1859; James Willis (May 18, 1840–February 22, 1929) m1 Elizabeth Lovina Olmstead (March 1839–April 4, 1908) in 1867 and m2 Jennie A. Francis Stevens (1875–October 7, 1848) on May 2, 1923; George Washington (1842–November 8, 1875) m1 Ann _____ (1850–*ca.* 1872) date unknown and m2 Marilda Ann Austin (1845–*post* 1892) *ca.* 1873;

Sophenia (August 1846–March 6, 1941) m1 James Hill (1846–January 31, 1893) *ca.* 1863, m2 Maurice S. Coe (1848–January 17, 1912) in 1870, and m3 Fredrick Joseph Lamkin (September 15, 1882–January 2, 1955) on September 16, 1918; Anna Olive (July 1849–March 20, 1906) married David Horan (December 1845–May 25, 1907) in 1884; Elvira Elizabeth (December 31, 1855–April 11, 1896) married Robert Beebes (March 6, 1851–October 26, 1930) *ca.* 1872.

Otis Pitcher was the first member of the family to join the Union cause, serving in Co. E, 81st Regiment and the Veteran Reserve Corps from October 11, 1861, to October 17, 1864. He was followed by James Willis, a soldier in Co. K, 94th Regiment from January 23, 1862, to August 10, 1863. He was wounded at Bull Run on August 30, 1862, and lost a leg.

In August and September 1862, Peter, William, and George Pitcher enrolled in the Black River Artillery which became the 5th NY HA. Peter and William served in Co. L and George, in Co. I. The regiment initially was detailed to protect various forts in New York City Harbor. Eventually it became attached to the Army of West Virginia and saw extensive action throughout the war.

It is difficult to believe that Peter Pitcher convinced the examining board that he was forty-five years old when he was actually sixty-one, but his muster card confirms that fact. Not until August 20, 1863, was he discharged for "disability" at Fort C. F. Smith, Virginia. That same month he made successful application for an invalid's pension.

Hiram Sherman Post No. 434 GAR, Vermillion, New York, was chartered on December 20, 1883. Peter "mustered in" on March 12, 1887, and at the time of his death was considered the oldest GAR member in New York State.

Peter Pitcher was a farmer his entire life, apparently moving from one rented farm to the next. Although he lived in Oswego County for several years, during which time some of the children were born, in 1850 the family resided in West Turin, Lewis County. By 1855 the family had moved to Montague, Lewis County, and was still there for the 1860 census. In 1865, everyone still at home lived in Palermo, New York. By 1875 the family had moved to New Haven, New York, where they lived in 1890.

Upon Pitcher's death of pneumonia in Palermo Center on April 9, 1894, at the age of ninety-three, a lengthy obituary lauded his service to the Union:

Mr. Peter Pitcher died after a brief illness of pneumonia last week, aged 94 [sic] years. His funeral occurred at the M. E. church on Wednesday and was largely attended. Post Sherman attended in a body and conducted the services at the grave. The Rev. John Fulford, also a member of the G. A. R., conducted the services . . . The deceased at the time of his death is said to have been the oldest member of the G. A. R. in the state. When his country called for volunteers, at the age of 63 years, he and his three [sic] sons enlisted and served faithfully to the close of the war . . . The deceased was an industrious, honest citizen, and moved with his father from Madison county in the year 1814. He leaves a wife, three sons, and two daughters.[409]

Figure 2.91. When Peter Pitcher died, he was the oldest member of the GAR in New York State. Author's collection.

Memorial resolutions published by Sherman Post No. 434 also alluded to his advanced age:

> Whereas, it has pleased our divine Commander to remove by death our brother, Comrade Peter Pitcher, whose head was crowned with the frosts of 94 winters, and who was the oldest G. A. R. man in the department of New York, and Whereas, by the death of our comrade we are reminded that our ranks are thinning, as one by one we lay our dear comrades in the grave to await the last bugle call which shall summon us to our rewards, therefore Resolved, That we extend to the sorrowing widow our heart-felt sympathy in being bereaved of one with whom she spent a long wedded life, whose joys and sorrows she shared. Resolved, that we also extend our sympathy to the three sons who gave some of the best years of their lives, with their father, in the service of our country in its great need.[410]

Margaret, a weaver, outlived her husband by many years. An interesting article about her appeared in 1890: "The most active woman in town is Mrs. Peter Pitcher. She is in her 80th year and is as active as most women at 50. It is no great trouble for her to walk seven or eight miles in a day or to do a good day's work in weaving carpets."[411] An obituary noted her long life:

> Mrs. Margaret Pitcher, said to be the oldest resident of Oswego county, died at the home of her son, Otis Pitcher, in Phoenix, Wednesday night. Mrs. Pitcher was born in Lafayette Square, Madison county, November 17, 1808, and was thus a little over one hundred years old. When a young girl she moved to Volney, where she has lived most of her life. Her maiden name was Margaret Blair. She married Peter Pitcher of Volney, in 1828, and from that union there are living three children, Otis Pitcher, aged seventy-six, of Phoenix, James Pitcher, aged seventy, and Mrs. Sophia Coe, aged sixty-eight, both residents of Fulton. Mrs. Pitcher has thirty-two grandchildren, twenty-three great-grandchildren and five great-great grandchildren.[412]

Figure 2.92. Margaret Blair Pitcher's grave marker contains only the word "Mother." Author's collection.

Peter Pitcher, Margaret Blair Pitcher, and his parents are buried in Sayles Corners Cemetery, Mexico, New York, east section.

William C. Raulston

Handsome, adventurous, assertive, and reckless, William C. Raulston embraced the ideals of his adopted country and paid the ultimate price in its defense.

Born on November 16, 1832, at Castlefinn, Donegal, Ireland, William C. was the eldest child of William Raulston (1809–April 1884) and Elizabeth "Eliza" Crawford (May 15, 1809–June 30, 1892). His sister, Elizabeth Jane (August 1836–March 1, 1902), was also born in Ireland. She married David H. McCoy (August 1820–February 12, 1901) in 1868. The youngest three children were born in Onondaga County, New York. John B. Raulston (June 14, 1839–February 28, 1893) married Mary Elizabeth Leversedge (October 1848–May 25, 1912) on July 23, 1879. James Alexander Raulston (July 21, 1841–September 17, 1862) was killed at the battle of Antietam. His body was returned to Oswego for burial. George F. Raulston (December 9, 1844–June 4, 1914) never married.[413]

The family moved to the United States *ca.* 1836 and was enumerated in DeWitt, Onondaga, New York, in 1850, the only time William's name appeared in a census. He was a blacksmith. The family moved to Oswego in 1851, according to the 1855 New York census. At some unspecified time between 1850 and 1855, William Raulston left New York State and moved to St. Louis, Missouri, where he found work in the mercantile industry. It is possible that his brother John accompanied him since neither name appeared in the 1855 census.

Exactly when the brothers returned to Oswego is unknown, although John was living with his parents in Southwest Oswego when the 1860 census was taken. With the approach of the war, they may have decided to leave Missouri, a slave state, before hostilities began. All this is conjectural. What is known is that on August 24, 1861, William Raulston enlisted in the 48th Militia in Oswego with the rank of captain. On August 29 his company (later designated Co. A) was organized at Fort Ontario in Oswego City.[414] His youngest brother, George, also enlisted on August 24. John joined them on September 17, 1861. Formal mustering occurred on September 14, 1861.[415] Not until December 10, 1861, was the regiment designated the 81st. Delays occurred until January 20, 1862, when the men, under the command of Colonel Edwin Rose (1807–January 13, 1864), traveled to Albany, New York. The Oswego contingent was consolidated with the Mohawk Rangers from Oneida County on February 18, 1862. After more delays the combined regiment finally left New York State on March 5, 1862, bound for Washington, DC.

Figure 2.93. William Raulston was fatally wounded in an escape attempt from Danville Prison. Courtesy of the Library of Congress.

Although inexperienced, the regiment participated in the battle of Fair Oaks, Virginia, from May 31 to June 1, 1862, in the course of which Lieutenant-Colonel Jacob J. DeForest was seriously wounded and Major John McAmbley was killed.[416] Because Colonel Rose was absent on sick leave, command of the regiment fell to Raulston as the senior captain.[417] Colonel Rose rejoined the regiment in June but was discharged for disability on July 7, 1862.[418] Raulston, who had been promoted to major effective May 31, 1862, now was advanced to the rank of lieutenant-colonel under the command of newly promoted Colonel DeForest.[419] Raulston held this rank until September 6, 1863, when he was discharged from the reconstituted veteran volunteer 81st Regiment.

Raulston was discharged for the express purpose of returning to Oswego to begin recruiting for a new regiment, subsequently designated the 24th New York Cavalry.[420] His brother John replaced him as lieutenant-colonel of the 81st.

The 24th Cavalry left New York State on February 23, 1864, under the command of Colonel William C. Raulston. It soon became embroiled in General Grant's Overland Campaign. The outfit suffered severe losses at Cold Harbor, Virginia, June 1–3, 1864, and still more at Petersburg on June 16.[421]

The 24th Cavalry was actively deployed in the Weldon Railroad Campaign. At the battle of Poplar Grove (Peebles's Farm) from September 30 to October 1, 1864, a part of that campaign, the Confederates captured Raulston. He ultimately became an inmate in Danville Prison, Virginia, where he and others plotted an escape. Alonzo Cooper, an eyewitness, recounted what occurred on December 10:

> Lieut. Cooper gives us definite information of the death of Col. Raulston. It seems that Gen. Duffie and the lamented Colonel were the prime movers in the attempted revolt. About four hundred Federal officers occupied a warehouse, 40 by 100 feet, the lower story of which was unoccupied except by a guard. Gen. Duffie and Col. Raulston, it was arranged, were to over power the guard, which consisted of only two rebels, secure their arms, give the signal to their companions above, and then rush out and overpower the guard in the prison yard. They performed their part of the programme, but unfortunately not before an alarm was given, and the door leading from the building was closed and locked before a rush could be

made. Seeing this, an attempt was made, but unavailingly, to batter down the door. In the meantime the rebel guard was formed outside, and it was seen that the attempt would prove a failure. The officers returned to the upper floor, Col. Raulston being the last one to ascend the stairs. He stopped to look from a window, and while standing there was fired upon by one of the guards, the ball entering his abdomen. He survived his wound five days, and was buried in the vicinity. Col. Raulston was the only officer wounded in the attempted escape. In fact, there was but one shot fired.[422]

The attempted escape and Raulston's death on December 15 made news in the southern press, even if it did smack of hyperbole:

Colonel Raulston, the leader of the plot among the Yankee officers to break out of prison at Danville, some ten days ago, and who was shot through the body in the melee, died of his wound Thursday night. He was colonel of the Twenty-fourth New York Cavalry. Raulston was represented by his associate prisoners, the Register says, to be a fearless, reckless character, insensible to consequences. He maintained, to his last breath, that his scheme for overpowering the guard, sacking the town, and making his escape, would have succeeded had not his colleagues flinched from the desperate nature of the work before them. He received a decent interment in the prisoners' burying ground.[423]

Before he died, Raulston dictated his will to Captain Albert Thomas, a fellow prisoner. He left a horse and tack to his brother, John. His mother received $2,000 and his sister, $1,000. To his fiancée, Miss Margaret Mary "Libby" Smith, daughter of Zachariah Smith of Oswego, he bequeathed $1,000 and the furniture and library currently in her care at the Welland House, Oswego City.[424]

Raulston's story does not end in the prisoner cemetery at Danville. In 1867 his brother John traveled to Danville to have the body exhumed and returned to Oswego. It arrived on February 8, 1867.[425] Because of a severe snow storm, the funeral, originally scheduled for Sunday, was postponed until Tuesday. In the meantime the body lay in state at the Doolittle House.

The local press detailed the plans for his elaborate funeral. The brothers of Oswego Lodge No. 127 F&AM, of which Raulston was a member, had a prominent role in the service.[426] Clergy from several denominations also participated in the funeral, after which the body was escorted to the cemetery:

> The procession moved at 12:30, amid the solemn tolling of bells, through densely crowded streets, and took its way to Riverside Cemetery. The body remained in charge of the military until the procession arrived at the gate of the Cem-

Figure 2.94. The inscription on the Raulston monument reads: "Died of wounds at Danville, Va. This distinguished soldier served during the war of 1861-5 as Capt., Major and L't Col. 81 Inf't'y and as Col. 24 Cavalry N. Y. Vol. Was twice severely wounded and became a prisoner of war. He fell leading a body of Union Soldiers in an attempt to escape from a military prison. He was a generous friend, a brave soldier and a true patriot." Author's collection.

etery, when the Masons took possession, and, with the usual impressive ceremonies of the order consigned it to the grave. Military honors were then paid, and all that is perishable of W. C. Raulston lay beneath the earth. "He sleeps his last sleep, he has fought his last battle," and none shall name him except as one who [so] loved his country that he laid down his life in her defense.[427]

Colonel William C. Raulston, his parents, James Alexander Raulston, Eliza Raulston McCoy, and David McCoy are buried in Riverside Cemetery, Scriba, New York, section L. A grave marker for John is also located in section L, but he and his wife, Mary Elizabeth Leversedge, are buried in Oak Woods Cemetery, Chicago, Illinois. Another marker erected in memory of "Freddie" has no dates. This stone in all likelihood memorializes George, commonly called Fred. He died in Republic, Ferry, Washington, and was buried in Ferry Cemetery.

Dr. Lawrence Reynolds

Standing on a gentle rise in St. Paul's Cemetery, Oswego City, a stark gray granite monument bears an equally stark inscription: DR. L. REYNOLDS/1803–1887. If not searching for the gravestone, one can easily pass by without noticing it. An inspection of the reverse of the huge monument reveals it was erected to memorialize members of the Ratigan family, prominent Oswegonians.

Why, then, was this man's name etched into the front with only the barest of information? The answer to that question begins in Ireland.

Lawrence "Larry" Reynolds was born in Waterford, Ireland, in 1803, the fourth and youngest son of Paul Reynolds (?–November 18, 1849) and an unidentified mother.[428] As the child of well-to-do parents he received an excellent education. For a time he joined his older brothers in the newspaper business, but dissatisfied with that occupation he moved to Liverpool, England, where he earned a medical degree and began a practice in that city.[429]

Reynolds supported efforts to gain Irish independence. In 1848 he abandoned his medical practice to take an active role in Young Ireland's crusade. He opened an iron works, and according to a speech published in the *Liverpool Albion*, he promised to provide swords to

Figure 2.95. The Ratigan family was prominent in Oswego's construction industry. Author's collection.

anyone wishing to have one. He avowed he did not advocate violence but reminded his audience that they had the right to own arms. Adding fuel to his oratorical fire, he said: "Remember, O mortal men before me, that you must die one time or another; and I would rather die leaving a glorious name behind me, of which neither country or family would be ashamed, than linger out a miserable old age."[430] Shortly thereafter the British government suspended habeas corpus in Ireland. As an Irishman, Reynolds was "accorded but little legal privileges." An arrest warrant charged him and others with "treasonable conspiracy in supplying arms to her Majesty's subjects."[431] When the authorities attempted to serve the warrant, however, they discovered that he had fled.

Somehow Reynolds managed to elude his would-be captors and secure passage to the United States. He was enumerated as a resident of Oswego City, New York, in 1850. For the next thirty-seven years he made the port city his home.

Reynolds established a practice in Oswego and was often summoned by those who could not afford to pay him, thereby earning him the nickname of "the poor man's doctor." Not infrequently his services went uncompensated.[432]

Very early in his residency he became involved in politics. He identified with the Whig and later the Democratic Party. He was called upon to speak at political rallies until shortly before his death, as witnessed by the following from the *Oswego Daily Palladium*: "Dr. Reynolds mounted the stage and for some little time poured hot shot into the dishonest and corrupt Republicans."[433]

When the Civil War began, Dr. Reynolds was forty-seven years old and legally exempt from military duty. He addressed the crowd gathered at a war meeting on April 16, 1861, to urge enlistments in the 24th Regiment:

> We are not going to fight the common people of the South; *we are to fight a Southern Aristocracy*. "Old Abe" is likely to become greater than Washington, inasmuch as Washington gave liberty to the whites only, while Mr. Lincoln will probably emancipate both white and black, and destroy the Aristocracy that has been the curse of the nation. For my part, I may safely promise that every Irishman will be found ready to shed his earth's blood in defense of American Freedom.[434]

To set an example, he enlisted the next day as an assistant surgeon.

His tenure with the 24th was short-lived. On February 26, 1862, he transferred to the 63rd Regiment, a part of the famous Irish Brigade, with the rank of surgeon.[435]

The Irish Brigade, composed of the 63rd, 69th, and 88th Regiments, participated in such battles as Fair Oaks, Fredericksburg, Antietam, Gettysburg, Wilderness, Cold Harbor, and the siege of Petersburg. The brigade's remnant was present at General Lee's surrender in April 1865.[436]

In charge of the Irish Brigade was General Thomas Francis Meagher, one of the conspirators rounded up in 1848. Meagher, who had been captured and sentenced to lifetime banishment in Van Diemen's Land, escaped and found his way to America. He and Reynolds were good friends, as Captain Edward Field of the 4th US Artillery was to learn. Captain Field described in an article titled "The Boys of Old Erin" how he came to know this fact:

> While riding through their [Rebel] abandoned camps, two of us, both youngsters, and about equally "green" came across a most curious figure, an old man with long white hair, and a

patriarchal, although sadly unkempt beard. He was dressed in a nondescript coat which looked as if it had begun life blue, then decided to be green, and finally hit upon a dirty drab. He nodded and rode by. We wondered who or what he could be. The more we thought about him the more suspicious he seemed, and we finally agreed that he must be a sort of rebel Rip Van Winkle, who had waked up to find his friends gone and was making the best of his way South. We felt proud of our acuteness, and only regretted that we had let him get such a start of us, that it was impractical to arrest him, or at any rate to satisfy our suspicion. A day or two after we met our old rebel riding along with General Meagher, chatting most amicably, and found out that it was Dr. Larry Reynolds, of the Sixty-third, familiarly and fondly known as "Old Larry," a poet of no mean performance, steeped to the eyes in Irish lore, honest as a looking glass, with the heart of a child and the growl of a mastiff—a Celtic Diogenes.[437]

Despite his age, Reynolds

was with the boys on all their weary marches, in all their bloody battles, aiding and cheering them. Men who fought with him have said that his cheerful disposition and encouraging words were as good to them as his physic, and many a soldier who spent many weary hours in the hospitals will bear testimony to the truth of this statement. We have also heard it said that Dr. Reynolds was a most fatherly man in the practice of his profession, and many a brave boy was spared a leg or an arm which other physicians would have taken off.[438]

He was universally admired for his strength and courage.

After the war Dr. Reynolds returned to Oswego. He was a member of John D. O'Brian Post No. 65 GAR and repeatedly held the office of surgeon. He was a popular speaker at conventions and campfires:

He thought one of his countrymen should be heard on this day, for they had fought gallantly for the blessings that had been talked about. He alluded to the excitement in Oswego when the news came that Fort Sumter was fired on, and pictured the alacrity with which the flower of the city—young men of every rank sprang to the rescue. He thought it well that we should look at those [regimental] flags and remember who has died for us. He thought if any city in the Union should be proud of her record it is the city of Oswego.[439]

Called upon for a toast at a campfire in Sodus, New York, Dr. Reynolds proposed one for "the Irish soldier, the adopted citizen."[440] He declared at a campfire sponsored by his own post "that America is the happiest spot in the world and we should all to be proud to live here."[441] He was present the night James McQuade, commander of the GAR of New York, was the guest of honor at a banquet in Oswego. His Irish humor shone through when asked to speak: "Dr. Reynolds who occupied a seat near the platform, was called upon, and after considerable urging arose. His first remark, that bashfulness, for which his countrymen were noted, prevented his saying much, put the house in convulsions of laughter."[442]

Dr. Reynolds also had other interests. He was a longtime member of the Father Matthew Temperance Society and the St. Patrick's Society which planned the annual St. Patrick's Day celebration. An interesting article revealed that an unnamed hypnotist had unsuccessfully attempted to hypnotize him at a performance the previous evening.[443] When Oswego's African American community celebrated the passage of the Fifteenth Amendment, Dr. Reynolds was invited to speak.[444]

He was known for his poetry. Called upon to write an original piece for the St. Patrick's Day celebration in 1863, he wrote one of his most famous poems, "Song of the Irish Brigade."[445] Others included "My Noble Irish Girl," "Hymn to the Blessed Virgin," "For God and Erin's Sake Unite," "The Oswego Quick Step," and "To John O'Mahony, H. C. F. B."

Dr. Reynolds's carelessness about finances led to a terrible swindle when he was almost eighty years old. A man calling himself John F. McDonald approached him, claiming that he owned 180 acres of land in Garfield, Kansas. He convinced Reynolds to give him money to buy adjacent land and plant eighty acres of wheat which would be ready for harvest soon after Dr. Reynolds arrived in Kansas: "He subsequently wrote that he had done so and sent a bill of $4 an acre for 80 acres, which sum Dr. Reynolds remitted. When he left here a few weeks ago he expected to find 80 acres of wheat on his Kansas farm. But arriving there he found no such man as McDonald, and none such had ever been known there."[446] Nearly destitute,

Dr. Reynolds contacted friends in Oswego who immediately set about raising money to bring him home. Among the fundraisers was a dramatic and musical entertainment.[447] An effort was also underway to place him in the National Soldiers' Home at Bath, New York, which evidently was unsuccessful, perhaps because Dr. Reynolds rejected the idea.[448] His arrival in March 1883 was eagerly anticipated:

> Geo. Morgan received a telegram yesterday stating that Dr. L. Reynolds would start from Chicago this (Wed.) afternoon and probably arrive in Oswego tomorrow (Thursday) afternoon. Dr. Reynolds has been absent from Oswego in the far west for about two years, and he will now be received at his former home with open arms. Some of his old friends feel like giving the warm-hearted old doctor a kind of an ovation, and it would not be inappropriate.[449]

Although the "warm-hearted doctor" resumed his practice, advancing years were taking their toll. Census records show that he boarded in many places in the city and apparently never owned a real home. He wrote his will about a month before he died, leaving everything to the woman who cared for him.

When Dr. Reynolds succumbed early in the morning of April 25, 1887, his death was widely noted in Central New York.[450] The best and most detailed obituary called him a "peculiar man in many ways" and reviewed his early education, flight from England, and life in Oswego, concluding:

> Dr. Reynolds was universally liked. He was possessed of a fund of humor which made his conversation at all times interesting. He was a man highly educated, of broad and liberal views, generous and kind-hearted to a degree not often witnessed, and withal an exemplary citizen. The people of Oswego, irrespective of nationality, will regret to hear of his death. The representatives of the Irish race cannot do him too much honor.[451]

Friends immediately began to solicit donations to buy Dr. Reynolds a suitable monument. The local papers reported a good response to the campaign, yet in 1895 the monument was still not erected—nor was it

Figure 2.96. Dr. Reynolds's grave lies somewhere in the Ratigan plot in St. Paul's Cemetery, Oswego. City. Author's collection.

ever. The only tangible evidence of Dr. Lawrence Reynolds's notable life is that brief inscription on someone else's monument.[452]

Dr. Lawrence Reynolds is buried in St. Paul's Cemetery, Oswego City, section B.

Daniel Falley Schenck

Born into a wealthy family in Fulton, New York, Daniel Falley Schenck exerted an influence over his hometown which extended far beyond his brief life. His character and devotion to country led to the formation of Daniel F. Schenck Post No. 271 GAR which existed until 1940.

Son of William Schenck (June 24, 1800–January 20, 1878) and Mary Falley Carrier (July 28, 1805–December 20, 1891), Daniel Schenck was born on October 28, 1836, and called Fulton home for his entire life. In adulthood he engaged in several types of commerce.

Allegedly unknown to his wife, William Schenck was actively engaged in the Underground Railroad, using his cellar to hide fugitive slaves on their way to freedom in Canada. It was probably not a surprise, then, when Daniel enlisted in the 50th Regiment NYSV on August 21, 1861, mustering in as a private. This unit quickly became the 50th NY Engineers.[453] As a trained engineer, Daniel swiftly rose through the ranks, eventually attaining the rank of captain.[454]

The 50th Engineers were famous among Union regiments as builders of fortifications and pontoon bridges, as well as destroyers of railroads. They first came to prominence at the battle of Fredericksburg, when under fire from Confederate sharpshooters they built a pontoon bridge across the Rappahannock River: "The pontooners had acceded [sic] in partially constructing the bridges when the rebels suddenly opened a very brisk and heavy fire of musketry from along the banks of the river and the windows of the houses, compelling a cessation of the work." After several attempts the bridge was finally completed late on the evening of December 11, 1862.[455]

The 50th Engineers were important participants at the battles of Chancellorsville, Wilderness, and Petersburg. A young man identified only as Henry proudly wrote to his father:

> The old men, those who have seen service from the Peninsula on through Pope's campaign, then Fredericksburg, (both battles) at Chancellorsville, in fact who have accompanied the

Figure 2.97. The construction abilities of the 50th New York Engineers were crucial for the Union Army's success. Courtesy of the Library of Congress.

Army of the Potomac in all its advances and retreats, they, with an esprit du corps unequalled, have to a man, almost, re-enlisted for the war . . . Do you wish a pontoon bridge built over the Potomac at a point 1,300 feet across? The 50th will do it in nineteen minutes. Try them if you don't believe it . . . It was a good choice that I made in enlisting, and not saying anything against other brave regiments that are in the field I will say no man can speak too highly of the 50th New York Engineers.[456]

After mustering out on October 21, 1864, Daniel Schenck returned to Fulton where he assisted in the family business and participated in local affairs. In 1874 he was appointed a notary public for the town of Granby.[457] He was active in the county's veteran soldiers' association which annually planned a reunion for all Civil War soldiers.[458]

As early as 1869, a Grand Army post was in operation in Fulton, named William C. Raulston No. 111 after the colonel of the 24th New York Cavalry who was fatally shot during an escape attempt from Danville Prison on December 10, 1864. (See Colonel Raulston's biography in this chapter for details.) In 1870 Raulston Post No. 111 participated in Decoration Day ceremonies in Fulton.[459] Newspaper accounts recorded names of several comrades, including Adolphus Bennett, John Palmer, Morris Highriter, Freeman C. Mosher, and Daniel F. Schenck.

Internal strife led to the post's demise in 1876 when its charter was revoked. Schenck's influence on the group's activities, however, was palpable, as evidenced by a speech delivered by Melvin F. Stephens on May 30, 1876:

For us, comrades, this is an occasion of unusual interest. We are today, for the first time, to place our floral offerings upon the grave of one who, since the first institution of this rite, has heretofore participated with us in its observance, and been foremost in recognition of our dead comrades' claim upon the grateful remembrance of their countrymen. The death of Comrade Daniel F. Schenck has left a void in our ranks that can never be filled. Remembering, as we will do, his kind heart, his worth and virtues as comrade, soldier, citizen and man, the flowers we place upon his grave today will be the heartfelt offerings of respect and esteem.[460]

Interest in the GAR did not wane and a new post, dubbed Daniel F. Schenck No. 271 in honor of their dead comrade, was established in June 1882: "It is proposed to name the G. A. R. in Fulton Post Schenck, in honor of Daniel F. Schenck, a brave man and thorough soldier who gave his life battling for the preservation of the Union. It would be a merited recognition also to one of the most patriotic families in this vicinity during the war."[461] This post, which had sixty charter members, would ultimately boast a membership of several hundred men and was only disbanded when the last member died.[462]

Daniel Falley Schenck died on December 7, 1875, in Fulton, reportedly of gastroenteritis acquired during the war.[463]

He was survived by his widow, Cornelia Smith Robinson (May 31, 1836–January 1, 1908), whom he had married on November 7, 1872. Schenck had never applied for a pension and Cornelia, aspiring to uphold her husband's honor, refused to apply for one for ten years: "It is due to truth to say that the applicant [Cornelia R. Schenck] in this case for all these years has been opposed to asking for any support, knowing the genuine patriotism of him who freely gave his life to his country, but failing strength and honest poverty prompted her to make the application."[464] Cornelia was in real need of a pension. When her petition to Congress for a special bill was vetoed by President Grover Cleveland on June 21, 1886, reaction was swift. Not only Schenck Post No. 271 but

Figure 2.98. Daniel Falley Schenck is buried in the family plot in Mt. Adnah Cemetery, Fulton, New York. Author's collection.

also Fairbanks Post No. 17 in Detroit, Wayne, Michigan, where Cornelia resided, petitioned members of Congress to override the president's veto.[465] Public opinion was definitely opposed to President Cleveland's action, as shown by the following: "The bill granting this delicate and helpless widow a pension of $20 a month was carefully examined by several Senators and a committee of the House and pronounced a just one. Yet the President thinks it necessary to hurl his veto at this poor woman and her little claim."[466] President Cleveland, who never served in the military during the Civil War, denied more pension bills than any previous president.[467]

Thanks undoubtedly to the influence of the GAR, Congress overrode the veto on July 31, 1886, and Cornelia obtained her pension.[468] She had moved to Detroit shortly after Daniel's death to live with her mother and two brothers. She succumbed to hemiplegia on January 1, 1908.[469]

Daniel Falley Schenck and other members of his family are buried in Mt. Adnah Cemetery, Fulton, New York, section 19. Cornelia Smith Robinson Schenck is buried in Elmwood Cemetery, Detroit, Michigan.

Elmina Pleiades Keeler Spencer

The daughter of pioneer settlers in the town of Mexico, New York, Elmina Pleiades Keeler Spencer rejected the feminine norm of remaining at home while men went off to war. Her direct efforts to aid the sick and wounded, often in the face of resistance from the male military hierarchy, confirm her position as a notable Oswego County Civil War veteran.

Elmina, eldest child of Darius Dunham Keeler (August 26, 1795–November 4, 1874) and Arethusa Powers (1797–July 17, 1875), was born on September 15, 1819. She obtained a good education for her time and sex and taught school for several years. On November 14, 1840, she married Robert H. Spencer (1818–November 24, 1873), sometime teacher and lake sailor.

When the 147th Regiment was formed in 1862, Robert Spencer, despite being too old to serve, enlisted as a hospital steward. Elmina Spencer, unwilling to part from him, also enlisted. During the next three years she aided thousands of soldiers by nursing them, consoling them, and distributing critical supplies and food.

She was first stationed in a hastily improvised hospital at Camp Chase, where she tended the sick and wounded while the men of the

147th performed more duty with shovels than with rifles. Discontent among the ranks became palpable, as numerous letters to the editor of the *Mexico Independent* demonstrate. Captain Reuben Slayton, for example, wrote: "We as a regiment are at work on a fort about a half mile from camp. We have not drilled much except with pick and shovel."[470] His and similar reports of soldiers' poor treatment were initially viewed as idle complaints, but confirming descriptions ultimately led the newspaper to issue a response.[471]

Amid that confusion and chaos, Elmina Spencer attempted unsuccessfully to obtain supplies through official channels. She recalled,

> It was impossible at this time to procure stoves, as our officers were unacquainted with the manner of making proper requisitions according to red tape, as it was called in Washington. Our men were suffering, dying, for the common comforts of life, and were refused because we did not present a proper requisition from the Sanitary Commissioner. We went away thoroughly disgusted and requested aid from the Christian Commissioner.[472]

Her position became stronger after she was appointed a New York State agent for the United States Sanitary Commission in the summer of 1863: "This gave her access to units at the front lines as well as the camps and hospitals where food, clothing, bedding, and medical supplies were needed, and sanitary conditions were evaluated and upgraded. The Agents requisitioned, organized, and managed supplies in the hospitals, and also made sure that the soldiers' families were contacted and kept informed as to their condition while there."[473]

Her reputation as an Oswego County hero was established when the 147th participated in the battles of Fredericksburg in December 1862 and Chancellorsville in May 1863. It was sealed at Gettysburg in July. On June 30, she was "on the Emmetsburgh Road eight miles from Gettysburgh," as she later remembered. Her role in the battle of Gettysburg was never forgotten by the men she aided during that bloody, three-day conflict: "I heard my husband call me. I went to him. He was very much excited, said, 'Mina, Genl. Reynolds is killed, the 14th Brooklyn all cut up and our Regt. almost destroyed. What will you do? Our train is ordered back 14 miles, will you go with them or go on to the fight?' I said, 'I will go to our suffering men.'" Her description continued:

[I] helped the attendants prepare nourishment. They had barely partaken of the food and coffee when orders came to remove the wounded and hospital stores back to a place of safety. As my husband and I went into the fight, we stopped at the foot of the hill where a fierce engagement was in full force and notwithstanding the flying missiles about us, made coffee for the stricken men. At dusk on Wednesday the first of July I helped to form [a] hospital at a little white church on the Baltimore Pike for the reception of sixty-four wounded men." Besides her hospital duties, over the next several days she rode her horse to superintend other makeshift hospitals and assist with amputations. She even helped locate and identify the dead still lying on the field: "I tied my handkerchief over my mouth and nose, found Haversacks and knapsacks on the field, placed them over the uncovered heads, then with a piece of board scraped up sufficient earth to cover them until the right parties could bury them properly."[474]

The men she aided never forgot her and their letters to relatives were full of gratitude and praise. Grove Dutton wrote:

I have neglected to mention Mrs. Robert Spencer, our nurse . . . No words of mine can do justice to the service of this patriotic woman. In this battle as in others after that she was on the firing line and ready and willing to aid all the sick and wounded soldiers, especially those from our regiment. She was not afraid to call on officers high in authority for luxuries and necessities for the disabled and always got the supplies if they could be had. No doubt she saved the lives of many and "smoothed the dying pillow" of others whose lives had to be yielded up in the field and hospital . . . The boys of the 147th and many others have a warm place in their heart for her.[475]

A correspondent known only as Spraker lauded her endeavors:

In visiting different regiments around Culpeper and Brandy Station, I found that they had been frequently visited by Mrs. Spencer, who, by the way, Oswego should be proud of, for she is the only lady that devotes her whole time to sick and needy soldiers. She is located at Brandy Station, the headquarters of the army, and her husband is Hospital Steward to the Medical Purveyor of the army. Oswego is well represented in them, for Mrs. S. mounts her horse with a bundle of needed things, and rides from camp to camp distributed upon personal inquiry, riding sometimes fifteen and twenty miles a day. In that way she succeeds in doing a vast amount of good. I saw soldiers who told me that she had saved their lives by her personal attention, especially after the battle of Gettysburgh, where for three weeks she nursed the wounded, and for which she has a complimentary letter from the Honorable John F. Seymour, Private Secretary to Gov. Seymour . . . Mrs. S. has an iron constitution, and has not been sick a day since she has been in the army. She told me she should stay as long as the war lasted if her health remained.[476]

A report she wrote on September 8, 1865, detailing her movements and activities from November 1864 to July 1865 provides graphic evidence of her importance for the war effort. She spoke of donations from the women of Oswego, of a visit by President Lincoln to the hospital where she was stationed, and of the misery attendant upon the siege of Petersburg. For March 26 and 27 she noted, "The wounded arrived in large numbers. My husband, myself, and a boy, staying with us, worked constantly for two days and nights with the wounded. During forty-eight hours one thousand five hundred wounded Union men were brought in; the rebel wounded were many also." One particularly telling entry described her arrival in the recently captured city of Richmond, Virginia:

> On the morning of the seventh we mounted our horses and proceeded on our way. Between one and two o'clock we reached the city. After eating our rations, resting and watering our horses, we passed on through some of the principal streets of the city, and finally paused in front of Libby Prison just in time to see the rebel prisoners taking the place within the walls so lately occupied by our noble, suffering patriots who had been *tortured, tantalized*[?], *underfed, robbed and destroyed* by these demons in human shape. There, within sight, and almost within reach of our starving men, were boxes of books, clothing

and food that had been sent by dear friends to relieve their wants and sufferings. Those boxes were allowed to moulder and perish within sight and almost within reach of the dying, (as I have before stated) with no other motive apparently but to torture to the utmost, and make their sufferings more excruciating. I must say that for the time, as I saw the Rebels entering the same prison where our men had been so horribly treated, I was sensible of a state of satisfaction that would be pronounced hardly Christian. At the same time I knew they would not be allowed to suffer as our men suffered.[477]

Elmina Spencer arrived in Oswego in mid-June. In November, when she and Robert celebrated their twenty-fifth wedding anniversary, a local newspaper reported that

> it is proposed by certain of their friends to make the occasion one for a call upon them, with substantial tokens of appreciation of their services in the army during the rebellion. We feel assured that the proposition will be heartily seconded by all who entertain a grateful remembrance of Mrs. Spencer's ministrations to our sick and wounded soldiers in camp, on the battle-field and in hospital. Every soldier will avail himself with alacrity of such an opportunity to reward the good deeds done by the Samaritan mother to himself or to even the least of his comrades. Let the donations be cheerful and generous; let the worthy pair be made as happy in the presence and gifts of friends as they were when twenty-five years ago, they first joined hands in the journey of matrimonial life.[478]

Robert, whose mental health was precarious in the best of circumstances, was unable to find steady work after the war and decided to try his hand at homesteading in Kansas, an occupation for which he was eminently unsuited. He and Darius Keeler, Elmina's father, went out to establish the claim in 1872. Elmina, her mother, and the elderly Spencers joined them in June 1873. By the end of 1874 all had died except Elmina. She attempted to remain in Kansas but when the grasshopper plague descended in late July 1874, she, like so many others, lost all her crops and became nearly destitute.[479] While efforts were underway to assist those in most need, Elmina went on a speaking tour to raise funds.[480] Later she gave talks about her wartime adventures and wrote articles for the *Great Bend Register* to support herself.[481] She eventually decided to return to Oswego.

On December 16, 1879, Elmina Spencer applied for a widow's pension. To supplement the meager eight dollars a month allotment, she gave piano lessons. An effort was made in 1885 to induce the federal government to increase the pension. According to the wording of House Resolution 7262, "She knew no fear. She was never too weary to minister personally to the wants of those who were sick or wounded; she never seemed conscious of weariness; the way was never too long or the roads too muddy for her . . . Her acts of devotion place her in the first rank of heroic women."[482] Yet those acts of heroism for which she was so justly praised were insufficient to recommend her for a pension of twenty-five dollars per month. That figure was reduced to twenty dollars, the amount she received for the rest of her life. In 1888 she discovered that she was eligible to claim Robert's federal bounty which had never been paid to him and proposed to do so. Her own "grateful" government

Figure 2.99. Grateful veterans recommended that Elmina Spencer's likeness be carved into the staircase of the New York State Capitol Building. Courtesy of the New York State Military Museum.

never gave her another raise, despite the fact that veterans of all gradations of invalidism obtained regular pension increases. Apparently even the Act of 1890, which rendered almost every living veteran eligible for a pension, was not applicable to her.

The veterans of Oswego County, however, did not forget Elmina Spencer. She was the only female member of John D. O'Brian Post No. 65 GAR. She was also a charter member and first chaplain of Post O'Brian's Woman's Relief Corps.[483] She went with the veterans when the regimental monument was erected at Gettysburg and was presented a veteran's medal, "the only lady present entitled to wear one."[484] She rode in parades, attended parties and banquets, and could always be counted on for an appropriate recitation or a wartime anecdote. For example, as reported in a local newspaper, "Then followed a recitation, 'The Grand Review in Washington,' by Mrs. R. H. Spencer."[485] On the formal recommendation of Henry H. Lyman, a veteran of the 147th Regiment, her bust was carved into the western staircase of the New York State Capitol Building.[486]

Elmina Spencer's last years might have been happier had it not been for an occurrence in March 1873, shortly before she was to move to Kansas. She and Robert had no children, but the 1870 census listed Ida, aged nine, as their adopted daughter. Ida, whose birth name was Rosencraft, was murdered in the family home in Syracuse, New York, on March 17, 1873, while Elmina was in Oswego.[487] Numerous newspapers reported that Elmina's nephew, Albert Keeler, had attacked the young girl, possibly because she rebuffed his sexual advances. Allegedly fearing Ida would tell Elmina, he beat her over the head with an iron bar, killing her almost instantly. Keeler then attempted to escape by jumping on a freight train. He lost his footing and fell onto the tracks, fracturing his skull.[488]

The two grandmothers were home when the murder occurred and a reporter interviewed Mrs. Keeler, who claimed to be an eyewitness to the crime.[489] Ida's body was taken to New York City and buried with her birth mother in Cypress Hills Cemetery.[490] That Elmina never mentioned the tragedy to friends or relatives speaks volumes about her grief. She did, however, reply to charges made against her by one of the boy's uncles that she had starved him. She hoped that such claims would be rendered baseless in days to come.[491]

In her final years Elmina Spencer lived with various female caregivers. Although bedridden for a long time, she retained her mental faculties and enjoyed visitors. The Woman's Relief Corps provided financial support to supplement her meager pension. Her health deteriorated significantly in 1912, the result of a wartime injury. On August 10, 1864, a boat loaded with ammunition exploded at City Point, Virginia: "Mrs. Spencer, belonging to one of the relief agencies, was riding by on horseback at the time, and was struck in several places by flying missiles, but was not badly hurt. Her bonnet string was cut by something which flew past her neck."[492] The injury was worse than thought, and in November 1912, Elmina was suffering from gangrene, which had extended halfway to her knee. When the leg hemorrhaged, the only way to save her life was to amputate.[493] Her impending death was announced the next day, but she survived until December 29, 1912.[494]

This death of this extraordinary woman was widely reported, but the obituary appearing in the *Syracuse Daily Journal* on December 30, 1912, is perhaps the most complete:

> Mrs. Elmina Spencer, 93 years old, of Oswego, who died yesterday in [Oswego], was born in a log cabin at Mexico . . . Her father was Darius Dunham Keeler, who with a party of French

Figure 2.100. The Woman's Relief Corps cared for Elmina Spencer in her later years. Courtesy of the New York State Military Museum.

Figure 2.101. This modest stone, on which her maiden name is misspelled, marks Elmina Keeler Spencer's grave in Rural Cemetery, Oswego Town. Author's collection.

Canadians, settled at Mexico, hewing their log cabins out of the virgin forest. A number of the descendants of these pioneers still live in and around Mexico. Mrs. Spencer's mother was a native of the Green Mountain state . . . Elmina Keeler married Robert H. Spencer and with him went to the War of the Rebellion. She was mustered into the One Hundred and Forty-seventh Regiment, New York Volunteers as hospital nurse and served until the close of the conflict. At City Point while ministering to the wounded she was struck in the side by grape shot . . . In the Army of the Potomac there was none better known at the close of the war than Mrs. Spencer and few generals elicited more cheers from the men when riding past than she as she rode her favorite horse "Pete." Generals, from Grant down, treated her with distinguished consideration and respect. Thousands of "New York boys" now way beyond their prime as well as veterans of other states remember her with gratitude for her ministrations to them. The state of New York some years ago honored Mrs. Spencer by placing her head and bust in bronze on the main stairway of the Capitol at Albany . . . Bedridden for years, but full of cheerfulness and hope, keen of mind, Mrs. Spencer had been cared for by the Woman's Relief Corps of the G. A. R. With her has passed away the last of the family.[495]

The Woman's Relief Corps paid her funeral expenses.

Elmina Pleiades Keeler Spencer is buried in Rural Cemetery, town of Oswego, section 4. Her husband, Robert Hamilton Spencer, lies in an unmarked grave in Great Bend Cemetery, Kansas.

Francis W. Squires

If the game of trivia had been in existence in the lifetime of Civil War soldier Francis W. Squires, he would have been a champion. His knowledge of the people and the places in Oswego County verged on encyclopedic. For his contributions to local history, he must be considered a notable veteran.

F. W. SQUIRES.

Figure 2.102. Francis W. Squires, avid writer and statistician, was well known in Oswego County for his extensive research into local history and biography. Courtesy of Crisfield Johnson, *History of Oswego County.*

Born in Lebanon, Madison, New York, on October 22, 1820, Francis Squires was one of seven children in the family of Pierce Squires (June 4, 1785–January 11, 1861) and Eunice Warriner (November 26, 1789–June 25, 1873).[496] After the family moved to Martinsburgh, Lewis, New York, in 1838, he attended Martinsburgh Academy, "walking two and a half miles every night and morning, in his zeal to acquire an education."[497] In 1846 Squires moved to New Haven, New York, where he taught school for several years.

Francis Squires married Sarah R. Rice, born in 1831, on October 9, 1851, and they became the parents of four children: Clarence A. (July 10, 1852–September 20, 1859); Harriet A. (May 1854–September 4, 1925) married Reuben Cyrus Coe (October 20, 1848–December 28, 1934) in 1875 as his second wife; Clara A. (October 24, 1856–December 22, 1916) married Clarence M. Gowdy (March 10, 1857–1937) on

Figure 2.103. Sarah Rice Squires was the mother of four children. Author's collection.

February 6, 1884; Frank C. (May 1859–August 27, 1948) married Jane "Jennie" E. Price (May 1866–1942) on October 30, 1880. Sarah died on March 8, 1860, of unknown causes.

In 1853 Francis and Sarah Squires moved to Volney where he was appointed postmaster in 1861, serving in that capacity until 1881 when the family moved back to New Haven.[498] He was a justice of the peace for twelve years and a longtime notary public. He was a staunch Republican, although not particularly active politically.

Squires was forty-four years old when he enlisted in the 184th Regiment on August 21, 1864, mustering into Co. A. He had kept a diary since 1843, so it is possible to learn details of his experiences during the year he spent in the army. On October 1, for example, he reported steady rain in the afternoon as he marched toward Harrisburg, Virginia, a distance of twenty-five miles. He noted, "Barns were on fire for the last 15 miles," a reference to General Sheridan's "scorched earth" policy in the Shenandoah Valley Campaign. On October 5, he wrote, "Pleasant day. Came to Newtown 23 miles & stopped early. I rode P.M. & fell from a wagon at night & nearly killed myself." He wrote on October 8, "Came to Martinsburg last night at 12:45 o'clock, 22 miles distant. I walked all the way as lame as I was. Very cold . . . Soldiers can scarcely keep comfortable."

Co. A was one of the four companies from the 184th involved in the battle of Cedar Creek on October 19. Colonel Wardwell G. Robinson remembered:

> The battle of Cedar Creek was the first engagement in which the detachment participated, and wherein it received its baptism of fire. It can truthfully be said that it sustained its part well, and materially aided in the final triumphant repulse and defeat of the Confederates. It must be remembered that at the time of the engagement, scarcely a month had elapsed since the members of the detachment had been drawn from the peaceful avocations of home life, and had but little or no acquaintance with military drill, tactics, or discipline.[499]

Squires made no entry concerning the battle of Cedar Creek, suggesting that the fall he had taken prevented him from participating in the struggle. On October 25 he wrote that he had been in the hospital again and on October 27 he "stood guard for 1st time today for 24 hours."

Later entries were revelatory. On March 4, 1865, he reported attending President Lincoln's inauguration. He met President and Mrs. Lincoln at the White House on April 12. His note for April 15 was terse: "President Lincoln was shot last night at 10 ½ o'clock and died this morning, at 22 minutes past 7 o'clock." On April 19 he wrote: "I have been to the funeral of President Lincoln. It was a grand affair." He was discharged on a surgeon's certificate on June 2, 1865. In 1890 he did not disclose the nature of his disability but when in later life he fell and injured himself severely, a newspaper article reported that he "was wounded in one of his legs in the late war."[500]

Like many regiments, the 184th formed a reunion association in which Francis was active. When the first reunion was held in 1889 he "read an interesting historical sketch of the regiment."[501] He also belonged to James Doyle Post No. 591 GAR in New Haven, serving as quartermaster in 1894.[502] On December 21, 1895, he transferred his membership to Melzar Richards Post No. 367 GAR in Mexico, New York.

Squires was interested in the spiritual wellbeing of his four children. Together with an unnamed concerned townswoman, he helped start and served as superintendent of a Sabbath school in an underserved section of North Volney, whose enrollment quickly rose from thirty to more than one hundred.[503]

He was a member of New Haven Grange No. 54, serving as its treasurer in 1888 and 1889.[504]

His greatest love, however, was the Old Settlers' Association which was founded on August 27, 1875. He was elected secretary-treasurer, a position he held until he died.[505] That founding date was also special to him for another reason. On August 29, 1875, he married Maria Louisa Vanderbilt Coe at Dempster Grove, where the association was formed: "A marriage was celebrated upon the grounds during the afternoon—that of F. W. Squires, Esq., to Mrs. M. S. Coe, both of North Volney."[506] Maria Vanderbilt's first husband was John Potter Coe (June 2, 1825–August 20, 1874), also a veteran of Co. A, 184th Regiment. They were the parents of four children.

The Old Settlers' Association met annually, and each year Squires, dubbed the leading statistician of the county, announced the names of those who had died during the previous twelve months. He also read the names of the oldest persons still living in the various towns.[507]

Squires was much more than a statistician, however, and no subject was too mundane for his consideration. He was a longtime correspondent for several regional newspapers, and in addition to reporting the news, he wrote interesting essays on items he had gleaned from recent editions. For example, he responded to an article concerning cannon balls which might have been used in the War of 1812: "The events aimed at happened before my remembrance, and if they had occurred since 1840 I might have been prepared to say something definite." He then described the battle of Fort Oswego, which occurred in the spring of 1814, concluding with: "I have made the history of this county quite a study, but I find there are many things yet to learn. I like to have questions come up in reference to early times, and will try and do my best to throw light where I can."[508] An article concerning Deacon Ezra Botsford elicited a response from Squires, in which he related that he had known the man fifty years earlier. Simultaneously he seized the opportunity to discuss some of the "leading men" of the time in Lewis County.[509]

Over the years Squires wrote about the town of New Haven, Groundhog Day, cold weather, the town of Mexico, and the early history of the New York State Legislature.[510] One particularly humorous piece described the current board of supervisors:

> F. W. Squires has just completed an interesting statistical table of the supervisors. From it we learn that the heavy weight of the board is Mr. Alport [sic] of Scriba who tips the beam at 200 pounds. Chairman Barrett and supervisors Selleck and Trimble are the feather weights each weighing 140 pounds. Supervisor Virgil of Mexico is the tallest man on the board, 6 feet 2 inches while Messrs. Hourigan, Selleck and Ross measure but 5 feet 6 inches.[511]

In the months preceding his death, Squires's ill health was mentioned numerous times in local news columns, though no precise sickness was named. He died on June 5, 1897, in the town of New Haven. An obituary paid tribute to his erudition:

> Mr. Squires was a local historian of accuracy and has collected much valuable [data] concerning the towns in which he has lived, besides a general sketch of almost all the towns of Oswego county. Since January 1st, 1843, he has kept a daily diary of events and many interesting anecdotes and facts will be gleaned from the now well-filled books. Mr. Squires was

Figure 2.104. It is ironic that the gravestone of Francis W. Squires, who compiled years of statistics and kept a diary for forty-three years, contains no biographical information. Author's collection.

a judicious collector of historical incidents, local and general, and his scrap-books, containing items of almost every description, were daily consulted as valuable records of by gone events. In his collection of data, Mr. Squires visited all parts of Oswego county and was, perhaps, better known than any other man in it.[512]

Maria outlived her husband by many years. She was involved in the Grange movement and in the Good Templars, a popular temperance organization. Upon her death on June 21, 1911, she was remembered as "a kind-hearted neighbor and a true friend, and many a tear will be shed at the remembrance of kindly deeds which she performed for those in trouble or sorrow."[513]

Francis W. Squires, Sarah R. Rice Squires, Maria L. Vanderbilt Coe Squires, and John Potter Coe are buried in North Volney Cemetery, old section.

Dr. James K. Stockwell

Any attempt to review the life and career of James K. Stockwell in a brief biography is fraught with challenges since the man lived a long life, most of it spent in Oswego City as a respected and knowledgeable physician. In addition to his practice, he was admired for his civic and political activities, and it was not uncommon to see his name in local newspaper columns.

James Stockwell, born on October 25, 1844, was the oldest of the five children of Ralph Stockwell (July 11, 1819–April 15, 1908) and Jane E. Streeter (1821–1859). At the time the family lived on a farm in Wilson, Niagara, New York. He attended the local common schools, entering Lockport Union School at the age of sixteen.[514] In 1863 he began his medical studies at Columbia University College of Medicine in New York City.

The Civil War had been raging for several years when the young man enlisted in the 23rd Independent Battery NY LA on September 3, 1864. The outfit by this time had been reorganized into a veteran volunteer regiment. Its entire tenure was spent in North Carolina and in April 1865 was attached to General Philip Sheridan's cavalry in the Shenandoah Valley Campaign. When the soldiers mustered out on July 14, 1865, Stockwell returned to New York State to continue his education. He completed his training at the University of Buffalo School of Medicine in 1870.[515]

In 1871 James Stockwell married Margaret Fleming, born in 1850 to John Fleming (1825–1905) and Margaret A. Miller (1826–1910). The daughter of immigrants, Margaret was born in Lewiston, Niagara County. The young couple moved to Oswego City where they resided for the rest of their lives.

James and Margaret were the parents of two daughters, Margery "Margie" (1877–March 14, 1887) and Helen M. (May 8, 1886–December 23, 1886). It is unknown what caused their deaths, but it is easy to speculate that the doctor's interest in the welfare of the city's children stemmed from the early deaths of his own little girls.

Dr. James Stockwell immediately became involved in the local medical community. As early as 1872 he was a member and recording secretary of the Oswego County Medical Society. In the ensuing years, he acquired more professional responsibilities. He was a surgeon on call for the New York, New Jersey, and New England Railroad, charged

Figure 2.105. James and Margaret Fleming Stockwell pose with members of the Fleming family in this 1895 portrait. They are the two people on the left in the back row. Courtesy of Keith O'Connell, https://www.ancestry.com.

with attending to patients in the event of a train derailment. He was the physician for the Oswego County Jail and a member of the local pension examining board.[516] Most important, perhaps, was his position as Oswego City's health officer.

Stockwell waged war against many diseases common in the late nineteenth and early twentieth centuries. Diphtheria, typhoid fever, smallpox, and polio ran rampant throughout the city annually, causing widespread deaths, especially among children. The newspapers were replete with stories of Dr. Stockwell's campaign to clean up the city, force business owners to maintain sanitary conditions, and close contaminated wells. Despite the fact that Oswego had begun to draw its water from Lake Ontario, many homes still relied on private wells. In a time when indoor plumbing was still reserved for the city's wealthier members, these wells were frequently contaminated by human and animal waste, which inevitably resulted in outbreaks of typhoid fever.[517]

Despite many demands on his time as a doctor and a surgeon, Stockwell found opportunities to become involved in local politics. He was a staunch Republican, supporting the local machine which in 1889 came to him with a problem. The incumbent mayor, Mr. McCaffrey, announced only days before the convention that he did not wish to run for reelection, throwing the party into chaos. After two other potential candidates declined to be considered, a committee was finally appointed to wait upon Dr. Stockwell and the subject was laid before him, as a matter of duty to the republican party and to the people of this city, and he was induced to enter the field . . . With only one day for organization the doctor entered the field, and the result was the victory which we have the pleasure of announcing today. The doctor won six out of the eight wards of the city . . . His election is both a personal and political triumph of which he and his friends may well be proud.[518]

His mayoralty lasted only one term. He did not wish to run again in 1890 but was prevailed upon by local Republicans who told him "he owed it to the public."[519]

Despite the fact that his administration was deemed efficient and honest, he was defeated by Edward Mitchell, a Democrat.[520]

Dr. Stockwell found other outlets for his abilities. He was a longtime trustee of the Oswego City Savings Bank. He was one of the founders of the Lake City Building and Loan Association in 1890 and was its longtime president.[521] He also was a member and president of the Riverside Cemetery Association.[522]

He was a charter member of May Humphrey Stacy Post No. 586 GAR and was its surgeon for several years. He later was a member of John D. O'Brian Post No. 65 GAR. His most significant membership, however, was in the Masonic fraternity.

James Stockwell was raised a Master Mason in Aeonian Lodge No. 679 F&AM in 1871, shortly after arriving in the city. He served as worshipful master from 1885 to 1892, a record at that time. He was appointed district deputy grand master in 1889 and grand standard bearer in 1892.[523] Additionally, Stockwell was a member of Lake Ontario Chapter No. 165 RAM, Lake Ontario Commandery, Kentucky, and Shrine Media Temple.

Such was his influence in these organizations that one newspaper reporter felt compelled to write: "James K. Stockwell . . . is the acknowledged leader among the Masonic fraternity in matters pertaining to the Grand Lodge. It is said he holds the same position in the Grand Lodge as do certain local Republican politicians in the State organization, and that no appointments are made unless they have his approval."[524]

Margaret Stockwell, like her husband, took an active role in local affairs. She was particularly interested in the city hospital and was a trustee for many years. She was a vice president and longtime board treasurer.⁵²⁵ Her name appeared frequently in the local newspapers as a donor of food and equipment for the facility. She served on the board of the city's Home for the Homeless (Ladies' Home) and participated in the activities of the Congregational Church to which she and her husband belonged.⁵²⁶ She belonged to the Oswego City Woman's Club and the Foreign Missionary Society.

Her death on April 14, 1924, elicited a lengthy obituary detailing her many civic accomplishments and describing her personally: "Mrs. Stockwell was loved and respected by all who came in contact with her during her long and useful life. She was a woman of quiet tastes and performed acts of kindness and benevolence with the least possible outward evidence. Her death will be deeply felt by those who knew her best."⁵²⁷

James Stockwell died on March 23, 1929, "after a long illness." An obituary referred to him as "the dean of the medical profession in Central New York" and reviewed his long career in Oswego City.⁵²⁸ In 1918, when his term as health officer was expiring, a newspaper article provided what might have been a fitting eulogy:

> Few officials have proved more efficient than Dr. Stockwell. Gifted with a most intimate knowledge of medicine and sani-

Figure 2.106. Margaret Fleming Stockwell took an active interest in Oswego Hospital. Author's collection.

Figure 2.107. Dr. James Stockwell was a tireless crusader in the struggle to improve the health of Oswego City residents. Author's collection.

tation, the result of twenty-five years of study and attention to his office, he has proven himself fearless in epidemics, fearless in going over the head of even the highest State authorities in his determination to give proper care to the health of a municipality . . . It has been the same in every epidemic that visited Oswego. Personal business has been thrown aside by the health officer, he has never been known to falter in his duties and he has been fearless.[529]

Dr. James Stockwell, Margaret Fleming Stockwell, and their daughters, Margery and Helen, are buried in Riverside Cemetery, Scriba, New York, section D.

John Wilson Sykes

When John Wilson Sykes died in Fulton, New York, on January 26, 1932, not one notice of his passing appeared in local newspapers. Such an interesting omission was in keeping with the many other mysteries surrounding this notable Civil War veteran.

John Sykes was born in Accrington, Lancashire, England, on April 19, 1841, to Harriet Barnes Sykes (1818–?) and an unknown father. That date is probably correct even though later Sykes claimed he had been born on August 19, 1841. In 1851 he was living with his mother and her husband, Henry Wilson, as well as several siblings, all Wilson's children. When John was baptized on May 21, 1854, his name was given as John Wilson, son of Harriet Sykes, a spinner. He sometimes claimed that Henry Wilson was his father when filling out marriage licenses but he probably did so to avoid embarrassment.

What compelled John Sykes to leave England is unknown, but he immigrated to the United States on the *City of Manchester*, arriving in New York City on September 16, 1863, shortly after the draft riots had taken place there. By September the battles of Gettysburg, Vicksburg, and Port Hudson had been fought. In January 1865 Sykes became involved in the struggle, but where he was and what he was doing up to that time is unknown.

On January 11, 1865, John Sykes, using the alias John Wilson, enrolled in the 10th NY Cavalry in Poughkeepsie, Dutchess County, New York, and was mustered into Co. A. Why he thought he needed to change his name is puzzling. Even though the war was nearly finished in early 1865, considerable hard fighting was ahead. The 10th, attached to the 1st Brigade, 2nd Division Army of the Potomac, participated in, among others, the engagements at Hatcher's Run, Sailor's Creek, and the Appomattox Campaign.

The 10th Cavalry was ordered to be consolidated with the 24th on June 17, 1865, although the order was not carried out until July 10 at Cloud's Mills, Virginia. The combined unit, renamed the 1st Provisional Cavalry, mustered out on August 3–4, 1865, at Syracuse, Onondaga, New York. John's muster card for the 1st Provisional carried the following note: "In confinement awaiting trial at muster out of company; no further record." A pension card reported that he had been discharged on July 19, 1865, at Cloud's Mills. This date was used when he was admitted to the National Soldiers' Home in Kennebec, Maine, on June 4, 1892. When he entered the Home in Bath, Steuben, New York, on April 12, 1918, he claimed to have been discharged in August 1865 in Syracuse.

From 1865 until 1882 Sykes's whereabouts are unknown. As a carpenter he probably had little trouble finding work and since his mother had been involved in the textile industry he was undoubtedly familiar with the equipment. Several documents listed his occupation as "loom fixer."

John Sykes's matrimonial odyssey began in Amesbury, Berkshire, Massachusetts, on January 23, 1882, when he married Hannah Lynch Glynn. Hannah was the daughter of Timothy Lynch (1810–?) and Mary _____ (1812–?). Born in Ireland *ca.* 1850, Hannah had previously been married to a man by the last name of Glynn, whose first name is lost to history. For some reason Sykes claimed he too was on his second marriage, and he may have been correct since in 1920 he said he had been twenty-two years of age when he contracted his first marriage. In 1882 he was almost forty-one years old.

What happened to this marriage is unknown but it is possible that the couple separated. In the 1890s a woman named Hannah Glynn "widow" lived in Amesbury.

Sykes's next matrimonial adventure began on December 26, 1896, in Manchester, Hillsborough, New Hampshire, when he married Harriet "Hattie" C. Grotton (October 6, 1844–November 23, 1899), a weaver. Both claimed to have been married once before. Hattie, whose parents were William Grotton (1800–1876) and Catherine Lessner (1804–1886), had been born in Washington, Knox, Maine. This marriage apparently did not last because when Hattie died of typhoid pneumonia she was buried with her parents in Marr Cemetery, Washington, Knox, Maine, and the name on her gravestone was Hattie C. Grotton.

In the meantime Sykes had moved on to his next marriage. His new wife was Fannie A. Jones Whitaker (September 21, 1849–September 26, 1920), born in Wells, York, Maine, whom he married on March 12, 1898, in Somersworth, Strafford, New Hampshire. Fannie's parents were Elias Jones (?–?) and Susan _____ (?–?). She had previously married George W. Whitaker (1848–?) on October 23, 1871, in Newburyport, Essex, Massachusetts. What happened to him is unknown. The significant point here is that John Sykes married Fannie while still married to Hattie. Their union was short-lived since she married Willard Grant (January 1874–February 23, 1963) on July 30, 1898. Perhaps Fannie discovered Sykes already had a wife and left him. She and Willard Grant were living together in 1900, claiming to have been married two years. By 1910, however, they had also parted company. Fannie succumbed to cancer and was buried in Riverside Cemetery, Lewiston, Androscoggin, Maine.

John Sykes entered the matrimonial arena again on March 24, 1900, when he married Mary Jane Guernsey Allen Oakes (June 7, 1850–March 26, 1914) at Rowley, Essex, Massachusetts. He again claimed this was his second marriage, as did Mary Jane. In 1910 both told the census enumerator truthfully they had been married three times. Mary Jane Guernsey first married Charles Allen (*ca.* 1845–?) *ca.* 1867 in Georgetown, Essex, Massachusetts, by whom she had a son, John L. (August 1869–September 7, 1925). She next married Orice C. Oakes (December 1837–May 12, 1913) *ca.* 1875. By 1900 the couple had separated and he was calling himself a widower. Mary Jane, daughter of Charles Guernsey (1817–June 20, 1864) and Elizabeth "Betsey" Taylor (1830–*post* 1880), was born in Oswego County, New York. She died in Haverhill, Essex, Massachusetts, after suffering a stroke. Her death record said she would be buried in Rowley, but her grave has not been located.

Seven months later, on December 17, 1914, at the age of seventy-three, John Sykes married Elizabeth Ann Slaver Moore (1876–December 7, 1938), the daughter of Lewis Slaver (March 1845–April 15, 1928),

Figure 2.108. John Wilson Sykes was a longtime soldier in the Salvation Army. Courtesy of the Salvation Army National Archives.

a veteran of the 10th Cavalry, and Mary Catherine Bell (February 23, 1839–May 27, 1913). Elizabeth had first married Irving Darwin Moore (September 24, 1872–May 17, 1954) on August 30, 1896, and by 1905 was the mother of three children, Raymond (July 9, 1897–April 26, 1973), Howard Roselle (May 22, 1898–December 8, 1962), and Doris Mildred (June 15, 1905–February 1, 1999). When she and Sykes procured their marriage license in Fulton, New York, she said she had been divorced from Moore on May 27, 1907, and did not know if he was alive or dead.[530] John and Elizabeth's wedding announcement stated that this was the groom's "third venture."[531]

Although John Sykes had earlier claimed to be a carpenter and loom fixer, at some point he became associated with the Salvation Army.

This affiliation was first noted in the 1900 census and again in 1910 when he and Mary J. were living in Kittery, York, Maine. John and Elizabeth's wedding announcement mentioned that he was an "envoy," an honorary title for retired noncommissioned members of the Salvation Army. When he was admitted to the Soldiers' Home, however, he made no mention of the Salvation Army, saying instead that he was a weaver. The couple resided in North Adams, Berkshire, Massachusetts,

Figure 2.109. Only this gravestone provides evidence that John Wilson Sykes died in Fulton and was buried in Mt. Adnah Cemetery. Author's collection.

in 1918 but had moved to Newport, Orleans, Vermont, by 1920 where he was an "officer" for the Salvation Army. In 1929 he and Elizabeth, living in Barry, Washington, Vermont, decided to return to Fulton. The newspaper article announcing this decision said: "He is also a veteran of the Salvation Army, having served in that organization for 45 years and recently retired with the rank of envoy."[532] If the number was accurate, he would have been associated with the organization since 1884.

Little else has been discovered about John Wilson Sykes. He does not appear in the 1890 Veterans' Schedules. He made a successful application for a pension in 1891 but Elizabeth never applied for a widow's pension. He joined Daniel F. Schenck Post No. 271 GAR but the date is unknown. And when he died at the age of ninety on January 26, 1932, his passing was not noticed in the newspapers.

Elizabeth outlived John by six years and died in Watertown, Jefferson County, New York. As with John, no announcement was made of her death.

John Wilson Sykes, Elizabeth Slaver Moore Sykes, and Elizabeth's daughter, Doris Moore Hansen are buried in Mt. Adnah Cemetery, Fulton, New York, section 10.

Figure 2.110. Elizabeth Slaver Moore Sykes and her daughter, Doris, are buried a short distance from John Wilson Sykes in Mt. Adnah Cemetery, Fulton, New York. Author's collection.

William A. Tillapaugh

A son of Mexico, New York, William A. Tillapaugh was born on May 4, 1838, to Solomon Tillapaugh (January 10, 1804–March 4, 1903) and Eliza A. Evarts (August 10, 1812–January 1, 1885), pioneer settlers in the area. His many adventures and misadventures distinguish him as a noteworthy Civil War veteran.

He was in the California gold fields when the Civil War began and enlisted in the 1st California Cavalry on May 27, 1863, mustering into Co. G on June 12.[533] This outfit saw extensive duty in Texas and New Mexico, primarily aimed at subduing various Native American tribes. He mustered out on May 27, 1866, at Santa Fe, New Mexico.

When exactly William Tillapaugh returned to Mexico is unknown, but in 1873 he was appointed a deputy sheriff, a position he held under three successive sheriffs. This job afforded him many adventures. The year 1875 started with a decided amount of excitement. On New Year's Eve a party was held at a hotel in Port Ontario which Simon Pierson "crashed." When told to leave, he refused. Tillapaugh, hired as a security guard that night, attempted to force him out. Guns were drawn and Tillapaugh shot Pierson in the head. Pierson went to Pulaski for treatment, then returned. He forced all the partygoers to flee except for the musicians, whom he ordered to play as he alleged he was going to die at any moment. While they played, he ransacked the dance hall. Another police officer, George Doane, finally placed Pierson under arrest. The next morning Tillapaugh was also arrested—for shooting Pierson. He made bail of $500,[534] and apparently nothing came of the charge against him.

The young deputy had other adventures. He was, for example, involved with Daniel McSweeney and the United States Secret Service in the investigation, arrest, and prosecution of the counterfeiting ring operating in Oswego County.[535]

In the same month, a prisoner attempting to escape from the jail in Pulaski attacked Tillapaugh: "While Deputy Sheriff Tillapaugh was taking him [St. Pierre] to his cell, he made a desperate effort to escape by seizing a heavy stick from the wood box, and attempting to strike Tillapaugh with it. The turnkey happened to be near, and with his assistance St. Pierre was locked up."[536]

In July 1883 three prisoners escaped from the Oswego jail, heading for parts unknown. Lawmen, including Tillapaugh, chased after them:

Deputy Sheriff Tillapaugh was on the look out at Mexico Point. Three men were seen to land a little distance west of the Point on Saturday afternoon and he with men, among whom were the life crew, went in search of them. As it was thought they were making their way to Texas, the officer acted accordingly and with the assistance of Sylvester Hemans, residing near the lake, he succeeded in capturing Nichols and Hunter, where the road leading to the lake turns from the State road. They showed a spirit of resistance but the sheriff was prepared for any emergency and they found this to be of no avail . . . Officer Tillapaugh, and all who assisted him, including the lifesaving crew, deserve much credit for their promptness and efficiency in capturing these jail birds.[537]

Tillapaugh made two unsuccessful attempts to run for sheriff in 1884 and in 1887.[538] Maurice L. Wright then appointed him court crier, a position he held from 1887 to 1888. Judge Merrick Stowell reappointed him in 1893.[539]

Even this job posed occupational hazards. One day after court recessed, lawyer Henry C. P. Benedict had a disagreement with the court crier and kicked him in the abdomen: "The Times says: 'A friendly feeling has not existed between Court Crier Tillapaugh and Attorney Benedict for a number of years, and for that reason believe many that the assault was not unintentional. Anyway, Mr. Tillapaugh is angry and expresses himself freely.'"[540] A contrite Benedict apologized after being hailed before Judge John C. Churchill, who thereupon suspended the sentence.[541]

For the next nine years Tillapaugh served in both the Oswego City and the Pulaski courts. Early in January 1909 the situation changed drastically when County Judge Louis Rowe abolished the post of court crier, reasoning that the job was an unnecessary expense.[542] Tillapaugh countered by claiming he could not be removed without cause because he was a Civil War veteran. His case was helped when Justice Scripture told Rowe he needed a court crier.[543]

On January 22, 1909, Rowe reversed himself and reinstated Tillapaugh. In his ruling Judge Rowe alluded to a bill passed by the state legislature in 1847 which abolished the post of court crier. He further stated that it had been permissible under later legislation "that the County Judge 'from time to time, may appoint and at pleasure remove a crier for the court of record in this county.'" He reiterated that he deemed the job of court crier obsolete, then referred to Tillapaugh's claim concerning his status as a Civil War veteran, considering it "doubtful." He stated that he was vacating his previous order "in deference to the request of said presiding Justice [Scripture] for a court crier."[544]

Tillapaugh's reinstatement was hotly contested the rest of the year. In February, George W. Rogers, Hannibal town supervisor, leveled charges against him, specifically that he "has on two occasions drawn double pay for the same day's service and that he has unlawfully taken money for mileage when in reality he is a resident of this [Oswego] city."[545] In response, Tillapaugh claimed, truthfully, that he was and always had been a resident of the town of Mexico.[546] Rogers demanded that Tillapaugh be charged for alleged "double dipping" and a hearing was held. Rowe presided, which caused Tillapaugh's attorney to object on the grounds of a conflict of interest. At the end of the two-day hearing, Judge Rowe announced he would reserve his decision until the conclusion of the current trial term.[547] Therefore, Tillapaugh would work each day while the term was in session.

This state of affairs evidently was unsatisfactory to Supervisor Rogers who went to court a few months later seeking permission to amend his original charges, now alleging he had uncovered five more specific allegations of misconduct. After a hearing, the judge granted the motion.[548] Rogers claimed that

> on April 27, 1908, he [Tillapaugh] obtained $26.20 for eight days' services as crier and $2.20 mileage at Pulaski and that while the term ran only 17 days, Mr. Tillapaugh is alleged to have received pay for 19 days . . . On Dec. 29, 1908, it is alleged that he received $4.80 for one day's service and 36 miles of travel while on the same day he received an order for $7.80 for two days' service and mileage at special term, the charge being that he received two mileages and two days' pay for serving in two courts on the same day.[549]

Again, Judge Rowe allowed the amendments to be entered. Despite a vigorous defense, Tillapaugh lost his case. In September Judge Rowe determined there were sixty-six rulings of fact and removed him from his position.[550] A. S. Wright, Tillapaugh's attorney, stated that he intended to appeal but apparently nothing ever came of that announcement. By that time Tillapaugh had other pressing problems.

William Tillapaugh and Harriet "Hattie" M. Tiffany (January 12, 1839–February 22, 1896) were married on February 16, 1870, and lived together for twenty-six years. They had no children. Upon her death Harriet was remembered thus:

> Mrs. Hattie M. Tillapaugh . . . died at her residence on Main street on Saturday morning, Feb. 22, 1896, after a brief illness of only about a week. Though so suddenly called to exchange worlds, death did not find her unprepared to go. She had anticipated the change that must come sooner or later to us all, and had wisely committed her interests for time and eternity into the keeping of her Saviour . . . Apparently without fear or dread she went down into the valley and shadow of death, fearing no evil, sustained by the glorious hope that to be absent from the body is to be present with the Lord. In the various relations of life as daughter, sister, a devoted wife, a kind neighbor and a sympathizing friend, she leaves behind her only pleasant memories.[551]

Tillapaugh's next attempt at connubial bliss was less satisfying. Florence C. Murphy was born in Mt. Vernon, Ohio, in March 1861. She married George D. Huntley (1862–December 25, 1894) in Kent County, Michigan, between 1883 and 1886. Their children, Helen Gladys (1891–?) and George Lovell (March 21, 1895–January 1969), were born in Chicago, Cook, Illinois. When George died, his body was transported to Mexico, New York, and buried in his family's plot in Mexico Village Cemetery.

On December 9, 1899, Florence married William Tillapaugh.[552] She and the children were living with him in 1900 and 1905. Florence became involved with the Woman's Relief Corps in Mexico. In 1903 she traveled to Montreal to see a childhood friend and sent a well-written, detailed letter to the editor of the *Mexico Independent* describing her delights in the Canadian city.[553]

Yet all was not well in the Tillapaugh household. By 1907 the couple had parted and William was ordered to pay for his wife's counsel and board until the parties finalized the separation.[554] In 1908 Helen was admitted to the Onondaga Poorhouse because she was ill. The admission form stated that her mother lived in Syracuse. In 1910 both children were living with their paternal grandparents, William and Nancy Huntley, in Mexico.

Therefore, while William Tillapaugh was fighting to retain his position as court crier, he was also dealing with domestic problems. Not until 1912 was he able to obtain a divorce. According to the terms, he was permitted to remarry but Florence was prohibited from doing so as long as William was alive.[555]

It must have come as a surprise when William discovered that Florence had married Julius Kosloski (June 1849–October 18, 1936) on November 4, 1914, in Utica, Oneida, New York. On the application for a marriage license Florence had used the surname of Huntley and alleged this was her second marriage. She also stated that her husband was dead. It is unclear when Kosloski discovered the truth, but a year later he was in court asking for an annulment. To bolster his case he

Figure 2.111. William and Harriet Tiffany Tillapaugh are buried in Mexico Village Cemetery. Author's collection.

brought Tillapaugh to court, bearing with him a certified copy of the divorce decree.[556]

The last known reference to Florence appeared in 1920. According to the census, she was living as a servant with a private family in New Hartford, Oneida, New York, and using the surname Huntley. It is possible that the woman named Florence Huntley, who was employed later in 1920 as the first matron of the Lutheran Home in Clinton, Oneida, New York, is the same person.[557]

By 1920 William Tillapaugh was almost finished with his life's adventures. He had been a staunch Republican throughout his adult life, supporting local candidates at caucuses and conventions. A charter member of Melzar Richards Post No. 367 GAR, he participated in its affairs for many years. He was also a brother in Mexico Lodge No. 136 F&AM and in 1925 was recognized for fifty years of membership.[558] When he celebrated his birthday in 1927, he was the lodge's oldest member.[559]

In his final years, Tillapaugh lived with the Van Arsdales in Mexico. He died there on October 8, 1928, after an illness of several months. His obituary paid tribute to his service to country and community and to his parents, especially his mother, Eliza Evarts, the first white girl born in the town.[560]

William A. Tillapaugh, Harriet M. Tiffany Tillapaugh, and Solomon and Eliza Evarts Tillapaugh are buried in Mexico Village Cemetery, section E.

Edmund Underwood

Sometimes serendipity plays a part in uncovering the story of a notable veteran. Thus it was that the lives of Edmund Underwood and his wife, Mary Beardsley, came to be investigated. Perched on a hillside overlooking Consecration Lake in Riverside Cemetery, Scriba, New York, their gravestones are easily missed. Only because a search was being made for another veteran's gravesite were theirs discovered beneath the limbs of a large tree.

Edmund Underwood was born February 22, 1828, in Dauphin County, Pennsylvania, the son of James M. Underwood (1789–1834), a well-known newspaper editor, and Catherine Goddard (1796–1875). Little is known about his childhood, but in 1846 he enlisted as a private in the US Army and served in the Mexican-American War. At the conclusion of his enlistment he accepted a commission as a second lieutenant in the Regular Army.⁵⁶¹ From 1848 to 1851 he was a soldier in the 4th United States Infantry stationed at Fort Ontario, Oswego, New York. For the next several years he was stationed with the 4th United States Regular Army (USA) in California. He was promoted to first lieutenant on March 24, 1853, and to captain on March 11, 1856.⁵⁶²

His wife Mary, who along with several other military wives also made the trip to California, described the voyage to a reporter many years later:

> We sailed from New York in the old frigate Ohio, and went to Aspinwall, now in the canal zone, and from there we went up the Chagres river in bongos, or native boats. There were six companies in the Fourth to make the trip, but four were to go around the Horn, leaving but two companies to go by way of the isthmus . . . At Panama cholera broke out, and we were there two weeks waiting for the steamer Golden Gate to sail . . . When we reached San Francisco I went with my husband and his company to Humboldt Bay, where we established a post, and there in a tent my oldest son was born, Commander E. B. Underwood, U. S. N. retired.⁵⁶³

Mary recounted in the same interview how she met Ulysses S. Grant at a party in New York City and how her husband and Grant, both stationed in the west, became good friends:

> My first introduction to General Grant was in 1848 in New York City . . . and during all the years of his life I had the pleasure of calling him my friend. I doubt if there is another living person who knew the hero of the civil war under more trying circumstances. General Grant was a brevet captain in those days . . . I again met General Grant, who had been detailed to the Puget Sound country, when he stopped to visit us at Humboldt. He and my husband were great friends and, after he had been assigned to Fort Redding in the Sacramento valley, where the Indians were troublesome, we met again.

The Underwoods spent many years in California, as Edmund's assignment was to protect pack trains in northern California from hostile Native Americans. Life changed dramatically when the Civil War began.

Underwood was promoted to major on May 14, 1861, and placed in command of the 2nd Battalion (Cos. F and S) of the 18th Regiment USA. He went to Columbus, Ohio, to train troops at Camp Thomas. On November 30, 1861, he led them to Louisville, Kentucky, where they came under the command of General Buell, who was organizing the Army of Ohio. Major Underwood never saw action with these soldiers. He was summoned before an army retiring board on February 25, 1862, and examined by two doctors, J. B. Smith and L. N. Holden, who reported to the board as follows: "I have carefully examined Maj. Underwood. I find he is afflicted with a light deponition [sic] of tubercules in the apex of the right lung and that in the beginning of January last he had a hemorrhage accompanied with profuse night sweats, from the debilitating effects of which he has nearly recovered—only suffering from a feeling of slight weakness."[564] On February 27, 1862, Major Underwood was formally retired from service.[565]

His military career, however, was not at an end. He and Mary were living in Oswego when he was summoned to Alton, Illinois, to be "president of a board of investigation. After these duties are finished the Major resumes active service in the field."[566]

His next assignment was announced the following year:

Major Underwood of the Regular Army returned to this city a day or two since, from Washington, which city he has been visiting for some weeks past. We are glad to learn from him that his health is now better than it has been for years previous. He has been appointed U. S. Mustering and Disbursing officer for the State. His office is located at Utica, for which city he will leave during the next week, to enter upon his duties.[567]

His assignment was of short duration.

According to the testimony of Dr. Charles B. Coventry, Major Underwood came under his care on July 11, 1863. He reported the man "had repeated attacks of hemorrhage from the lungs and that his death was caused by Tubercular Disease of the lungs."[568]

Major Underwood died on September 5, 1863, at Utica, and his remains were returned to Oswego for burial. His death was widely reported.[569]

Figure 2.112. Major Edmund Underwood was a career soldier in the US Army. Author's collection.

Mary Beardsley, the daughter of Joseph Beardsley (May 26, 1792–July 6, 1841) and Elizabeth Eddy (November 7, 1794–March 14, 1888), was born on December 28, 1828, in Monticello, Otsego, New York. An obituary revealed how she met Edmund Underwood:

> Mrs. Underwood first came to Oswego in 1846 to attend school here and to make her home with her sister, the late Mrs. S. H. Lathrop. On that occasion she made the trip from Syracuse here on a canal packet, there being no railroad connections in those days. While here she met Lieutenant Underwood, U. S. A., then a young officer stationed at Fort Ontario, and they were married June 2d, 1852, immediately thereafter leaving for California.[570]

Edmund and Mary were the parents of three sons. Edmund Beardsley (March 5, 1853–April 12, 1928) married Charlotte Hamilton (1859–February 18, 1935) in 1880. He won an appointment to the Naval Academy at Annapolis, Anne Arundel, Maryland, in 1869, graduating in 1873. He rose to the rank of captain and had a very successful naval career. Both are buried in the Naval Academy Cemetery, Annapolis. James Beardsley, born in Richfield, Otsego, New York, in November 1855, died in July 1860. Champlin Louis (September 23, 1859–November 30, 1926) was a longtime employee of the railroad in Pennsylvania. He married Deborah Cresswell (September 25, 1861–June 10, 1926) on February 27, 1889. They are buried in West Laurel Hill Cemetery, Bala Cynwyd, Montgomery, Pennsylvania.

Soon after Major Underwood died, Mary applied for a widow's pension. The file details her husband's illness and death. As the widow of an officer, she was granted a monthly pension of twenty-five dollars. By the time she died in 1917, that figure had risen to seventy-five dollars per month. She never remarried and spent the rest of her life in Oswego City.

Throughout her fifty-four years of widowhood, Mary Beardsley Underwood remained active. She was a member of Christ Church and the Red Cross. Perhaps her greatest contribution was her role in establishing the Home for the Homeless.

According to Mary's recollections, the idea for the project was born in Mrs. Theodore Irwin's parlor. Mrs. William H. Wheeler opined that "there ought to be a home established in Oswego for ladies of gentle birth who were destitute of means and home."[571] Alida Littlejohn, wife of Congressman DeWitt Clinton Littlejohn, dove into the work enthusiastically. Many local church women attended a public hearing on the proposal. Mary recalled, "Ladies were appointed from each church to solicit contributions and it was resolved that a home should be opened somewhere by May 1st of that year, 1872." Mrs. Littlejohn's untimely death delayed the grand opening by one day.

The organizers first used the Eagle House on West Second Street for their shelter. That was replaced by the facility located on East Utica Street, completed in 1876 at a cost of $20,000. Over the years, the women in charge of running the Home employed a variety of ways to solicit funds for the residents' upkeep. Social events, such as an Easter Tea and a Martha Washington Tea, complete with dinner, dessert, and a "fancy

Figure 2.113. Mary Beardsley Underwood was instrumental in the construction and management of the Home for the Homeless (Ladies' Home) in Oswego City. Author's collection.

table" with donated items for sale, were popular.[572] Individual donations were always gratefully accepted, and the newspapers were frequently used to convey thanks to contributors.[573] The Home for the Homeless was eventually renamed the Ladies' Home. It was open until 2019 when financial difficulties and other factors forced its closing. Listed in the Registry of National Landmarks, the building is being renovated for other purposes.

When Mary Beardsley Underwood died on August 9, 1917, several interesting obituaries noted her passing.[574] Perhaps the most affecting was that contributed by an anonymous friend, which said, in part:

> And thus a remarkable life rounded to almost the extreme limit of human existence has ended here. But what tender loving memories cluster around that life. With all the advantages of high breeding, she possessed what is rarer than the purest lineage, a vigorous intellect. With an intellectual culture kept up to the last, a memory that never lost its hold upon events that have passed into the province of the biographer and his-

Figure 2.114. Mary Underwood is buried next to her husband in Riverside Cemetery, Scriba, New York. Author's collection.

torian. She was rich in garnered experience and beautiful with the beauty of venerable age . . . Triumphing over apparently insurmountable obstacles with ever a word of cheer for those in sorrow, a willing ear and open hand for those in sickness and distress, we cannot but rejoice, while we sorrow, over a life so full, so completed.[575]

Major Edmund Underwood and Mary Beardsley Underwood are buried in Riverside Cemetery, Scriba, New York, section N.

Dr. Mary Edwards Walker

Intelligent, skillful, and brave yet flamboyant and controversial, Dr. Mary Edwards Walker rarely conformed to the nineteenth-century view of femininity. Her contributions to the Union cause and to women's rights earn her a place among notable Oswego County Civil War veterans.

Mary Walker, a daughter of Alvah Walker (April 9, 1798–April 9, 1880) and Vesta Whitcomb (April 5, 1801–February 25, 1885), was born in the town of Oswego, New York, on November 26, 1832. She attended the local school which her family had financed and Falley Seminary in Fulton.

After completing her studies, Mary Walker taught school, but she had higher ambitions. She used her teacher's salary to pay tuition for Syracuse Medical College from which she graduated in 1855, the only woman in her class. She married Dr. Albert Miller (1831–April 21, 1913) on November 19, 1855, and the couple established a medical practice in Rome, Oneida, New York. Walker insisted on using her maiden name for business.[576] The marriage failed when she learned of Miller's numerous adulteries.[577] His shocking response to her accusations was to suggest that "if she would not get a bill of divorce she might have the same privileges" of relationships outside the marriage.[578] Learning that Iowa divorce laws were less stringent, Walker went there in an unsuccessful attempt to dissolve her marriage.[579] She returned to New York shortly before the Civil War commenced.

Dr. Mary Walker offered to work in one of the federal hospitals set up subsequent to the outbreak of the conflict but was initially rebuffed, primarily because she was a woman. By November 1861, however, she had succeeded in finding work at Indiana Hospital, housed in the United States Patent Office in Washington, DC, as she reported in a letter to her family dated November 13, 1861:

> I am Assistant Physician Surgeon in this hospital. We have about 80 patients now. We have 5 very nice lady nurses, and a number of gentlemen nurses. We have several cooks, and a dispenser to put up and prepare the medicines, after our orders. Every soul in the Hospital has to abide by my orders as much as though Dr. Green gave them & not a soldier can go out of the building after stated hours, without a pass from him or myself.

Dr. Walker was in Virginia in December 1862 at the battle of Fredericksburg, treating wounded Union soldiers. When she finally obtained a position in the Union army, the following is one example of how it was reported: "Miss Mary E. Walker, of Oswego, a graduate of the female

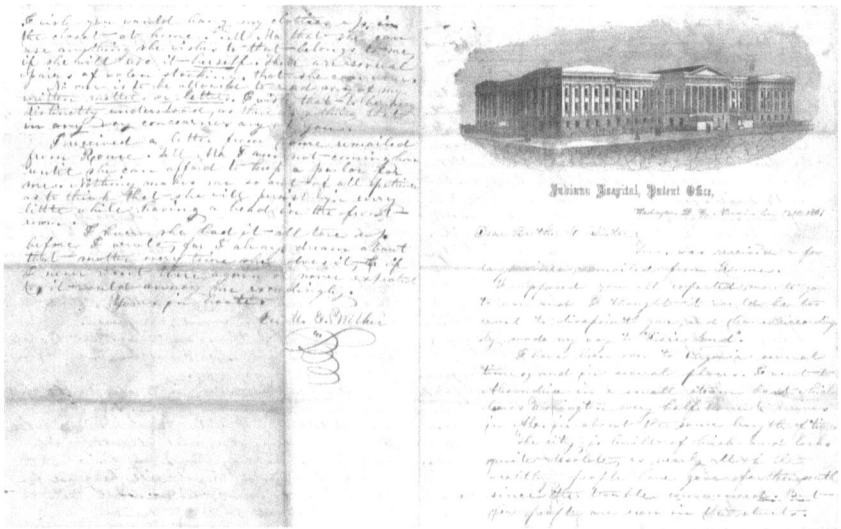

Figure 2.115. Dr. Mary Walker's letter to her family described her position in the Patent Office Hospital in Washington, DC. Courtesy of the Oswego County Historical Society.

medical college, and very pretty young lady, has been ordered to report for duty in Col. McCook's brigade of the Western army."[580] She was in fact attached to the 52nd Ohio Regiment, Army of the Cumberland, as a contracting assistant surgeon. While attending to local civilians and sick or wounded soldiers in Georgia, she was captured by the Confederates as a spy.[581] After a short stay in Libby Prison, Richmond, Virginia, she was transferred to another prison in that city, Castle Thunder.[582]

Walker was incarcerated four months, during which time her health deteriorated significantly. Nevertheless, she only agreed to be exchanged for a soldier of "equal rank."[583] After her release she obtained a position of acting surgeon in the Union army and was assigned to the female military prison in Louisville, Kentucky.[584]

While she was imprisoned, her husband obtained a divorce and then married Vesta Delphene Freeman (1844–February 23, 1908) in 1865. Walker retaliated in 1866 by asking the New York State Legislature to set aside the divorce on the following grounds: "Mrs. Mary declares that she had no notice of the proceedings, and that the decree

Figure 2.116. Two Union army generals recommended Dr. Mary Walker for the Medal of Honor. Courtesy of the Oswego County Historical Society.

of divorce was, therefore, irregularly obtained."[585] She finally obtained a divorce on January 2, 1869, during a special session of the New York State Supreme Court.[586]

Walker's trailblazing efforts were recognized on November 11, 1865, when President Andrew Johnson awarded her the Medal of Honor, an action President Lincoln had reportedly planned before his assassination.

The official citation read, in part, "That Dr. Mary E. Walker, a graduate of medicine, has rendered valuable service to the Government, and has devoted herself with much patriotic zeal to the sick and wounded soldiers, both in the field and hospitals, to the detriment of her own health, and has also endured hardships as a prisoner of war four months in a Southern prison while acting as a contract surgeon." She was the sole woman ever so honored and wore the medal constantly.[587]

She must have been shocked when in 1917 Congress organized a commission to review all Medal of Honor winners in an attempt to ensure that only enrolled soldiers whose combat performance was "above and beyond the call of duty" would be allowed to retain their medal. Anyone not entitled to the medal was liable to arrest on a misdemeanor charge if caught wearing or displaying it. Walker's name, along with

910 others, was stricken from the rolls and she was ordered to return the medal. Walker "remained defiant. She wrote a bristling letter to the Adjutant-General saying she would wear her medal the all [sic] remaining days of her life."[588] Years later Ann Walker, a distant descendant, worked tirelessly to have the medal restored, alleging the reasons for its withdrawal were "social and political."[589] She claimed that Mary Walker had been wronged and in 1978 President Jimmy Carter agreed, formally restoring the medal to her.[590]

Considering herself a Civil War veteran, Dr. Walker applied for a pension on March 8, 1873, based on "disease of eyes lungs and dig[estive] organs" according to a pension payment card.[591] Her original claim resulted in a monthly payment of $8.50. In 1898, that amount was increased to $20 by act of Congress:

> If Dr. Mary E. Walker had been nothing more than a nurse we would not have increased her pension beyond $12 unless under exceptional circumstances. But Dr. Walker was not only a nurse, but a skilled surgeon; she went upon the field

Figure 2.117. The reverse of Dr. Walker's medal reads: "The Congress / To / Dr. Mary E. Walker / A.A. Surgeon, U. S. A. / Nov. 11th / 1865." Courtesy of the Oswego County Historical Society.

of battle; she went into the hospitals; she was there night and day . . . She has supported herself until the present time; but she is now failing. It is but proper and just that we give her enough to insure her reasonable support during the remainder of her days, not in luxury, but in a reasonable manner.[592]

Making a living was crucial. Like scores of others, Walker sought government positions through political favor. In one instance she was actually hired as a clerk in the United States Treasury Department for an annual salary of $900. The treasury secretary, however, was unwilling to put her to work because he disliked her mode of dress. Although she was never permitted to do the job for which she had been hired, in 1882 she finally received her pay.[593] She also obtained a short-lived position in the Pension Bureau.[594]

Figure 2.118. During the Civil War, Dr. Walker adopted a mode of dress intended to identify her as a military doctor. Courtesy of www.Freethought.com.

In another attempt to obtain employment Walker applied to the mayor of Washington, DC, for a position as physician.[595] She also embarked upon a less than successful lecture tour in England. During the next few years she hit the lecture circuit in the United States, speaking about marriage, women's suffrage, and dress reform.[596]

Mary Walker's exotic dress made headlines everywhere and was a focus of her numerous obituaries. As a girl living on a farm she had worn garments appropriate for working in the fields and barns. Her parents, particularly her father, objected to the custom of corseting, considering it unsanitary and unhealthful. She adapted her clothing to permit her to work in the hospital and on the battlefield unhampered by voluminous skirts. Pictures taken during this period show her in a short dress and military jacket over pantaloons.

Later she completely adopted men's clothing, including top hat and tails: "The two most striking costumes at the President's reception

Figure 2.119. Dr. Mary Walker's crusade for dress reform was personal, leading her eventually to wear only male attire. Courtesy of the Library of Congress.

Notable Civil War Veterans of Oswego County | 223

at the White House, New Year's day, were worn by Capt. De Lachere of the Austrian Embassy, and our own Dr. Mary Walker . . . attired in a full black suit, furbound overcoat and plug hat."[597]

Society, both male and female, was unwilling to accept this "outlandish" and allegedly illegal form of dress and Walker found herself constantly harassed or, worse, arrested when she appeared on the street. She invariably produced a piece of paper purporting to be an act of Congress giving her explicit permission to wear pants.[598] As historians have pointed out, however, no evidence of that legislation has been found.[599]

Because Walker was such a flamboyant character, newspapers everywhere delighted in making jokes at her expense. The following are a few of the less offensive examples: "Dr. Mary Walker is writing a book on the condition of her sex. She probably argues that a woman is as good as any other man."[600] Her marital status was a constant source of humor: "The report that Dr. Mary Walker is to be married has been contradicted. It is said now that the man has escaped."[601] Another referred to the same topic: "Dr. Mary Walker thinks of marrying and settling down, but the name of the prospective bride is not given."[602] Her efforts to find employment were mocked: "Dr. Mary Walker is the only self-made man in Washington today."[603] A rumor that she wanted a particular government appointment prompted this sarcastic comment: "Dr. Mary Walker wants Secretary Fish to give her an appointment in Alaska. Everybody hopes he will do it."[604]

Politically, Dr. Walker was a Democrat. In 1880 she failed in an attempt to vote in the national election. After being insulted about her attire she responded accordingly: "Some pert young fellow in the crowd said if she was going to vote, they might as well dress up all their women folks in men's clothes and bring them down and vote them. 'I don't wear men's clothes,' retorted Dr. Walker, 'I wear my own clothes.'"[605] Her reproof, taken out of context, was maliciously quoted in numerous newspapers.[606]

She also attempted to run for public office. In 1881 she petitioned to run for a state senate seat.[607] She announced her candidacy for Congress in 1890.[608] Her support of Belva Lockwood's campaign for the presidency garnered more scurrilous commentary.[609]

Walker supported woman's suffrage but ran afoul of mainstream doctrine that a constitutional amendment was necessary to achieve it:

> "Why," said the Doctor warmly, "the women of the country are laboring under the delusion that they have no rights under the Constitution of the United States, and can never have until the same be accorded by an amendment . . . I claim that women already have all the rights that men have, but what I am laboring for is their protection in their rights . . . The Constitution did not commence, 'We the men,' but 'We, the people . . . It is, therefore, evident enough that our forefathers intended to make this a pure Republican Government, instead of a half-jointed one as at present."[610]

This was her stance to the end of her life.[611] She died shortly before the Nineteenth Amendment to the Constitution was ratified and thus was denied the suffrage she had so long advocated.

Dr. Walker, who outlived most of her contemporaries, was a figure of both awe and ridicule as she entered her final years. She once prophesied:

> I have got to die before people will know who I am and what I have done. It is a shame that people who lead reforms in this world are not appreciated until after they are dead; then the world pays its tribute by piling rocks over the grave of the reformer. I would be thankful if people would treat me decently now instead of erecting great piles of stone over me after I am dead. But then, that's human nature.[612]

Far advanced in her thinking, she clung to her beliefs and principles and stubbornly endured society's ridicule.

Her death on February 21, 1919, was widely reported.[613] The most informative obituary, however, appeared in a hometown newspaper:

> Dr. Mary E. Walker, Oswego's widely known advocate of women's rights and dress reform, in which latter movement she set an example by wearing male attire, died at the home of Frank Dwyer, in Oswego Town, near the old Walker homestead, at eight o'clock last night in her eighty-seventh year. Two years ago last Winter she fell in Washington and her illness dates from that accident. She was able to return to her home on Bunker Hill in the Spring, but a little later was taken seriously

ill and in the Fall was removed to the General Hospital at Fort Ontario, where she underwent treatment. She had been living alone at Bunker Hill, and when she was able to be removed was taken to the home of Mr. Dwyer to be cared for. She wanted to die in the shadow of her old home . . . Dr. Walker's career has been a most picturesque and exceptional one. Among other distinctions she was the first woman in the world to hold a commission as an assistant army surgeon, she having served in that capacity in the Civil War. At the beginning of the war she served as assistant in the Patent Office Hospital in Washington, and in 1862 and 1863 served at the front, before she was regularly in the service, having been appointed by surgeons in charge because of efficiency and was finally employed regularly . . . At the beginning of her professional career Dr. Walker adopted what she called the American reform costume, but later dressed in full male attire and never discarded it. Attired in a man's frock coat, man's trousers, wearing a man's silk hat, and carrying a man's cane, she was a leading topic of discussion during the years she toured the country lecturing upon the proper dress for women. She did not dress in male attire for notoriety's sake. She dressed as she did because she believed that such was the sensible way for women to dress. She had the courage of her convictions and was willing to pay the cost . . . Although always an ardent advocate of equal suffrage, she was not in sympathy with the modern method of bringing about the reform. Several years ago she wrote a pamphlet called The Crowning Constitutional Argument, which she sent to every prominent personage in the country. It was her idea that the women under the Constitution had the right to vote and she was much disgusted that the suffragists didn't go en masse to vote and then carry their case to the United States Supreme Court . . . She was a prolific writer, well informed on all current topics and for years contributed articles to The Palladium on every conceivable topic. She had no patience with the fads and fancies of some of the medical practices of today, and was a firm believer in the theory that good air and good food were all that was necessary to preserve life. The Doctor's passing marks the end of one of the most remarkable characters that ever resided in Oswego, in fact, in the country. Small and

Figure 2.120. Mary Walker was buried in the family plot in Rural Cemetery, Oswego Town. Author's collection.

frail, she nevertheless had wonderful energy and vitality, and up [to] about two years ago, when she began to fail, no task was too great for her to attempt. Her nervous energy kept her continually on the move, physically and mentally. Dr. Walker is gone, but it will be long before she is forgotten.[614]

Dr. Mary Edwards Walker is buried with members of her family in Rural Cemetery, section Acre.

Granville Sharp Woodall

This is the story of Granville Sharp Woodall, a foolish young boy who wanted to play at war and paid for his folly with his life. He was a younger brother of my great-great grandfather, John Joseph Woodall.

John Woodall (June 1, 1817–May 5, 1877) and Jane Wray Woodall (1818–November 3, 1868) immigrated to the United States in 1842, settling in New Haven, New York, where John was a tailor. They were already the parents of Elizabeth "Libby" Jane (June 1839–May 8, 1921) and William (May 30, 1841–September 26, 1867). John Joseph (August 7, 1844–October 2, 1914), the first child born in America, was followed by Granville Sharp (January 20, 1847–June 7, 1864) and Robert Kelsey (May 7, 1850–October 30, 1879).

Granville Woodall and his siblings attended the local common school and the Congregational Church. Like many young boys, he probably perceived the Civil War as a grand adventure, not understanding or caring to understand the attendant misery of sickness, injuries, and death.

In late December 1863 and early January 1864, recruiting was taking place for the 24th Cavalry. Although not yet sixteen, Granville sneaked away from home on January 5, 1864, to enlist. It is difficult to

Figure 2.121. Although only fifteen years old, Granville Woodall put on a Union soldier's uniform and marched off to war. Author's collection.

believe that the recruiting agent did not realize Granville was a minor. A photograph of him in his uniform clearly shows he was a child.

Nevertheless, the medical doctor on site certified that he had closely examined the volunteer and found him fit for duty. By 1864 the draft was in full force and it was becoming increasingly difficult to find men willing to enlist, bounty or no bounty. If the volunteer was breathing, he was generally accepted. Granville Woodall mustered into Co. M on January 26, 1864. His horrified parents could have approached the local provost marshal to have their wayward son discharged on account of his age. Unfortunately, they did not do so, perhaps out of ignorance or, more likely, misguided pride. Instead, they turned to John Joseph for a solution.

John Joseph Woodall had already served in the 26th "Oneida" Regiment, enlisting on May 13, 1861, and mustering into Co. I on May 21. This outfit was organized for ninety days, but on August 2, shortly after the disastrous first battle of Bull Run, the soldiers heard the unhappy news that their unit had been federalized and they would be required to serve two years.[615] By that time, both the Union and the Confederacy had realized the war would not end speedily. It is quite certain, therefore, that the elder Woodalls were fully aware of the hazards of warfare in January 1864.

At the end of his two years of service, John Joseph Woodall returned home to his wife, Catherine Purdy, who would shortly become pregnant with her first child. He probably believed his warring days were over and was none too happy when his father and mother pressured him to enlist in the 24th Cavalry "to look after Granville." According to the *Adjutant-General's Report* for the 24th Cavalry, John Joseph Woodall enlisted on February 25, 1864, and mustered into Co. K the next day.

The 24th Cavalry was noted for one conspicuous lack in its kit: horses.[616] Not until late October 1864 did the men finally receive mounts. Until that time, the 24th was used as an infantry unit. It participated in the battle of the Wilderness and then marched with General Grant's Army of the Potomac to Cold Harbor, Virginia, a place long reviled due to its bloodletting. Between June 1 and June 12, Union losses were estimated at thirteen thousand, of which 9,042 were killed or wounded. The missing numbered over two thousand. It was, General Grant revealed in his memoir, the single battle he would not care to refight: "I have always regretted that the last assault at Cold Harbor was ever made . . . At Cold Harbor no advantage whatever was gained to compensate for the heavy loss we sustained."[617]

John Joseph Woodall most certainly remembered Cold Harbor with bitterness, for it was there that Granville died of typhoid fever on June 7, scarcely six months after he had enlisted. He was fortunate enough to die in a bed in the 9th Army Corps Hospital, not on the battlefield where his body might or might not be collected for burial.

A grief-stricken John wrote a letter on June 8, addressed ostensibly to his parents. Since he asked that the letter be published in the *Mexico Independent*, however, it is evident that he was sending a subtle message to other would-be Granvilles to stay home where they belonged:

> My dear parents: Granville, my dear brother, is no more. He died yesterday, the 7th inst. about 1 o'clock p.m. He was in much pain during the morning hours, but he became quiet and easy and died without a struggle or a groan. He was tranquil and happy in his mind during his sickness. Towards the last hours he was not able to speak, but by his looks and actions he appeared willing to go, and I have no doubt he is better off now than if living. But what shall compensate me for my loneliness and solitude here?
>
> I have succeeded in having his body embalmed, and have an order to send it home. It will leave here tomorrow morning en route for home. Mrs. Spencer, the New York agent, advanced the money for me to get his body embalmed and to send it home. . . . I tried hard to get a furlough to accompany his body home, but could not. I shall probably stay here a day or two longer, and then return to my regiment. I would like to have published in the Mexico Independent that it was only through the kindness and benevolent exertions of Mrs. Spencer that I was enabled to get the body embalmed and sent home. She is doing a great deal for the soldiers here, and her kindness and attention have given her the praise of all the living of the poor wounded soldiers; and many a life has been saved by her care that would otherwise have been lost. Many die through neglect and exposure, and if there were many such women in the field there would be proportionate decrease of death. Give my love to all my brothers and sisters at home, and all kind friends, and may this affliction be a warning and a lesson to all dear Granville's friends.[618]

Figure 2.122. Thanks to the efforts of Elmina Spencer, John Woodall succeeded in having Granville's body shipped home for burial. Author's collection.

Granville Woodall's death was reported in a local newspaper: "Mr. A. Osborn, of this city has received the body of Granville S. Woodall, of New Haven, who was killed in battle before Richmond. He belonged to the 24th Cavalry and was but 17 years old."[619] Perhaps it sounded nobler to say that Granville died in battle rather than in a hospital bed after contracting typhoid fever, but it did not lessen the family's pain. It was unfortunate too that his age was given incorrectly, an error repeated on his gravestone.

Other errors exist. Crisfield Johnson,[620] for example, stated that the boy died on June 4, 1864, at the age of seventeen. His muster card provided an age of eighteen and a death date of June 4, 1864. His surname was incorrectly spelled Woodhof in a death notice.[621] The Civil War monument standing inside New Haven Rural Cemetery contains perhaps the most egregious error, mistakenly assigning him to Co. K, 26th Cavalry.

Figure 2.123. Granville's regiment and company are erroneously carved into the Soldiers' Monument in New Haven, New York. Author's collection.

This boy's death was not glorious or noble, nor was it beneficial to the Union. If that recruiter had told him in no uncertain terms to go home and stay there, how much different the Woodall family history would have been.[622]

Granville Sharp Woodall, his parents, and his brother, William, are buried in New Haven Rural Cemetery, row 11, lot 197.

Notes

Notes to Chapter 1

1. Judith Wellman, "'Bound by Duty': Abolitionists in Mexico, New York, 1830–1842," *Thirty-Fourth Annual Publication of the Oswego County Historical Society, 1973* (Oswego, NY: Beyer Offset, 1974), 4–5.

2. No headline, *Oswego Palladium*, September 30, 1835.

3. "The Abolitionists," *Oswego Palladium*, September 30, 1835.

4. Crisfield Johnson, *History of Oswego County, New York* (Philadelphia: L. H. Everts, 1877). Portrait and biography following page 146.

5. Elizabeth Simpson, "Two Famous Abolitionists of Oswego County," *Fourth Annual Publication of the Oswego Historical Society* (Oswego, NY: Palladium-Times, Inc., 1940), 81–91. See also Charles M. Snyder, *Oswego From Buckskin to Bustles* (Port Washington, NY: Ira J. Friedman, 1968), 154–64.

6. "Oswego County Anti-Slavery Society Annual Meeting: January 17, 1839," Freethought Trail, https://freethought-trail.org/historical-events/event:1839-anti-slavery-meeting/. The date of the meeting is erroneously given in this article as January 13, 1839.

7. Dwight L. DuMond, *Anti-Slavery: The Crusade for Freedom in America* (Ann Arbor: University of Michigan Press, 1961), 292.

8. Cong. Globe, 25th Cong., 3rd Sess. 355 (1839) (appendix). The American Colonization Society advocated purchasing land in Africa and settling it with slaves whose owners had willingly turned them over for that express purpose.

9. "Seneca, Oswego, Jefferson," *Impartial Citizen*, November 21, 1849, http://www.libraries.udmercy.edu/archives/special-collections.

10. Woody Jones, "In Their Own Words: Stephen Elliott 'That the Past May Be Vindicated,'" *Meridiana* (blog). *The Roberson Project*, March 24, 2020, http://meridiana.sewanee.edu/2020/03/24/in-their-own-words-stephen-elliott-that-the-past-may-be-vindicated. Stephen Elliott (1806–1866) was the thirty-seventh bishop of the Protestant Episcopal Church in America and the first bishop of Georgia.

11. Quoted in Bruce Chadwick, *1858: Abraham Lincoln, Jefferson Davis, Robert E. Lee, Ulysses S. Grant and the War They Failed to See* (Naperville, IL: Sourcebooks, 2008), 26.

12. Charles McCool Snyder, *Oswego County, New York in the Civil War: 1962 Yearbook* (Oswego, NY: Oswego County Historical Society, 1962), 1.

13. "An Apology for Slavery," *Oswego Commercial Times*, February 7, 1861, 1–2. On the second page is an editorial sharply criticizing Reverend Schuyler's sermon. Shortly after the Emancipation Proclamation was published, the local newspaper published an editorial again supporting abolition, saying, in part, that the "existence of slavery is incompatible with the safety of the Union." See "A Talk with the Albany Journal," *Oswego Commercial Times*, January 15, 1863.)

14. "Early Days of Chester S. Lord in Up-State," *Fairport Herald-Mail*, May 4, 1933, 1, 4. For an interesting description of the perspective other Oswego churches took in this debate, see Charles McCool Snyder, "The Antislavery Movement in the Oswego Area," *Eighteenth Publication of the Oswego County Historical Society* (Oswego, NY: Palladium-Times, Inc., 1955), 10–11.

15. Snyder, *Oswego County, New York in the Civil War*, 1.

16. "Letter from the 110th Regiment," *Mexico Independent*, October 23, 1862.

17. "Letter from a Member of the 110th Reg't.," *Mexico Independent*, August 6, 1862, 1.

18. "Letter from New Orleans," *Oswego Commercial Times*, September 16, 1864, 1.

Notes to Chapter 2

1. "Oswego Times," *Oswego Palladium-Times*, November 20, 1945, 16.

2. Wisconsin Historical Society, "Wisconsin Genealogy Trails," https://www.wisconsinhistory.org/Records/Article/CS2332.

3. Wisconsin Historical Society, "23rd Wisconsin Infantry History," accessed January 14, 2022, www.wisconsinhistory.org/Records/Article/CS2332.

4. "Oswego Times."

5. No headline, *Mexico Independent*, May 26, 1880.

6. "His 80th Birthday," *Oswego Daily Palladium*, February 28, 1921, 2.

7. "John B. Alexander, Many Years Times Editor, Passes Away at his Home Here Early this Morning," *Oswego Daily Times*, March 19, 1925, 7.

8. "Postmaster Alexander," *Oswego Daily Palladium*, September 19, 1898, 8.

9. "Postmaster Alexander"; see also "Mrs. Alexander Is In Charge," *Oswego Daily Palladium*, November 1, 1898, 5. John Alexander was last appointed post-

master in 1911 by President Howard Taft. See "Chosen Again as Postmaster," *Syracuse Post-Standard*, February 1, 1911. He retired from the position in 1916.

10. "Certainly a Dismal Failure," *Oswego Daily Palladium*, June 30, 1888. Rpt. from *The Fulton Patriot*.

11. "Mr. Dowdle Says No," *Oswego Daily Palladium*, February 27, 1893, 5.

12. "A Board of Architects," *Oswego Daily Times*, May 16, 1890, 1.

13. "In the Soup at Last," *Oswego Daily Palladium*, May 17, 1891, 1.

14. "The Criminal Libel Case," *The Oswego Times*, May 19, 1890.

15. "That Stove Pipe Hole," *Oswego Daily Times*, May 17, 1890.

16. "Recorder's Court," *Oswego Daily Times*, August 2, 1890.

17. "Talked About New Hospital," *Oswego Daily Palladium*, October 18, 1904, 8. See also "Mrs. Mary Place Alexander," *Oswego Palladium-Times*, January 28, 1928, 5. Later she was to serve as the board's secretary. See "Election of Officers," *Oswego Palladium-Times*, October 24, 1910, 8.

18. "The Baptists Meet," *Oswego Daily Palladium*, June 1, 1892, 8.

19. "A Delightful Entertainment," *Oswego Daily Palladium*, September 29, 1896, 5.

20. "Municipal Playgrounds," *Oswego Daily Palladium*, June 2, 1909, 5.

21. "Winter Club Guest Night," *Oswego Palladium-Times*, January 31, 1928, 5.

22. "D.A.R. Meeting," *Oswego Daily Palladium*, October 15, 1915, 3. See also "D.A.R.'s Met Yesterday," *Oswego Daily Palladium*, September 14, 1917, 5.

23. "Mrs. Shepherd is Re-Elected," *Oswego Daily Palladium*, May 8, 1925, 5.

24. "Ready for the Historians," *Oswego Daily Palladium*, September 18, 1913, 3.

25. "Against Oswego," *Oswego Daily Palladium*, April 25, 1911, 6.

26. "List of Signers of Petitions," *Oswego Daily Palladium*, May 18, 1918, 3.

27. "Campaign for Irish Relief," *Oswego Daily Palladium*, April 7, 1921, 4.

28. "John B. Alexander, Many Years Times Editor, Passes Away at His Home Here Early this Morning."

29. "Postmaster Alexander Is Very Strong for It," *Oswego Daily Palladium*, March 29, 1915, 11.

30. "The Oswego Times Is Sold," *Watertown Daily Times*, June 17, 1922, 4.

31. "Friends Pay Tribute to J. B. Alexander," *Oswego Daily Times*, March 19, 1925, 7.

32. "Our Venerable Editor John B. Alexander Gone," *Pulaski Democrat*, March 25, 1925, 2.

33. "John B. Alexander," *Oswego Daily Palladium*, March 19, 1925, 10.

34. See "Mrs. Mary Place Alexander," *Oswego Palladium-Times*, January 28, 1928, 5; "Mrs. Mary P. Alexander," *Buffalo Evening News*, January 30, 1928, 27; "Dr. Savage Officiated," *Oswego Palladium-Times*, January 31, 1928, 5.

35. See Natalie Joy Woodall, *Men of the 110th Regiment: Oswego's Own* (Denver: Outskirts Press, 2016), 6–9.

36. Howard Hunter, "Unionist Troops in Louisiana," 64 Parishes, accessed January 14, 2022, https://www.64parishes.org.

37. Chris Graham, "More Steam Shovel History," Heritage Machines, March 20, 2021, https://heritagemachines.com/plant-machinery/more-steam-shovel-history/.

38. "List of Patents," *Hudson Daily Register*, January 13, 1873.

39. "Business," *Oswego Daily Palladium*, May 2, 1873, 4; "Improved Friction Clutch," *Scientific American*, May 17, 1873, 312.

40. "Brooklyn's Reservoir Suit," *New York Herald*, October 26, 1876, 9.

41. "Neighboring Towns," *Syracuse Daily Standard*, January 24, 1878.

42. "Fulton Items," *Oswego Daily Times*, January 21, 1878.

43. "Northern and Central Counties," *Utica Morning Herald*, January 17, 1878.

44. "Neighboring Towns," *Syracuse Daily Standard*, March 6, 1878.

45. See, for example, "Northern and Central Counties," *Utica Morning Herald*, June 2, 1881.

46. "County Towns," *Oswego Daily Palladium*, September 8, 1881. Although it is not identified, the Masonic lodge to which he belonged was undoubtedly Hiram 145.

47. "The Late Samuel B. Alger," *Oswego Daily Palladium*, September 13, 1881.

48. No headline, *Mexico Independent*, April 30, 1884.

49. See, for example, "A Telegrapher's Error," *Maysville [KY] Evening Bulletin*, April 29, 1884, 1; "Charged With Bigamy," *New York World*, April 28, 1884, 1.

50. "A Telegrapher's Error."

51. "William E. Waugh," *Syracuse Sunday Herald*, April 27, 1884, 1.

52. "The Fulton Scandal," *Oswego Daily Times and Express*, April 28, 1884.

53. "The Fulton Scandal."

54. "William E. Waugh."

55. "Deserted Wife," *Syracuse Daily Journal*, March 26, 1904, 8; "Many Estates Before Surrogate," *Oswego Daily Times*, May 23, 1911, 4.

56. "Obituaries," *Syracuse Daily Journal*, June 22, 1931, 22.

57. "Advertisement," *Troy Daily Whig*, 1844.

58. "Large Contract," *Utica Gazette*, October 31, 1848.

59. "Personal Mention," *Syracuse Daily Journal*, February 6, 1866, 8; "Laws of New York—By Authority," *Albany Morning Express*, May 20, 1868.

60. See, for example, "Syracuse Northern Railroad," *Mexico Independent*, June 3, 1868; "Baldwinsville & Mexico Railroad," *Oswego Daily Palladium*, October 19, 1871; "Railroad Meeting at Phoenix," *Oswego Weekly Commercial*

Advertiser, November 1, 1871; "Vanderbilt to the Rescue," *Syracuse Daily Courier*, March 30, 1878, 1; "Various News Items," *Oswego Daily Palladium*, June 11, 1881; "Port Byron," *Auburn News and Bulletin*, October 22, 1881; "Railroad Items," *Rome Daily Sentinel*, March 6, 1885; "Gen. Burt's Railroad Operations," *Weekly Saratogian*, February 23, 1882.

61. These are only a few of the articles printed during that time: "The Darien Expedition," *Watertown Daily Times*, December 1, 1870; "The Darien Surveying Party," *New York Daily Herald*, April 27, 1871, 7; "Darien Surveying Expedition," *Watertown Daily Times*, May 4, 1871; "Darien Canal," *New York Daily Herald*, July 14, 1871, 5. The last article provides a detailed account of the work completed during the survey.

62. "The Siege of Port Hudson," *New York Times*, June 11, 1863, 8.

63. "Important From New Orleans," *Albany Morning Express*, June 3, 1863.

64. No headline, *Mexico Independent*, September 17, 1863. The letter was dated August 10, 1863, and sent from Port Hudson, Louisiana.

65. For a detailed study of Port Hudson's importance for the Union, see Edward Cunningham, *The Port Hudson Campaign, 1862–1863* (Baton Rouge: Louisiana State University Press, 1963).

66. "From Captain Barnes' Battery," *Oswego Commercial Times*, April 25, 1864. These men, though Barnes did not know it at the time, were sent to Andersonville. One of them was Daniel McSweeney, whose story is detailed below.

67. "A New Grand Army Post," *Oswego Daily Palladium*, March 22, 1880; "A New G. A. R. Post," *Syracuse Daily Standard*, March 22, 1880. See also "Joe Gould Post," *Phoenix Register (Centennial Edition)* 1958, 36; "Phoenix Members of D. U. V. Group Honor Veterans," *Oswego Palladium-Times*, December 12, 1933, 4.

68. Frances Caroline Morse's actual date of birth is disputed. A family history claims she was born on January 1, 1830, but other sources place her birth year as 1824. The inscription on the family monument is 1826. See Henry Dutch Lord, *Memorial of the Family of Morse, Compiled from the Original Records for the Hon. Asa Porter Morse* (Cambridge, MA: Harvard Printing Company, 1896), 290.

69. "Brief Locals," *Syracuse Weekly Express*, December 5, 1889, 1; "Social and Personal," *Baldwinsville Gazette and Farmers' Journal*, December 5, 1889.

70. Edgar Luderne Welch, *Grip's Historical Souvenir of Phoenix* (Pulaski, NY: Seamans Press, 1902), 20.

71. "Oldest Phoenix Resident Dead," *Syracuse Journal*, July 10, 1905, 5; "Phoenix," *Syracuse Herald*, July 10, 1905, 3.

72. An excellent example of this behavior occurred on April 12, 1864, in what is known as the Fort Pillow Massacre. After laying down their arms, almost 200 black soldiers were clubbed, shot, and bayoneted by enraged Confederate soldiers whose officers had lost control of them. See, for example, "The Fort Pillow Massacre," *New York Times*, May 3, 1864, 9; W. C. King and W. P. Derby, eds., "The Fort Pillow Massacre," *Camp-Fire Sketches and Battle-Field Echoes of*

61-65 (Springfield, MA: King, Richardson, & Co., 1888), 288–91. For a different, equally horrific, description of Civil War atrocities, see "The Barbarities of Port Hudson," *Oswego Commercial Times*, June 23, 1863.

73. "Levi Bird," *Sandy Creek News*, May 25, 1899.

74. Egbert E. Covey (November 4, 1835–September 2, 1913) originally enlisted in Co. B, 7th NY Cavalry, a northern New York organization. His was a checkered military career, involving injury, desertion from a hospital, and enlisting in another outfit without permission. See "Egbert E. Covey," *Sandy Creek News*, September 11, 1913; "Egbert E. Covey," *Sandy Creek News*, September 18, 1913. Covey died in Lacona, New York.

75. "Lacona," *Pulaski Democrat*, October 19, 1882; "Lacona," *Sandy Creek News*, September 10, 1885. See also "Ridge Road," *Sandy Creek News*, June 19, 1890, 1.

76. "Town Talk," *Sandy Creek News*, October 8, 1885.

77. See, for example, "Ridge Road," *Sandy Creek News*, March 15, 1888; "Ridge Road," *Sandy Creek News*, December 24, 1891, 1; "Ridge Road," *Sandy Creek News*, October 27, 1892, 1; "Here About," *Sandy Creek News*, April 1, 1897, 1.

78. "Lacona," *Pulaski Democrat*, November 23, 1882.

79. "Levi Bird."

80. "Lacona," *Sandy Creek News*, March 15, 1900.

81. "Recall Days When Tiles Were Made in Pulaski Plant," *Oswego Palladium-Times*, September 10, 1951, 7.

82. "Mrs. Anna Brockman, 89, of 200 Cedar Street, Dies," *Watertown Daily Times*, January 14, 1929, 14.

83. Frank I. Brockman married Maud S. Reiss in Pulaski on December 21, 1895. They were the parents of John W. Brockman (August 17, 1897–August 23, 1940), a longtime New York State trooper. Frank and Maud separated in 1902 and eventually divorced. He died in Watertown on May 3, 1940, and was buried in North Watertown Cemetery. See "Frank Brockman," *Oswego Palladium-Times*, May 4, 1940, 3.

84. "Melancholy Event," *Washington Evening Star*, September 2, 1854, 3; "Death of Charles Preuss," *Washington Sentinel*, September 3, 1854, 3.

85. See, for example, Edgar Luderne Welch, *Grip's Historical Souvenir of Pulaski and Vicinity* (Pulaski, NY: Seamans Press, 1902), 15; "Pulaski," *Oswego Daily Times*, November 7, 1900, 7; "Recall Days when Tiles Were Made in Pulaski Plant."

86. See "An Interesting Career," *Oswego Daily Palladium*, May 14, 1901, 8.

87. "John Brockman," *Pulaski Democrat*, May 15, 1901.

88. "Board of Trustees," *Pulaski Democrat*, May 12, 1881.

89. "Death of a Fighter," *South New Berlin Bee* (?), May ?, 1901.

90. "Resolutions," *Pulaski Democrat*, May 29, 1901.

91. "Personal Mention," *Pulaski Democrat*, September 12, 1923, 5.

92. "Orwell," *Pulaski Democrat*, April 15, 1908, 1.

93. According to the *Adjutant-General's Report*, Carpenter enrolled in Co. K, 186th Regiment on September 1, 1864, at Rodman, Jefferson, New York, and mustered in on September 9, on which day he also deserted. His muster card noted he had enlisted in the 186th on August 17, 1864, at Watertown, mustered at Sackets Harbor on September 9, and deserted the same day. Despite claiming to be seventeen, he was only sixteen. In 1890 he told the enumerator he had been a drummer in the 193rd Regiment, but there is no evidence to support that statement.

94. "Orwell," *Sandy Creek News*, February 4, 1897, 1.

95. "Board of Supervisors," *Sandy Creek News*, December 24, 1891.

96. "Orwell," *Sandy Creek News*, July 13, 1893, 1.

97. "For Member Assembly," *Sandy Creek News*, May 26, 1898.

98. "Vorea," *Sandy Creek News*, November 20, 1902, 1; "Would Remove Carpenter," *Sandy Creek News*, November 5, 1903, 1.

99. "Vorea," *Sandy Creek News*, July 13, 1893, 1.

100. "Orwell," *Sandy Creek News*, September 30, 1897, 1; "Orwell," *Pulaski Democrat*, January 9, 1901.

101. "DeWitt Carpenter," *Sandy Creek News*, April 16, 1908, 5.

102. "Resolutions," *Pulaski Democrat*, April 15, 1908, 1.

103. "Orwell," *Sandy Creek News*, April 16, 1908, 1.

104. "Orwell," *Pulaski Democrat*, April 15, 1925, 1; "Orwell," *Pulaski Democrat*, April 22, 1925, 1.

105. "Col. Cooke's Funeral Sunday at 3 O'Clock," *Oswego Daily Times*, March 4, 1921, 10.

106. "Letter from Lieut. E. A. Cook," *Oswego Commercial Times*, June 17, 1864. The letter was dated June 11, 1864, and sent from Headquarters "in the field."

107. "From the 81st Regiment," *Oswego Daily Palladium*, October 10, 1864. The letter was dated October 3, 1864.

108. "National Guard—Twenty-Fourth Brigade," *Syracuse Daily Journal*, December 13, 1872.

109. "Military Examining Board," *Syracuse Daily Standard*, December 16, 1872.

110. "Reunion of the Eighty-First," *Oswego Daily Times*, August 11, 1914, 8; "Tells Men How Fort Harrison Was Captured," *Syracuse Post-Standard*, August 19, 1915, 8.

111. "Eighty-First Will Hold Reunion," *Oswego Daily Times*, July 9, 1917, 5.

112. John D. O'Brian Post No. 65 was chartered on August 5, 1878. The original descriptive book has been lost.

113. "The Firemen's Convention," *Oswego Daily Times*, June 16, 1894.

114. "News in Brief," *Oswego Daily Palladium*, June 15, 1889.

115. "Wedded in Dansville," *Oswego Daily Palladium*, November 26, 1889.

116. See, for example, "Has Served Oswego Twenty-Six Years," *Syracuse Sunday Herald*, May 15, 1904, 19; "Colonel E. A. Cooke, Oswego, Employed By City 40 Years," *Syracuse Post-Standard*, January 30, 1914, 10.

117. "Col. Edward A. Cooke, War Veteran, Is Dead," *Syracuse Post-Standard*, March 4, 1921, 12.

118. "Col. Edward A. Cooke," *Oswego Daily Times*, March 3, 1921, 8.

119. "Flag at Half-Mast," *Oswego Daily Palladium*, March 4, 1921, 4.

120. "Road Plans Passed On," *Oswego Daily Palladium*, March 8, 1921, 3.

121. "Deaths," *Oswego Palladium-Times*, July 2, 1942, 17.

122. John Churchill, *Landmarks of Oswego County, New York* (Syracuse, NY: D. Mason & Co., 1895), "Family Sketches," 198; "Dr. S. J. Crockett," *Sandy Creek News*, May 3, 1906; DC Caughey, "Samuel J. Crockett, 1st U. S. Cavalry," Regular Cavalry in the Civil War, January 15, 2021, https://regularcavalryincivilwar.com//?s=Samuel+J.+Crockett%2C+1st+U.+S.+Cavalry&search=Go.

123. Crockett described his experiences during the battle of Gettysburg to J. B. Bachelder in a letter dated December 27, 1882. See Edward L. and Audrey J. Ladd, eds., *The Bachelder Papers: Gettysburg in Their Own Words* (Dayton, OH: Morningside House Publishers, 1994–1995), 2:915–17.

124. Letter posted by joyandmark on Ancestry.com on November 18, 2016.

125. "Dr. S. J. Crockett." For a graphic description of the conditions endured by Union soldiers confined in Pemberton Prison, see Michael Dougherty, *The Prison Diary of Michael Dougherty: Union Survivor of Two Years' Confinement in Confederate Prisons* (Bristol, PA: Chas. A. Dougherty, 1908). Dougherty, a soldier in the 13th PA, was captured in February 1863.

126. Crockett had been elected surgeon of Post Bailey in 1870. See "G. A. R.—Post Bailey," *Oswego Daily Press*, July 18, 1870.

127. "The New Grand Army Post at Sandy Creek," *Oswego Daily Palladium*, May 17, 1881.

128. "Pencilings," *Sandy Creek News*, July 23, 1891.

129. "Town Talk," *Sandy Creek News*, July 18, 1889.

130. "Wednesday Club Is 70 Years Old," *Sandy Creek News*, July 23, 1964, 9; "Church and Society," *Sandy Creek News*, April 9, 1896.

131. "Dr. S. J. Crockett." See also "A Tribute to Comrade Crockett," *Sandy Creek News*, May 31, 1906.

132. "Mrs. Frances C. Crockett," *Sandy Creek News*, September 2, 1926, 5.

133. Cate Lineberry, "The Boys of War," *New York Times Opinionator*, October 4, 2011, http://opinionator.blogs.nytimes.com/2011/10/04/the-boys-of-war.

134. "Joined Army at Age of 14," *Syracuse Post-Standard*, April 17, 1911.

135. Natalie Joy Woodall, *The Men of the 110th Regiment: Oswego's Own, A Biographical Supplement* (Oswego, NY: Port City Printing, 2021), 105–6.

136. "For a Soldiers' Monument," *Oswego Daily Palladium*, August 31, 1904, 4.

137. Although frequently spoken of, that monument did not become a reality until 1932. It stands in East Park, Oswego City.

138. "Interesting Exercise," *Oswego Daily Times*, May 31, 1906, 7.

139. "Appointments Made by Pulaski Trustees," *Syracuse Post-Standard*, March 31, 1909, 11.

140. "Freeman H. Cross," *Pulaski Democrat*, April 19, 1911, 1.

141. "Delia G. Cross," *Pulaski Democrat*, June 1, 1927, 1.

142. John Joseph May, *Danforth Genealogy, Nicholas Danforth and William Danforth and Their Descendants* (Boston: Charles H. Pope, 1901), vii–xii.

143. "Rev. H. M. Danforth," *Lowville Journal and Republican*, April 20, 1905, 5.

144. Edgar Luderne Welch, *Grip's Historical Souvenir of Camden, N.Y* (Camden, NY: Camden Advance-Journal, 1902), 126–27. This information can be found in the chapter titled "Rev. Horace M. Danforth."

145. "Rev. H. M. Danforth," *Northern Christian Advocate*, December 14, 1864.

146. "Personal," *Rome Daily Sentinel*, September 19, 1885.

147. "Caroline W. Danforth," *Oswego Daily Times-Express*, November 5, 1885. See also "Death of Mrs. H. M. Danforth," *Rome Citizen*, November 13, 1885, according to which article she died "after a long and painful illness."

148. "Local Intelligence," *Lowville Journal and Republican*, July 11, 1889. See also "Marriage Notice," *Northern Christian Advocate*, July 11, 1889.

149. "Camden Items," *Rome Citizen* [?], March [day unknown], 1872.

150. "Brief Mention," *Lowville Journal and Republican*, October 12, 1899, 5.

151. *Grip's Historical Souvenir of Camden*, 127.

152. "Rev. H. M. Danforth," *Lowville Journal and Republican*, April 20, 1905, 5.

153. "The Rev. H. M. Danforth," *Oswego Daily Palladium*, April 18, 1905, 5. See also, for example, "Past Away Last Night," *Camden Advance-Journal*, April 15, 1905; "H. M. Danforth," *Watertown Daily Times*, April 14, 1905, 12; "Death's Harvest in the Towns," *Utica Herald-Dispatch*, April 14, 1905, 8.

154. "The Rev. Horace Melvin Danforth," *Northern Christian Advocate*, July 27, 1906.

155. "Elder Danforth's Funeral," *Oswego Daily Palladium*, April 17, 1905, 1.

156. "Camden," *Syracuse Daily Journal*, August 16, 1905, 6.

157. "Mrs. Sarah B. Danforth Dies in Holyoke," *Watertown Daily Times*, February 22, 1910. See also "Funeral of Mrs. Danforth," *Oswego Daily Palladium*, February 23, 1910, 8.

158. "Lone G. A. R. Man Has Unique War Charm," *Camden Advance-Journal*, April 24, 1930, 6.

159. See, for example, "Body of Morse Found At Last," *Oswego Daily Times*, August 12, 1912, 1.

160. "Business Change in Cleveland," *Camden Advance-Journal*, August 16, 1917, 3.

161. "New Chamber of Commerce," *Oswego Daily Palladium*, April 21, 1917.

162. Deans' name was frequently mentioned in marriage announcements. See, for example, "Hoyt-Taber," *Oswego Palladium-Times*, August 23, 1928, 11.

163. See, for example, "Captured Fish Pirates," *Camden Advance-Journal*, August 31, 1916, 3; "Received at Jail," *Oswego Palladium-Times*, October 2, 1925, 5.

164. "Cleveland Water Company," *Camden Advance-Journal*, March 9, 1916, 2.

165. See "Sunday School Officers Elected," *Camden Advance-Journal*, January 5, 1928, 3; "Methodist Church at North Bay Now Under Interior Improvements," *Camden Advance-Journal*, November 29, 1923, 6.

166. "Masonic Elections," *Oswego Daily Palladium*, December 30, 1903, 6; "Cleveland Lodges," *Camden Advance-Journal*, January 9, 1913, 6; "Cleveland Lodge F. and A. M.," *Camden Advance-Journal*, December 28, 1916, 7; "Final Cleveland Veteran Is Dead," *Oswego Palladium Times*, May 9, 1935, 2.

167. "Post Reorganization," *Camden Advance-Journal*, June 1, 1916, 6; "Final Cleveland Veteran Is Dead."

168. "Only 23 Veterans in County G. A. R.," *Oswego Palladium-Times*, May 11, 1932, 7.

169. "Cleveland Fetes Veteran of War," *Oswego Palladium-Times*, May 27, 1931. See also "Final Cleveland Veteran Is Dead."

170. "Mrs. Thos. D. Deans," unsourced obituary; "Cleveland," *Rome Daily Sentinel*, August 3, 1897.

171. "Cleveland," *Rome Daily Sentinel*, October 13, 1897; "Charles Kime," *Rome Daily Sentinel*, February 11, 1898, 2; "Constantia," *Oswego Daily Palladium*, February 16, 1898, 6.

172. "Cleveland Chapter O. E. S.," *Camden Advance-Journal*, December 21, 1916, 7.

173. "Was Native of Camden," *Camden Advance-Journal*, December 30, 1920, 3.

174. "Mrs. Deans, Formerly of Rome, Dies," *Rome Daily Sentinel*, December 19, 1957, 26.

175. "News Notes," *Rome Daily Sentinel*, April 30, 1935, 5.

176. See "Thomas D. Deans Dies at Age of 87," *Rome Daily Sentinel*, May 8, 1935, 9; "Death Claims Last GAR Vet at Cleveland," *Utica Observer-Dispatch*, May 9, 1935, 36; "Final Cleveland Veteran Is Dead."

177. "Cleveland," *Rome Daily Sentinel*, May 13, 1935, 3. See also "Cleveland," *Rome Daily Sentinel*, May 31, 1935, 1.

178. "Obituary Notes," *Oswego Daily Palladium*, December 3, 1877.

179. "A Partisan Militia," *Oswego Commercial Times*, August 20, 1863.

180. "Sad Accident at Oswego," *Oneida Morning Herald*, July 16, 1850.

181. "Presentation of a Sword to Capt. Doyle," *Oswego Commercial Times*, August 22, 1862.

182. "Col. James Doyle," *Oswego Daily Palladium*, December 1, 1882; "Capt. Doyle of the 116th," *Oswego Commercial Advertiser*, February 18, 1865. The number in the headline should be 110th.

183. "Letter from the 110th," *Oswego Commercial Advertiser*, April 10, 1865.

184. "From the 110th Regiment," *Oswego Commercial Times*, March 17, 1865. See also "Items From the Telegraph," *Syracuse Daily Journal*, March 15, 1865, 1; "Southern Battle," *Richmond County Journal*, March 10, 1989, 3.

185. "Deserved Promotion," *Oswego Daily Palladium*, October 17, 1868.

186. See "A Faithful Officer," *Oswego Advertiser and Times*, March 16, 1867.

187. "Sheriff of Oswego County," *Syracuse Daily Standard*, November 4, 1869. See also "Man About Town," *Oswego Daily Times*, November 6, 1909, 5.

188. No headline, *Oswego Daily Palladium*, August 3, 1871.

189. No headline, *Pulaski Democrat*, January 16, 1873. Rpt. from *Syracuse Standard*.

190. "Col. James Doyle," *Oswego Morning Post*, December 1, 1882. The day was mistakenly given as Thursday. See also "A Veteran Gone," *Buffalo News*, December 1, 1882, 1.

191. "Tribute to a Comrade," *Oswego Morning Post*, December 4, 1882. See also "Col. Doyle's Funeral," *Oswego Morning Post*, December 4, 1882.

192. "Mrs. Margaret Doyle," *Oswego Daily Palladium*, November 3, 1917, 5.

193. Very little is known about Peter C. Dutcher. He apparently was a career soldier who saw duty during the American Indian Wars. After marrying Laura he reenlisted only to desert and be dishonorably discharged. What happened to him following the birth of his second son is unknown. See Natalie Joy Woodall, *Oswego County and the Civil War: They Answered the Call* (Charleston, SC: History Press, 2013), 101–2.

194. "War Memories," *Oswego Daily Palladium*, April 6, 1898, 6.

195. Deposition of February 28, 1888.

196. Deposition of February 28, 1888.

197. Deposition of February 27, 1888.

198. Deposition of February 28. 1888.

199. See Gilbert Dutcher's letter to the commissioner of pensions dated April 29, 1886.

200. Deposition of March 31, 1888.

201. "A Handsome Badge," *Oswego Times and Express*, January 3, 1885, 8.

202. "Public Installation," *Oswego Daily Palladium*, January 8, 1898, 5.

203. See, for example, "Decoration Day," *Oswego Times and Express*, May 3, 1884, 1; "Memorial Day," *Oswego Daily Times*, April 3, 1890.

204. "Veterans at Fulton," *Oswego Daily Palladium*, June 7, 1889.

205. "Gilbert C. Dutcher," *Oswego Daily Times*, July 25, 1898, 8.

206. "Funeral of Gilbert C. Dutcher," *Oswego Daily Times*, July 27, 1898, 8.

207. "Died," *Oswego Palladium-Times*, January 22, 1929, 5; "Mrs. Helen V. Dutcher," *Oswego Palladium-Times*, January 23, 1929, 10.

208. Two of these sons would also serve in the Civil War. Lieutenant Jason DeVillo Ferguson (1839–April 7, 1862), Co. D, 12th IA, died of wounds received in action at Pittsburg Landing (Shiloh), Tennessee, on April 6 and was buried in Shiloh National Cemetery. J. D. Ferguson Post No. 31, Nevada IA, was named for him. Hiram Fitch Ferguson (April 14, 1843–April 30, 1929) was a member of Co. B, 2nd IA Cavalry from August 31, 1861, to September 19, 1865.

209. "Taps Sounded for Maj. W. D. Ferguson," *Syracuse Daily Journal*, May 18, 1915, 5.

210. Norman Cooper, "History of the 24th N. Y. Infantry, Continued," *Fulton Times*, July 10, 1912, 6. The letter, which Cooper explained had never before been published, was dated January 17, 1863, and sent from Belle Plain, Virginia. It was signed by nineteen officers who all demurred on any claim they might have on the colonelcy.

211. "Met a Soldier's Fate," *Oswego Daily Palladium*, November 30, 1897, 8.

212. "Taps Sounded for Maj. W. D. Ferguson."

213. "Northern and Central Counties," *Utica Weekly Herald and Courier*, October 30, 1866, 1.

214. See, for example, "Around the Mess Table," *Oswego Daily Palladium*, May 18, 1889; "Veterans' Reunion," *Oswego Daily Palladium*, June 8, 1899, 8.

215. "A Good Appointment," *Oswego Weekly Advertiser*, June 7, 1871.

216. "W. D. Ferguson Retires," *Pulaski Democrat*, December 27, 1911, 1. See also "Fulton," *Oswego Daily Palladium*, December 23, 1911, 12.

217. "Order United American Mechanics," *Fulton Times*, June [?], 1906.

218. "Borrowed Time Club," *Pulaski Democrat*, July 16, 1912, 2.

219. For more information about Major Ferguson's postwar activities, see "Maj. William D. Ferguson," *Sandy Creek News*, May 27, 1915, 1.

220. No headline, *Pulaski Democrat*, March 15, 1911, 4.

221. In 1916 Nettie Ferguson received thirty dollars from the City of Fulton, no reason provided. See "Recommends Bond Issue To Cover Deficit," *Fulton Evening Times*, January 26, 1916, 4.

222. "Taps Sounded for Maj. W. D. Ferguson." See also "Major W. D. Ferguson Died Today; Age 84," *Fulton Evening Times*, May 18, 1915, 1; "Sandy Creek Veteran Dies," *Watertown Daily Times*, May 1915, 8; "Major W. D. Ferguson," *Sandy Creek News*, May 20, 1915, 2.

223. "The Oswego High School," *Oswego Daily Times*, May 25, 1894, 5.

224. "A Legal Tender," *Oswego Commercial Times*, September 25, 1862.

225. "Letter From Williamstown," *Oswego Commercial Advertiser*, October 26, 1864. George McClellan, here referred to as "Mackeral," was a favorite among soldiers, who considered him a fine officer and excellent presidential candidate. The term "Villain-Dames" was intended to mock Clement Laird Vallandigham (1822–June 17, 1871), a former Democratic member of Congress from Ohio who supported slavery and openly advocated ending the war and dividing the country into four sections. After delivering what became widely known as the King Lincoln speech in Mount Vernon, Ohio, on May 1, 1863, he was arrested, tried, and convicted by a military court in for violating General Ambrose Burnside's General Order No. 38, which stated that "all persons found within our lines who commit acts for the benefit of the enemies of our country will be tried as spies or traitors, and if convicted, will suffer death." Lincoln, realizing that executing or imprisoning the man would do more harm than good for the North, had him handed over to Confederate authorities. They did not want him either and enabled his escape to Canada, where he continued his anti-war campaign. He returned to the United States in 1864, still full of anti-war fury, and even spoke at a rally in Syracuse in August 1864. See Woodall, *Men of the 110th Regiment: Oswego's Own*, 123–25.

226. "General Election," *Oswego Daily Palladium*, November 21, 1866, 1.

227. "The Election," *Mexico Independent*, November 13, 1867.

228. No headline, *Oswego Daily Palladium*, October 15, 1864. See also "Sudden Death," *Oswego Commercial Advertiser*, October 14, 1864, in which the cause of death was described as "convulsions."

229. "Death of Recorder Gary," *Oswego Daily Press*, July 28, 1870.

230. For more information on Captain Gary, see Natalie Joy Woodall, *Of Blood and Battles: Oswego's 147th Regiment* (Denver: Outskirts Press, 2019), 220–22. For the story surrounding the discovery of Delos and Kate's graves, see Natalie J. Woodall, "Lost and Found: Captain Delos Gary's Grave," *Oswego Palladium-Times*, May 28, 2019, 1.

231. Letter written by Dr. W. H. Rice, dated February 25, 1865, and sent from Fulton, New York.

232. Letter written by Dr. E. M. Allen, dated March 17, 1865, and sent from General Hospital, Fortress Monroe, Virginia.

233. "Death of a Soldier of the 81st," *Oswego Commercial Times*, September 12, 1864.

234. "Marriages," *Syracuse Daily Journal*, March 13, 1866, 5.

235. "Has Decorated the Graves of Confederates for Forty-two Years," *Oswego Daily Times*, May 29, 1908, 4.

236. "The Enlarged Welland Canal," *Oswego Daily Palladium*, February 5, 1914, 5. Hirschbolz was nicknamed Major because he had been a drum-major while in the service.

237. "'Wild' Night in Oswego Over Lee's Surrender," *Watertown Daily Times*, April 9, 1915, 10.

238. "Major Andrew J. Hirschbolz," *Oswego Daily Palladium*, December 16, 1915, 5.

239. "An Indignant German Citizen," *Oswego Daily Palladium*, March 3, 1894, 5.

240. "People's Convention," *Oswego Daily Times*, October 27, 1875.

241. Johnson, *History of Oswego County*, 166. The church's cornerstone was laid in 1862.

242. "The First German Organization," *Oswego Daily Times*, January 5, 1880.

243. "Has Decorated the Graves of Confederates for Forty-two Years."

244. "Decorates the Confederate Graves," *Oswego Daily Times*, May 29, 1914, 7.

245. "Part Oswego Took in Parade," *Oswego Daily Palladium*, June 21, 1910, 5; "Major Andrew J. Hirschbolz."

246. "Lethia Kingsley Hirschbolz," *Oswego Daily Times*, October 22, 1902. See also "Aletha Kingsley Hirschbolz," *Oswego Daily Palladium*, October 22, 1902, 1.

247. "Major Hirschbolz's Big Reception," *Oswego Daily Times*, September 12, 1910, 8; "In the Fatherland," *Oswego Daily Palladium*, October 13, 1910, 3; "Major Hirschbolz in His Old Home," *Oswego Daily Times*, November 14, 1910, 8.

248. "Introduces Bride Upon Return from Europe," *Syracuse Post-Standard*, November 21, 1910, 15. Although called Elizabeth in this announcement, Louise was the bride's correct name.

249. "Major Andrew J. Hirschbolz."

250. See "Mrs. Louise Hirschbolz," *Oswego Daily Palladium*, October 26, 1923, 5. Since Louise died in Orwell, New York, it is likely that she died of tuberculosis at the sanitarium.

251. "Old Politician Dies at Mexico," *Watertown Daily Times*, April 16, 1915, 2.

252. Churchill, *Landmarks of Oswego County* "Biographical," 55–57.

253. See, for example, an advertisement in the *Mexico Independent*, June 22, 1892, 1.

254. No headline, *Mexico Independent*, December 27, 1893. See also "Walks and Talks Among the Business Interests of Mexico," *Mexico Independent*, May 12, 1880, 1.

255. "An Agreeable Surprise," *Mexico Independent*, January 23, 1895.

256. "Melzar Richards Post," *Mexico Independent*, February 8, 1893.

257. See "List of Soldiers of the War of 1861–1865," *Mexico Independent*, June 20, 1888, 1.

258. "A Memorable Day for Mexico," *Mexico Independent*, July 10, 1889. The same issue contains the final list of Union men from the town of Mexico as well as a drawing of the monument.

259. "Reunion of the Brave Twenty-Fourth," *Mexico Independent*, July 26, 1899.

260. See, for example, "Masonic Installation," *Mexico Independent*, January 13, 1892; "Election of Officers," *Mexico Independent*, December 19, 1894.

261. "Mexico Academy," *Mexico Independent*, May 18, 1892; "Here and There," *Mexico Independent*, April 19, 1899; "Thief Detective Society," *Mexico Independent*, January 23, 1901.

262. No headline, *Mexico Independent*, September 14, 1881; "The Election," *Mexico Independent*, November 9, 1881.

263. "Here and There," *Mexico Independent*, December 28, 1898; "Here and There," *Mexico Independent*, May 10, 1899; "Shrievalty Race Much Simplified," *Mexico Independent*, June 21, 1899.

264. Mexico Historical Society, "Mexico Electric Light Heat and Power Company," accessed January 14, 2022, http://www.mexiconyhistoricalsociety.com.

265. See "Electric Lights," "Mr. Editor," and "Unfounded Reports," *Mexico Independent*, January 1, 1890.

266. "Light Heat and Power Company," "Here and There," *Mexico Independent*, October 12, 1887; "Here and There," *Mexico Independent*, December 11, 1888; "Here and There," *Mexico Independent*, May 11, 1893; "Here and There," *Mexico Independent*, May 9, 1900. See also Churchill, *Landmarks of Oswego County*, 593.

267. No headline, *Mexico Independent*, March 7, 1894.

268. "Edwin L. Huntington," *Pulaski Democrat*, April 21, 1915, 3. See also "Funeral Tomorrow for Captain E. L. Huntington," *Syracuse Post-Standard*, April 15, 1915, 12.

269. "Mrs. Huntington Buried Monday," *Mexico Independent*, October 14, 1943, 1.

270. See Frank W. Blackmar, *A Cyclopedia of State History, Embracing Events, Industries, Counties, Cities, Towns, Prominent Persons, etc.* (Chicago: Standard Publishing, 1912), 2:130. See also *Appleton's Cyclopedia of American Biography, 1600–1889* (New York: D. Appleton & Co., 1889), 3:656.

271. "From the Department of the Gulf," *New York Daily Tribune*, May 27, 1864, 8.

272. See "The New Orleans Riot," *Philadelphia Inquirer*, August 21, 1866, 2. This article quotes Lee's account.

273. Albert Lindley Lee II (May 11, 1868–November 10, 1946) was a successful author and playwright. He was married twice: (1) Carrie B. Coit (1872–*post* 1900) on May 22, 1895, by whom he was the father of Norman Coit (June 13, 1896–November 17, 1973), and (2) Ada Delamater (May 29,

1888–January 6, 1986) on October 20, 1909, by whom he was the father of Barbara (May 13, 1913–April 1, 1994).

274. Grace Lynch, "The Way it Used to Be," *Fulton Patriot*, March 21, 1963.

275. "Notice," *Wall Street Journal*, January 7, 1908, 5.

276. "Our State Ticket," *Kansas Chief*, September 22, 1864; "Louisiana in the Senate," *Washington Evening Star*, June 5, 1868.

277. "A Wall Street Type," *Wall Street Journal*, January 3, 1908, 1. See also "Death of General Lee," *Iola Index*, January 2, 1908, 4; "Gen. A. L. Lee Dead," *New York Times*, January 1, 1908, 9; "Gen. Albert L. Lee," *Rutland Daily Herald*, January 1, 1908, 2; "General Albert Lindley Lee," *New Orleans Times-Picayune*, January 1, 1908, 2; "General A. L. Lee Is Dead," *Salina Semi-Weekly Journal*, January 3, 1908, 1.

278. "Fulton Briefs," *Syracuse Daily Herald*, January 3, 1908, 3.

279. "Tribute to Gen. Lee," *Fulton Times*, January 29, 1908, 1. The article was originally a letter written to Dr. Charles Lee, a cousin.

280. "Memorial Hospital," *Syracuse Daily Herald*, April 4, 1908, 3; "Munificent Gift to Fulton," *Fulton Times*, April 8, 1908, 1. Lee's burial occurred on June 7, 1908. See "Gen. Lee's Monument," *Fulton Times*, June 14, 1908, 1.

281. "Lee Memorial Hospital Dedicated," *Fulton Times*, April 13, 1910, 1.

282. "Mrs. Lee's Will," *Fulton Patriot*, January 22, 1919, 1; "Author's Children Get Estate," *New York Clipper*, September 3, 1919, 4; "Rare Jewels Go On Sale," *New York Sun*, November 30, 1919, 15. See also "Widow of Gen. A. L. Lee Left $192,000 Estate," *Brooklyn Standard Union*, November 13, 1921, 3.

283. "Mrs. Victoria Lee Dead," *Kansas City Star*, January 1, 1919, 3.

284. "James H. Lee Was Hero of the Civil War," *Oswego Palladium-Times*, August 31, 1948, 13.

285. See Rossiter Johnson, "The History of the Alabama," *Camp-Fire Sketches and Battle-Field Echoes of 61-65*, 442–44.

286. James Lee, unpublished diary, June 19, 1864. See also Norman C. Delaney, "Victory Has Perched on Our Banners," *Naval History* 28, no. 3 (June 2014), 32–38; Ves Levshiz, "Medal of Honor Recipient Remembered for Heroic Actions Aboard Union Ship," *Oswego Palladium-Times*, July 17, 2000, 1.

287. According to Dr. Jesse Kraft, assistant curator of American Numismatics, Lee's medal formerly belonged to well-known collector Jonas Coolidge Hills (October 18, 1851–November 8, 1913) of Hartford, Connecticut. When Hills died the collection first went to Wadsworth Athenaeum. It was given to the American Numismatic Society in 1967 (Dr. Jesse Kraft, email communication with author).

288. "Albany Correspondence," *Lowville Journal and Republican*, January 8, 1872; "Death of a Cayugan of Kearsarge Fame," *Auburn Morning News*, August 15, 1877; "Cayuga and Oswego In It!" *Cayuga Chief*, March 5, 1899.

289. "Oswego County Celebrates National Grange Week," *Valley News*, April 19, 1990, 23.

290. "Secret Session of the Grangers," *Auburn Morning News*, March 1874, 1; "Oswego County Foremost in Grange Work," *Fulton Patriot*, February 19, 1931, 1; L. L. Allen, "Pioneer Granger Was Hero of Kearsarge Crew in Civil War Battle," *Watertown Daily Standard*, April 9, 1927, 9.

291. "Oswego County Celebrates National Grange Week."

292. See an advertisement in *Oswego Daily Times*, May 3, 1876.

293. "Obituary–James H. Lee," *Oswego Daily Palladium*, August 13, 1877. See also "Masonic," *Oswego Daily Times*, August 13, 1877.

294. "Obituary–James Lee"; Deposition of May 21, 1890.

295. Deposition of August 10, 1889.

296. Deposition of June 27, 1889.

297. "Julia E. Lee," *Oswego Daily Times*, May 20, 1895, 4. See also "Funeral of Mrs. Julia E. Lee," *Oswego Daily Times*, May 23, 1895, 8.

298. "Death of One of the Heroes of the Kearsarge," *Oswego Daily Times*, August 13, 1877.

299. Anne Derousie, "The Rome-Oswego Plank Road," *Thirtieth Publication of the Oswego County Historical Society* (Phoenix, NY: Phoenix Press, 1969), 52–53.

300. Letter dated February 25, 1860, posted on https://www.Fold3.com.

301. "Veterans of the 81st Regiment," *Oswego Commercial Times*, January 11, 1864.

302. "The Battle of Cold Harbor," *Oswego Daily Times*, June 3, 1910, 4. See also Crisfield Johnson, 78–81.

303. "Keys of Rebel Prisons in City," *Oswego Palladium-Times*, November 20, 1945, 9; "Northern and Central Counties," *Utica Weekly Herald*, September 12, 1865, 4.

304. Letter posted on https://www.Fold3.com.

305. Churchill, *Landmarks of Oswego County*, "Family Sketches," 64; "Political Notices," *Albany Evening Times*, July 21, 1874; "Work Well Done," *Albany Argus*, February 10, 1886, 1; "Work on the Albany Capitol," *Oswego Daily Palladium*, July 19, 1895, 2.

306. "G. A. R.," *Oswego Morning Herald*, March 22, 1879.

307. He died in office in 1910. See "In Memoriam," *Oswego Daily Times*, July 9, 1910, 7.

308. "The G. A. R.," *Mexico Independent*, June 24, 1903, 1; "Veterans Are Home," *Oswego Daily Times*, June 19, 1903, 4.

309. "G. A. R. National Council of Administration," *Grand Rapids Herald*, August 22, 1906, 4.

310. "Oswego is Represented," *Oswego Daily Palladium*, February 27, 1886.

311. "Republican Town Caucuses," *Oswego Daily Times*, August 26, 1878; "Political," *Albany Times*, September 21, 1889.

312. "Obituary," *Oswego Daily Palladium*, June 18, 1910, 5.

313. "Veteran Volunteer Association," *Oswego Daily Times*, September 7, 1896, 4.

314. See "The Mattison Case," *Oswego Daily Palladium*, November 15, 1878; "Charged with Improperly Opening Letters," *Oswego Daily Times*, November 14, 1878; "The Rights of Wives," *Utica Morning Herald*, November 16, 1878; "A Case That Interests Married People," *Mexico Independent*, November 28, 1878; No headline, *Terre Haute Weekly Gazette*, December 5, 1878.

315. "Opening a Wife's Letters," *Syracuse Sunday Times*, December 8, 1878; "Discharged," *Syracuse Daily Journal*, December 24, 1878.

316. "Oswego Matters," *Syracuse Morning Standard*, October 1, 1879, 1.

317. "Brevities," *Oswego Morning Express*, August 13, 1881.

318. "Died," *Oswego Daily Times*, September 1, 1891.

319. "Funeral of Mrs. Mattison," *Oswego Daily Times*, March 17, 1909.

320. See, for example, "Col. L. V. S. Mattison Dead," *Brooklyn Daily Eagle*, June 19, 1910, 8; "Old General Dies," *Elmira Telegram*, June 19, 1910, 1. Both incorrectly reported that Mattison was an attorney.

321. "Obituary." See also "Col. Mattison Buried With Military Honors," *Oswego Daily Times*, June 20, 1910, 1.

322. William Patrick McKinley served in Co. G, 110th Regiment and later as lieutenant-colonel in the 184th Regiment. After the war he and his family settled in New Orleans where he and his sons worked on the railroad. See Woodall, *Men of the 110th Regiment: Oswego's Own, A Biographical Supplement*, 278–79.

323. "Enlist Now and Save Your Bounty," *Oswego Commercial Times*, September 2, 1862.

324. "Wants a Special Agency," *Oswego Daily Times-Express*, June 17, 1885. The reporter noted, "He would make a good officer."

325. "Appointed to Auburn Prison," *Oswego Daily Palladium*, October 7, 1887.

326. "Captain McKinley's Appointment," *Oswego Daily Palladium*, February 2, 1888.

327. "A Clever Crook," *Rome Daily Sentinel*, May 26, 1888, 1; "Here and Hereabout," *Seneca County News*, May 29, 1888; "Scaling a High Prison Wall," *Homer Republican*, May 31, 1888, 1; "In the Warden's Clothes," *Auburn Weekly Democrat*, May 31, 1888; "News from Everywhere," *Otsego Farmer*, June 2, 1888, 8.

328. "A Keeper Suspended," *Oswego Daily Palladium*, June 4, 1888.

329. See, for example, "Noted Veteran Dies," *Ithaca Daily News*, October 26, 1905, 7.

330. "Captain James A. McKinley," *Oswego Daily Palladium*, October 26, 1905, 1.

331. "Veterans All for Hancock," *Oswego Daily Palladium*, June 26, 1880. Other prominent Democrats in Oswego supporting this effort included Alexander R. Penfield, Thomas Kehoe, and James Doyle.

332. "Second Annual Ball," *Oswego Daily Times*, October 3, 1853. The event was being held to purchase hats for the firemen.

333. "Fire Department—Election of Chief Engineer and Assistants," *Oswego Commercial Times*, March 10, 1862.

334. "The Common Council," *Oswego Times and Express*, April 29, 1885.

335. See "Veterans' Association," *Oswego Morning Herald*, May 16, 1879, 1; No headline, *Oswego Daily Times*, August 1, 1896, 4.

336. "Going to Gettysburg," *Oswego Daily Palladium*, June 26, 1886.

337. Local newspapers published detailed travel plans and descriptions of the dedication service. See, for example, "The 147th at Gettysburg," *Oswego Daily Palladium*, May 31, 1888; "Bound for Gettysburg," *Oswego Daily Palladium*, June 30, 1888, 1. For years, controversy raged over the accuracy of the placement of the monument and a marker on Culp's Hill. See, for example, "Culp's Hill at Gettysburg," *Oswego Daily Times*, December 20, 1899, 2. Much has been written about the 147th Regiment's role in the battle of Gettysburg. See Thomas Ebert, *147th Infantry, September 22, 1862-June 7, 1865* (Clovis, CA: T. J. Ebert, 2009). Ebert's bibliography includes H. H. Lyman, adjutant for the 147th. H. H. Lyman wrote "Historical Sketch of the 147th Regiment," *Monuments Commission for the Battlefields of Gettysburg and Chattanooga* (Albany, NY: J. B. Lyon Co., 1900), 997–1010. See also Natalie J. Woodall, "On to Glory: Oswego's 147th Regiment at Gettysburg," *Oswego Palladium-Times*, July 1, 2019, 1.

338. "Now to Gettysburg," *Oswego Daily Palladium*, July 17, 1893, 4.

339. "A Tribute to Captain McKinley," *Oswego Daily Palladium*, October 26, 1905, 1. The writer was identified only as "Veteran."

340. "Mrs. Jane McKinley," *Oswego Daily Palladium*, March 19, 1917, 8.

341. "St. Patrick's Society," *Oswego Daily Palladium*, March 9, 1874.

342. See, for example, "Making the Queer," *Syracuse Daily Courier*, January 23, 1880; "Bonnell's Examination," *Oswego Daily Times*, January 23, 1880; "Bogus Financiers," *Oswego Weekly Palladium*, January 28, 1880, 1; "Oswego's Queer Gang," *Syracuse Morning Standard*, January 31, 1880, 1; "Part of the Loomis Gang," *New York Sun*, February 2, 1880; "Oswego's Wicked Gang," *Syracuse Daily Standard*, February 7, 1880; "The Counterfeiters," *Oswego Daily Times*, February 9, 1880; "The Counterfeiters," *Mexico Independent*, February 11, 1880; "The Counterfeiters' Cases," *Oswego Weekly Palladium*, February 25, 1880, 1; "The Famous Eleven," *Oswego Daily Palladium*, March 30, 1880; "The Counterfeiters' Cases," *Mexico Independent*, March 31, 1880; "Thomas Jefferson Towsley," *Oswego Daily Palladium*, May 13, 1880.

343. "Oswego Matters," *Syracuse Morning Standard*, April 26, 1880, 1. The reporter may be excused if he exaggerated the facts slightly.

344. "Secret Service," *New York Press*, April 1, 1894.

345. "An Oswego Officer Helping to Maul Counterfeiters," *Oswego Daily Palladium*, March 12, 1881.

346. "Our Portraits," *National Police Gazette*, November 7, 1885, 2.

347. "A Farmer's Bad Crop," *Watertown Daily Times*, March 26, 1891, 1.

348. "For Circulating Counterfeit Money," *Oswego Daily Palladium*, April 20, 1893, 5.

349. "Dynamiters Arrested," *Ithaca Morning Herald*, November 16, 1894, 1; "The Detective Muddle," *Scranton Tribune*, June 22, 1895, 2. See also "Damaging Evidence Against Farrell," *Atlantic City Daily Union*, June 24, 1896, 1.

350. See "That Detective Bill," *Scranton Tribune*, August 24, 1896, 8.

351. "Mrs. Daniel McSweeney," *Oswego Daily Times*, February 9, 1918, 8.

352. "To Bring Body from Pittsburgh," *Syracuse Daily Journal*, April 10, 1919, 21.

353. "Fall Down Mine Shaft Fatal," *Pittsburgh Post-Gazette*, August 8, 1920, 13.

354. "Daniel J. McSweeney," *Oswego Daily Palladium*, August 9, 1920, 10. See also "The Death Roll," *Pittsburgh Post-Gazette*, August 9, 1920, 2.

355. "Civil War Experiences of Late Oliver B. Mowry Noted," *Mexico Independent*, December 26, 1940, 6–7.

356. "Mexico Couple at Anniversary," *Oswego Palladium-Times*, July 22, 1933.

357. "Oswego Co. Holstein Club Banquet," *Mexico Independent*, April 12, 1934, 1.

358. "Oliver W. Mowry Gets Invitation to Gettysburg," *Mexico Independent*, May 26, 1938, 1.

359. "'Pie Wagon' Thrill," *Kingston Daily Freeman*, July 15, 1938, 6.

360. "91 and 84, Mates Still Happy," *Albany Times-Union*, July 24, 1938, 6-A.

361. "Civil War Vets Meet in Oswego," *Mexico Independent*, September 30, 1937, 1.

362. "Mexico Man Is Sole Survivor," *Oswego Palladium-Times*, February 6, 1928, 3.

363. "Mexico Couple Will Be Married 67 Years Friday," *Mexico Independent*, July 21, 1938, 1.

364. "Mrs. O. B. Mowry," *Oswego Palladium-Times*, March 26, 1940, 7; "Mrs. O. B. Mowry," *Oswego Palladium-Times*, March 29, 1940, 3.

365. "County's Last Civil War Veteran Given Full Military Rites," *Mexico Independent*, October 29, 1940, 1. See also "O. B. Mowry Dead at 92 in Mexico," *Syracuse Herald-Journal*, October 19, 1940, 14; "Oliver B. Mowry Dead at Mexico," *Oswego Palladium-Times*, October 19, 1940, 7.

366. For an interesting article on the North Country's reaction to the recruitment of the 186th and the promised financial incentives, see Will Hickox,

"The Civil War's 11th—Hour Soldiers," *New York Times Opinionator*, April 6, 2015. Bounties were supposed to increase enlistments and diminish the necessity of local drafts. See also "More Troops," *Oswego Commercial Times*, July 15, 1862; "Drafting," *Oswego Commercial Times*, July 31, 1862.

367. "Sudden Disappearance," *Mexico Independent*, June 23, 1869.
368. No headline, *Mexico Independent*, June 30, 1869.
369. "Mrs. Lawson R. Muzzy," *Pulaski Democrat*, July 8, 1908.
370. "Passing of the 'Plug' Hat," *Watertown Daily Times*, June 22, 1920, 13.
371. No headline, *Pulaski Democrat*, October 12, 1895.
372. "Mrs. Lawson R. Muzzy."
373. "Pulaski," *Syracuse Herald*, November 6, 1911, 2.
374. "L. R. Muzzy Dead," *Kenosha Evening News*, November 19, 1912, 1.
375. "Pulaski," *Oswego Daily Times*, November 20, 1912, 7.
376. "The Funeral of Lawson Read Muzzy Was a Real Demonstration in Honor of Man Who Loved Pulaski," *Pulaski Democrat*, November 27, 1912, 1.
377. No headline, *Jefferson County Journal*, November 27, 1912, 4.
378. Statement signed by Orimel B. Olmstead on September 5, 1863. This statement was attached to Samuel's muster card. It also appeared on the reverse of Samuel's carte-de-visite.
379. Olmstead's statement of September 5, 1863.
380. "Orimil B. Olmstead," *Pulaski Democrat*, October 23, 1884.
381. "Orimil B. Olmstead."
382. "Minutes of the Board of Supervisors," *Mexico Independent*, December 18, 1862. This statement was reprinted in Captain Olmstead's obituary.
383. "Orwell's Big Day," *Pulaski Democrat*, July 11, 1894.
384. Churchill, *Landmarks of Oswego County*, 476.
385. "Letter from a Volunteer," *Oswego Commercial Times*, May 20, 1861.
386. "The Twenty-Fourth Regiment," *Oswego Commercial Times*, August 24, 1861.
387. Deposition of January 31, 1869.
388. Deposition of May 6, 1869.
389. Deposition of December 31, 1868.
390. "Letters from the 147th Regiment," *Mexico Independent*, November 13, 1862, 1. The letter written by "a volunteer" was dated October 29, 1862.
391. "He fought at Gettysburg," *Oswego Daily Palladium*, April 11, 1898, 6. See also "The Killed, Wounded and Missing of the 147th Regiment," *Oswego Commercial Times*, July 20, 1863.
392. Dorothy Kincheloe Hendrix, ed., *A Leaf from Army Life: The Background and Experiences of a Civil War Soldier* (independently published, 1995), 125–26. See also "From the One Hundred and Forty-Seventh Regiment," *Oswego Commercial Times*, May 23, 1864; "The 147th in Action," *Oswego Daily Palladium*, June 14, 1864, 1–2.

393. "N. Y. Conference Veterans at the Annual Camp Fire," *Poughkeepsie Daily Eagle*, March 30, 1910, 1.

394. Deposition of March 26, 1885.

395. Deposition of March 26, 1885.

396. Edward F. Roberts, *Andersonville Journey: The Civil War's Greatest Tragedy* (Shippensburg, PA: Burd Street Press, 2000), 59–60.

397. Samuel Eliot, "A Diary of Prison Life: Andersonville and Florence, SC," PA-Roots, accessed January 14, 2022, https://www.pa-roots.com/pacw/reserves/7thres/eliotdiary.html. See also John McElroy, *Andersonville: A Story of Rebel Military Prisoners* (Toledo, OH: D. R. Locke, 1879); John Worrell Northrop, *Chronicles from the Diary of a War Prisoner in Andersonville and Other Military Prisons in the South* (Wichita, KS: published by the author, 1904).

398. Deposition of July 30, 1885.

399. Deposition of July 31, 1882.

400. Deposition of July 31, 1883.

401. Deposition of May 26, 1885.

402. "North Scriba," *Oswego Daily Times*, February 19, 1877.

403. See "GAR," *Oswego Daily Palladium*, April 3, 1871; "Obituary Resolutions," *Oswego Daily Times*, August 26, 1879.

404. See "Town Meetings," *Oswego Daily Times*, March 3, 1880; "Returns of the Towns," *Oswego Daily Palladium*, March 8, 1882; "Result of Town Meetings," *Oswego Daily Times and Express*, March 5, 1884.

405. Francis Pease, deposition of August 21, 1883; Byron Earl, deposition of July 31, 1883.

406. Deposition of June 12, 1886.

407. "Catherine B. Dutcher," *Oswego Daily Palladium*, January 23, 1904, 4. See also "Mrs. Catherine B. Dutcher," *Oswego Daily Times*, January 23, 1904, 5.

408. "Celebrates 95th Birthday," *Oswego Daily Palladium*, November 28, 1917, 2.

409. "Palermo," *Oswego Daily Times*, April 17, 1894, 6. See also "An Old Man Gone," *Oswego Daily Palladium*, April 10, 1894, 8; "Sala," *Oswego Daily Times*, April 13, 1894, 6; "Clifford," *Mexico Independent*, April 18, 1894; "North Volney," *Mexico Independent*, April 25, 1894, 1.

410. "Memorial Resolutions," *Oswego Daily Times*, May 5, 1894, 4.

411. "New Haven," *Oswego Daily Times*, April 8, 1890.

412. "Oldest Woman Dead," *Oswego Daily Palladium*, February 19, 1909, 4.

413. See "Raulston Family of Oswego Town Set War Record," *Oswego Palladium-Times*, June 24, 1942, 11.

414. "Sworn In," *Oswego Commercial Times*, August 29, 1861.

415. "Mustering in the Forty-Eighth," *Oswego Commercial Times*, September 14, 1861.

416. "Letter from Capt. Steele," *Mexico Independent*, June 12, 1862. The letter was dated June 2. See also "81st Regiment, N. Y. V.," *Sag-Harbor Express*, June 12, 1862.

417. No headline, *Mexico Independent*, June 5, 1862.

418. "The Eighty-First Regiment," *New York Reformer*, June 25, 1862.

419. See "Promotions," *Mexico Independent*, August 14, 1862.

420. "The Twenty-Fourth Regiment to be Re-Organized," *Mexico Independent*, August 27, 1863. See also "Avoid the Draft," Mexico *Independent*, December 31, 1863. Raulston's advertisements detailed the numerous benefits of enlisting in the new regiment.

421. "From the Army of the Potomac," *Buffalo Daily Courier*, June 10, 1864. This letter was written by H. W. F., who died of "disease" on September 11, 1864. See also "From the 81st Regiment," *Oswego Commercial Times*, June 20, 1864. This article detailed the role the 81st Regiment played at Cold Harbor.

422. "Lieut. A. Cooper," *Oswego Commercial Times*, March 9, 1865. For a fuller account of the escape plot, see also Lieut. A. Cooper, *In and Out of Rebel Prisons* (Oswego, NY: R. J. Oliphant, 1888), 222–27.

423. "Dead," *Richmond Dispatch*, December 24, 1864. See also "Thirty-Six Years Ago, Reminiscences of the War of the Rebellion," *Oswego Daily Palladium*, December 15, 1900, 4.

424. See "First Will Executed Ninety-Six Years Ago," *Oswego Daily Times*, May 25, 1912, 4. Margaret Mary Smith (August 1842–February 5, 1937) married Dr. Giles Clark Decker (1843–1902) on August 25, 1869, in Wayne County, Michigan. She died in Binghamton, Broome, New York. She and Dr. Decker, a dentist, are buried in Oak Hill Cemetery, Owasso, Shiawassee, Michigan.

425. "The Late Col. Raulston," *Oswego Daily Palladium*, February 9, 1867.

426. "Masonic—," *Oswego Daily Palladium*, February 9, 1867.

427. "William C. Raulston," *Oswego Daily Palladium*, February 12, 1867. Raulston was later honored by Civil War veterans residing in Fulton, New York, who organized William C. Raulston Post No. 111 GAR *ca.* 1870.

428. "Death of Paul Reynolds, Esq.," *Oswego Commercial Times*, January [?], 1850. Rpt. from *The Irish Paper*.

429. Michael Cavanaugh, *Waterford Celebrities* (Waterford: C. P. Redmond & Co., 1902), 4; Waterford Civil War Veterans, "Surgeon to the Irish Brigade," accessed January 14, 2022, http://www.waterfordcivilwarveterans.wordpress.com.

430. Cavanaugh, *Waterford Celebrities*, 5.

431. Cavanaugh, *Waterford Celebrities*, 6.

432. Jay Knox, "Do You Remember?" *Oswego Palladium-Times*, May 31, 1945, 15.

433. "A Rousing Meeting," *Oswego Daily Palladium*, October 4, 1876. See also "Third and Fourth Wards," *Oswego Daily Palladium*, October 31, 1857; "Fulton Democrats," *Oswego Daily Palladium*, October 2, 1884.

434. "The Voice of a Patriot!" *Oswego Commercial Times*, October 25, 1862. This editorial was written to persuade Republicans to support the war effort by invoking Dr. Reynolds, a staunch Democrat.

435. See "Oswego Volunteers," *Oswego Commercial Times*, April 3, 1862.

436. For a thorough examination of the 63rd Regiment, see Patricia Vaticano, "A Defense of the 63rd New York State Volunteer Regiment of the Irish Brigade" (2008), (master's thesis, 703), https://www.semanticsscholar.org.

437. Captain Edward Field, "The Boys of Old Erin," quoted in Cavanaugh, *Waterford Celebrities*, 10.

438. "Lawrence Reynolds," *Oswego Daily Palladium*, April 25, 1887.

439. "Decoration Day," *Oswego Daily Press*, May 31, 1879.

440. "Peace Hath Her Victories," *Oswego Daily Palladium*, April 9, 1880.

441. "Post O'Brian's Camp Fire," *Oswego Daily Palladium*, March 10, 1881.

442. "G. A. R.," *Oswego Daily Times*, August 20, 1879.

443. "Dr. Reynolds and the Mesmerizer," *Oswego Daily Times*, May 1, 1877.

444. "The Fifteenth Amendment," *Oswego Daily Press*, April 22, 1870.

445. Captain D. P. Conyngham, *The Irish Brigade and Its Campaigns* (Glasgow: Cameron & Ferguson, 1868), 187–88.

446. "Dr. Reynolds Badly Swindled," *Oswego Daily Palladium*, August 26, 1881. Dr. Reynolds had departed from Oswego on July 28, 1881. See "News from Reporters' Books," *Oswego Daily Palladium*, July 27, 1881.

447. "For Doctor Reynolds," *Oswego Daily Palladium*, June 14, 1882; "The Entertainment for Dr. Reynolds," *Oswego Daily Palladium*, June 15, 1882. See also "Dr. Lawrence Reynolds," *Oswego Morning Express*, May 10, 1882.

448. See "Dr. Lawrence Reynolds," *Oswego Daily Palladium*, February 10, 1883.

449. "Personal," *Oswego Morning Post*, March 21, 1883.

450. See, for example, "Dr. Lawrence Reynolds," *Syracuse Daily Journal*, April 26, 1887, in which he was described as "a remarkable man in many ways."

451. "Lawrence Reynolds," *Oswego Daily Palladium*, April 25, 1887.

452. See, for example, "A Monument for Dr. Reynolds," *Oswego Daily Palladium*, April 28, 1887; "The Reynolds Monument Fund," *Oswego Daily Palladium*, April 29, 1887; "What People Say," *Oswego Daily Palladium*, May 28, 1895.

453. William and Mary sent another son to the war in 1862. William Penn Schenck (March 10, 1840–July 27, 1863), a member of Co. D, 147th Regiment, was severely wounded at the battle of Gettysburg. Since it was thought he would survive, his father traveled to Gettysburg to visit him. The young man died soon thereafter after and his body was taken home to Fulton

for burial. See Woodall, *Of Blood and Battles: Oswego's 147th Regiment*, 417–18.

454. "Post Schenck Has a New Flag," *Syracuse Daily Journal*, September 30, 1903, 10. Fred Schenck, Daniel's brother, presented the post with a flag in his memory and spoke briefly about his military service.

455. "Bombardment of Fredericksburg," *Oswego Commercial Times*, December 13, 1862. See also "The Taking of Fredericksburg," *Rochester Evening Express*, December 12, 1862.

456. "Army Letters," *Rochester Evening Express*, March 17, 1864. The letter, dated March 13, 1864, was sent from Washington, DC.

457. "Notaries Public," *Mexico Independent*, March 26, 1874.

458. "Soldiers' Re-Union," *Mexico Independent*, May 27, 1875.

459. "Decoration Day at Fulton," *Oswego Daily Press*, June 1, 1870.

460. "Address Delivered on Decoration Day, May 30, 1876, at Fulton, N. Y, by Melvin F. Stephens," *Fulton Times*, May 31, 1911, 4.

461. "Grand Army Notes," *Oswego Morning Express and Post*, May 27, 1882; "Post Daniel F. Schenck," *Fulton Times*, June 7, 1882; No headline, *Baldwinsville Gazette and Farmers' Journal*, June 15, 1882, 1.

462. "Schenck Post To Be Disbanded," *Oswego Palladium-Times*, March 28, 1940, 15; "Last Survivor Gone; Post Is Disbanded," *Fulton Patriot*, April 4, 1940, 1.

463. "Briefs," *Mexico Independent*, December 16, 1875; "A Special Pension," *Auburn Bulletin*, July 3, 1886, 1.

464. "Fulton," *Syracuse Standard*, July 7, 1886, 6.

465. "A Special Pension," "In the Senate," *Lancaster Intelligencer*, July 27, 1886, 1.

466. "The Cruelty of a Pension Veto," *National Tribune*, July 15, 1886, 7.

467. See, for example, "Grover and His Vetoes," *Hillsboro News-Herald*, October 13, 1892, 4. For the story of how Cleveland avoided military service, see Woodall, *Of Blood and Battles: Oswego's 147th Regiment*, 523–24.

468. 49 Cong. Rec., 1st Sess. 7786 (1886).

469. "Died," *Fulton Times*, January 29, 1908, 1. The obituary mistakenly stated she had succumbed to typhoid fever. Her death certificate specified that she died of hemiplegia of the left side.

470. "Letters from the 147th Regiment," *Mexico Independent*, November 13, 1862, l.

471. See "Can It Be Possible?" *Mexico Independent*, December 4, 1862; "Letter from the 147th Regiment" written by "a volunteer" on the same page.

472. *Recollections*, quoted in Joyce Hawthorne Cook, *Elmina Spencer: Oswego's Civil War Battlefield Nurse* (Syracuse, NY: Avalon Document Services, 2017), 15–16.

473. Cook, 17.

474. *Recollections*, quoted in Cook, 21–22.

475. Hendrix, *A Leaf from Army Life*, 122. See also "Letter from the 147th Regiment," *Mexico Independent*, July 21, 1864, written by Lt. Ernest Richard Esmond. These examples represent only two of many laudatory letters written by grateful soldiers.

476. "The Army in Virginia," *Oswego Daily Palladium*, March 1, 1864.

477. "Mrs. Spencer's Service in the Hospital Department of the Army," *Oswego Daily Palladium*, November 30, 1865.

478. "Silver Wedding," *Oswego Daily Palladium*, November 10, 1865.

479. "Destitution in Kansas—Mrs. E. H. Spencer a Sufferer," *Oswego Daily Times*, October 20, 1875. See also "Grasshopper Plague of 1874," Kansas Historical Society (October 2016), https://www.kshs.org/kansapedia/grasshopper-plague-of-1874/12070#.

480. "Select Reading Last Night," *Leavenworth Times*, June 2, 1877, 3.

481. See, for example, "An Extract from Mrs. R. H. Spencer's Life Sketches During the War," *Great Bend Register*, January 11, 1877, 1; "An Extract from Mrs. R. H. Spencer's Life Sketches During the War," *Great Bend Register*, January 18, 1877, 1; "Town County and State," *Osage County Chronicle*, May 3, 1877, 3; "Today's Local Notices," *Lawrence Daily Journal*, May 15, 1877, 4.

482. A Report to Accompany H. R. 7262, 48th Cong., 2nd sess., *Cong. Rec.* 1371.

483. "Had a Gay Old Time," *Oswego Daily Palladium*, April 6, 1900, 6.

484. "Mrs. Spencer Honored," *Oswego Daily Palladium*, July 7, 1893, 5.

485. "The Old Vets," *Oswego Daily Palladium*, November 25, 1893, 5.

486. See "G. A. R. Encampment," *Watertown Daily Times*, May 18, 1899, 1, 8; "Governor and Legislature," *Oswego Daily Palladium*, May 24, 1899, 3; "Destroyed With Capitol," *Oswego Daily Palladium*, March 29, 1911, 5.

487. "The Last Syracuse Tragedy," *Troy Weekly Times*, March 22, 1873.

488. See, for example, "News by Mail," *Ithaca Daily Journal*, March 18, 1873, 1; "Murder at Syracuse—Death of the Murderer," *Ogdensburg Daily Journal*, March 19, 1873.

489. See "The Keeler Murder," *Rochester Democrat and Chronicle*, March 21, 1873.

490. "The End of a Love Tragedy," *New York Sun*, March 22, 1873, 1.

491. See "Mrs. Spencer and the Keeler Tragedy," *Oswego Daily Palladium*, March 25, 1873.

492. "Frightful Explosion," *Mexico Independent*, August 18, 1864.

493. "Mrs. Spencer's Leg Amputated," *Oswego Daily Palladium*, November 13, 1912, 5.

494. "Mrs. Spencer is Dying," *Oswego Daily Palladium*, November 14, 1912, 8.

495. See "The Death of Mrs. Spencer," *Oswego Daily Palladium*, December 20, 1912, 3; "Sons of Veterans Bearers at Mrs. Spencer's Funeral," *Watertown Daily Times*, December 31, 1912, 3.

496. "Oswego County," *Lowville Journal and Republican*, November 5, 1891.

497. Churchill, *Landmarks of Oswego County* "Biographies, 254–55.

498. "Francis W. Squires," *Lowville Journal and Republican*, June 10, 1897. See also "North Volney," *Mexico Independent*, May 4, 1881.

499. Wardwell G. Robinson, *History of the 184th Regiment, New York State Volunteers* (Oswego, NY: R. J. Oliphant, 1895), 13–14.

500. "Here and There," *Mexico Independent*, October 7, 1885.

501. "Here and There," *Mexico Independent*, June 12, 1889.

502. "G. A. R. Officers Elected," *Oswego Daily Palladium*, December 6, 1893, 3.

503. "North Volney Sabbath School," *Mexico Independent*, May 30, 1877; "The Sunday School in the Woods," *Mexico Independent*, October 10, 1877.

504. "Demster," *Mexico Independent*, January 11, 1888; "Here and There," *Mexico Independent*, December 11, 1889.

505. "Old Settlers' Association," *Pulaski Democrat*, August 31, 1893.

506. "Dempster Grove," *Mexico Independent*, September 2, 1875.

507. See, for example, "Settlers of Oswego County," *Oswego Daily Palladium*, August 25, 1880; "Old Residents of Oswego County," *Mexico Independent*, July 2, 1884. See also No headline, *Pulaski Democrat*, July 14, 1887.

508. "War of 1812," *Mexico Independent*, July 24, 1888.

509. "Oswego County," *Lowville Journal and Republican*, February 11, 1897.

510. "Town of New Haven," *Mexico Independent*, January 21, 1875; "It Cuts No Figure," *Sandy Creek News*, February 15, 1884; "November Cold Snap," *Sandy Creek News*, December 6, 1888, 1; "Old Mexico," *Mexico Independent*, October 6, 1886; "Vote on Senator," *Pulaski Democrat*, November 15, 1883.

511. "The Board of Supervisors," *Oswego Daily Palladium*, December 31, 1884.

512. "Francis W. Squires," *Oswego Daily Palladium*, June 5, 1897, 8. See also "Francis W. Squires," *Mexico Independent*, July 9, 1897; "Francis W. Squires," *Lowville Journal and Republican*, June 10, 1897; "The Late F. W. Squires," *Lowville Journal and Republican*, June 24, 1897; "Memorial Resolutions," *Mexico Independent*, July 21, 1897.

513. "Maria L. Squires," *Oswego Daily Palladium*, June 22, 1911, 5.

514. "James K. Stockwell," *Sandy Creek News*, April 4, 1929, 6.

515. "Directory of Deceased American Physicians card file," https://www.ancestry.com.

516. "Pension Examiners Retired," *Sandy Creek News*, January 25, 1900.

517. See, for example, "Charges Preferred," *Oswego Daily Times*, January 30, 1897; "Meat Markets Must Be Kept Clean," *Oswego Daily Times*, September 13, 1910, 4; "General Health of City Probed," *Syracuse Post-Standard*, April 24, 1914, 12; "Stockwell After Milk Peddlers," *Oswego Daily Times*, January 13, 1915, 5; "Sanitary Survey Will Be Made," *Oswego Daily Palladium*, June 8, 1915, 3; "Inspector Hoey Busy," *Oswego Daily Palladium*, June 23, 1915, 4; "Child Dies; Whole Family Ill at Oswego," *Syracuse Post-Standard*, September 10, 1915, 12.

518. "Mayor Stockwell," *Oswego Daily Times*, March 6, 1889, 1.

519. "Dr. Stockwell and the Mayoralty," *Oswego Daily Times*, March 3, 1890.

520. See "Election Notes," *Wilmington Evening Journal*, March 5, 1890, 1.

521. "To Name New Officers," *Oswego Daily Times*, January 28, 1925, 2.

522. "Let Contract on New Modern House," *Oswego Daily Times*, April 6, 1925, 4.

523. See "To Rule the Masons," *Albany Argus*, June 24, 1889, 1; "Appointments Made by the Grand Master of Masons," *Utica Weekly Herald*, June 28, 1892, 1.

524. "Mr. Shepherd Gets the Place," *Oswego Daily Palladium*, June 8, 1903, 4.

525. See, for example, "Officers for the Hospital," *Oswego Daily Palladium*, October 20, 1914.

526. See, for example, "Congregationalists," *Oswego Daily Palladium*, May 20, 1904, 8; "Dr. Campbell Is Supply Here," *Oswego Daily Palladium*, December 21, 1916, in which it was announced that Margaret had been elected a deacon in the church for the following year.

527. "Mrs. Margaret Fleming Stockwell," *Oswego Daily Palladium*, April 15, 1924, 5.

528. "Dr. James K. Stockwell," *Sandy Creek News*, April 4, 1912, 6. See also "Dr. Stockwell, 84, Former Resident, Passes at Oswego," *Lockport Union-Sun*, March 27, 1929, 16.

529. "Dr. Stockwell's Term Expires," *Oswego Daily Times*, December 15, 1917, 4.

530. Moore was very much alive, dying in 1954 in California. He and his second wife, Cora Mae _____ (1874–April 2, 1962), are buried in Lakewood Memorial Park, Hughson, Stanislaus, California.

531. "Wedding Occurred at Mount Pleasant Yesterday," *Fulton Evening Times*, December 18, 1914, 6.

532. "Local Happenings," *Fulton Patriot*, June 5, 1929.

533. "Oldest Public Official in County of Oswego," *Mexico Independent*, May 18, 1904, 1. Rpt. from *Syracuse Post-Standard*, May 8, 1904.

534. "Shooting in Port Ontario," *Mexico Independent*, January 7, 1875.

535. "Here and There," *Mexico Independent*, February 4, 1880; "The Counterfeiters," *Mexico Independent*, February 11, 1880.

536. "Here and There," *Mexico Independent*, February 18, 1880.

537. "Escaped From Jail and Captured," *Mexico Independent*, July 11, 1883.

538. "Here and There," *Mexico Independent*, August 6, 1884; "Here and There," *Mexico Independent*, July 13, 1887.

539. See "A Practical Joke," *Mexico Independent*, October 12, 1887; "Here and There," *Mexico Independent*, May 2, 1888; "Here and There," *Mexico Independent*, January 11, 1893.

540. "Here and There," *Mexico Independent*, January 12, 1898.

541. "Here and There," *Mexico Independent*, January 19, 1898.

542. "Court Crier Tillapaugh Is Out," *Oswego Daily Palladium*, January 2, 1909, 1; "The Tillapaugh Case," *Oswego Daily Palladium*, January 5, 1909, 1; "Court Crier Unnecessary Expense," *Lowville Journal and Republican*, January 13, 1909, 5.

543. "Tillapaugh Serves," *Watertown Daily Times*, January 5, 1909, 4; No headline, *Sandy Creek News*, January 7, 1909, 4.

544. "Tillapaugh Holds Job," *Oswego Daily Palladium*, January 23, 1909, 5; No headline, *Sandy Creek News*, January 28, 1909. 4.

545. "Tillapaugh Must Answer," *Oswego Daily Palladium*, February 20, 1909, 5.

546. "Mr. Tillapaugh Makes Answer," *Oswego Daily Palladium*, February 25, 1909, 5.

547. "The Tillapaugh Hearing Today," *Oswego Daily Palladium*, February 26, 1909, 8; "Tillapaugh Hearing," *Oswego Daily Palladium*, March 1, 1909, 1; "The Tillapaugh Case," *Oswego Daily Palladium*, March 5, 1909, 5; "The Tillapaugh Case," *Oswego Daily Palladium*, March 12, 1909, 8.

548. "For Reopening Tillapaugh Case," *Oswego Daily Palladium*, June 8, 1909, 1.

549. "Charges Against the Court Crier," *Watertown Daily Times*, June 9, 1909, 5.

550. "Answer Filed in Tillapaugh Case," *Watertown Daily Times*, June 23, 1909, 4; "Court Crier Removed," *Watertown Daily Times*, September 27, 1909, 5.

551. "In Memoriam," *Mexico Independent*, March 4, 1896. See also "Here and There," *Mexico Independent*, February 26, 1896.

552. See "Mexico," *Syracuse Evening Herald*, December 13, 1899, 3.

553. "My Impressions of Montreal," *Mexico Independent*, September 30, 1903.

554. "The Tillapaugh Case," *Mexico Independent*, November 27, 1907.

555. "Final Decree of Divorce," *Oswego Daily Times*, Mary 18, 1912, 1; "Divorce for W. A. Tillapaugh," *Watertown Daily Times*, May 20, 1912.

556. "In Special Term," *Utica Herald-Dispatch*, November 16, 1915, 3.

557. See "Lutheran Home at Clinton to Open Tomorrow," *Utica Morning Telegram*, December 10, 1920, 15.

558. No headline, *Sandy Creek News*, June 4, 1925, 1.

559. "Has Enjoyed Many Birthdays," *Mexico Independent*, May 5, 1927, 1.

560. "William A. Tillapaugh," *Mexico Independent*, October 11, 1928, 1.

561. No headline, *Troy Daily Whig*, March 22, 1848.

562. "Promotions and Appointments," *Washington Evening Star*, September 6, 1856, 1.

563. "Knew Grant When He Was a Captain," *Syracuse Herald*, April 28, 1912, 8-C.

564. Minutes of the Retiring Board, February 25, 1862.

565. "The Retired List," *New York Daily Tribune*, February 28, 1862, 5; "From Washington," *Albany Argus*, February 28, 1862, 1; "On the Retired List," *New York Herald*, February 28, 1862, 1; "Army and Navy Intelligence," *Journal of Commerce Junior*, March 1, 1862; No headline, *Boston Daily Advertiser*, March 5, 1862.

566. "Major Underwood," *Oswego Commercial Times*, August 30, 1862.

567. "Mustering and Disbursing Officer," *Oswego Commercial Times*, June 4, 1863.

568. Deposition of September 24, 1863.

569. For example, see "Death of Major Underwood," *Oswego Commercial Times*, September 7, 1863; "Death of Major Underwood," *Albany Morning Express*, September 7, 1863; "Death of Major Underwood," *New York Daily Tribune*, September 7, 1863, 5; "Death of Major Edmund Underwood," *Philadelphia Inquirer*, September 7, 1863, 1; No headline, *Alexandria Gazette*, September 7, 1863, 1; No headline, *Troy Daily Times*, September 8, 1863; No headline, *Louisville Daily Journal*, September 11, 1863, 1; "Death of Major Underwood," *Sacramento Weekly Union*, October 3, 1863, 5.

570. "Mrs. Mary Beardsley Underwood," *Oswego Daily Palladium*, August 9, 1917, 4.

571. "The Founding of the Home," *Oswego Daily Times*, October 13, 1894, 5.

572. "'Easter Tea' at the 'Home,'" *Oswego Daily Times*, March 30, 1891, 6; "Home for the Homeless," *Oswego Daily Times*, February 9, 1897, 6.

573. See, for example, "Acknowledgments for the Home," *Oswego Daily Times*, June 5, 1906, 6.

574. See, for example, "Death Came Suddenly," *Oswego Daily Times*, August 9, 1917, 8.

575. "Mrs. Mary B. Underwood," *Oswego Daily Times*, August 10, 1917, 5.

576. No headline, *Sugar Planter*, January 5, 1856, 2; No headline, *Salem Register*, December 20, 1855, 2.

577. "Mary Edwards Walker," *Civil War* (blog), November 21, 2013, http://civilwaref.blogspot.com/2013/11/mary-edwards-walker-born-november-26.html.

578. Quoted in Theresa Kaminski, *Dr. Mary Walker's Civil War* (Guilford, CT: Lyons Press, 2020), 11–12.

579. "A Strong-Minded Woman," *Troy Daily Times*, June 9, 1869, 1. Rpt. from *Dubuque Times*.

580. No headline, *Cazenovia Republican*, April 6, 1864.

581. Kaminski, *Dr. Mary Walker's Civil War*, 123–24. Some truth may be attached to that accusation since both General William T. Sherman and General George H. Thomas recommended her for the Medal of Honor.

582. "From Georgia," *Mexico Independent*, April 28, 1864; "Personal Items," *Herald of Progress*, May 28, 1864, 5. See also "She Asks Correction Fifty Years After War," *Richmond Times Dispatch*, September 6, 1914, 7.

583. No headline, *Buffalo Morning Express*, November 1, 1864. See also "Rebel News," *Dansville Advertiser*, August 18, 1864; "Secesh Items," *Troy Weekly Times*, August 30, 1864.

584. "Personal," *Troy Weekly Times*, December 10, 1864. See also No headline, *Oswego Daily Palladium*, December 17, 1864; No headline, *Newport Mercury*, December 24, 1864, 2.

585. "Won't Stay Divorced," *New York Daily Reformer*, November 21, 1867. See also "Mrs. Dr. Walker and Divorce," *Oswego Daily Palladium*, April 2, 1866.

586. Sharon Harris, *Dr. Mary Walker: American Radical, 1832–1919* (New Brunswick, NJ: Rutgers University Press, 2009), 107.

587. "Dr. Mary Walker," *Muskegon Chronicle*, November 28, 1893, 1.

588. Lester A. Halpin, "Only Woman to win 'Medal' wouldn't give it back," *Oregonian*, June 30, 1944, 104.

589. "Relative Seeks Restoration of Medal of Honor to 'Dr. Mary,' Only Woman to Receive it," *Arkansas Gazette*, August 1, 1976, 5.

590. "She Wins Fight for Kin's Medal," *Boston Herald*, August 20, 1978, 3.

591. Dr. Walker's pension file is available online: Jessie Kratz, "Dr. Mary E. Walker," Pieces of History, March 22, 2019, https://prologue.blogs.archives.gov/2019/03/22/dr-mary-e-walker/.

592. "Dr. Mary Walker's Pension," *Evening Star*, June 18, 1898, 11.

593. "Dr. Mary Walker in Luck," *Mexico Independent*, February 16, 1881; "Washington News," *Potsdam Courier & Freeman*, March 10, 1881.

594. No headline, *Buffalo Evening News*, May 3, 1882; "Gritty Mary Walker," *Albany Argus*, July 14, 1883, 5; "Dr. Mary Walker's Ideas," *Evening Gazette*, June 18, 1884, 1.

595. "Wishes a Position," *Newport Mercury*, February 13, 1869, 2.

596. See, for example, "For and About Women," *Buffalo Evening News*, November 22, 1881.

597. "What is Going On in Society," *Albany Argus*, January 6, 1884, 5. See also "Dr. Mary Walker, the Man Woman," *Morning Star*, August 19, 1904, 4.

598. See, for example, "Dr. Mary Walker, Civil War Veteran, Wearer of Men's Attire, Succumbs," *Muskegon Chronicle*, February 22, 1919, 9.

599. George W. Stimpson, "You'd Be Surprised," *Corpus Christi Times*, July 18, 1940, 6.

600. "Floating Humor," *Oneida Dispatch*, April 11, 1884. This statement is a corruption of her own words: "The majority of men have no high moral standard, but without shame assert that they are as good as any other men." See Mary Walker, *Unmasked: The Science of Immorality* (Philadelphia: Wm. H. Boyd, 1878), 2.

601. No headline, *Chenango American*, May 7, 1885.

602. "Humorous," *Franklin Gazette*, April 21, 1882.

603. "Quiet Smiles," *Niagara County News*, April 18, 1884.

604. No headline, *New Orleans Times-Picayune*, July 2, 1873, 2.

605. "Dr. Mary Walker at Polls," *New York Sun*, November 8, 1880, 1.

606. See, for example, "Personal–Home and Abroad," *Catskill Recorder*, November 26, 1880.

607. "The Latest News," *Plattsburgh Sentinel*, July 1, 1881.

608. "Dr. Mary Walker for Congress," *Saginaw News*, October 11, 1890, 1.

609. Belva Ann Bennett Lockwood (October 24, 1830–May 19, 1917) was one of the first female attorneys in the United States and the first woman admitted to the Bar of the Supreme Court. She ran for president in 1884 and 1888 representing the National Equal Rights Party.

610. "Dr. Mary Walker," *Chicago Daily Tribune*, August 15, 1880, 13.

611. "She Sees No Need for Suffrage Law," *Washington Times*, April 8, 1913, 5.

612. Quoted in Steve Yablonski, "Hundreds Turn Out to Pay Tribute to Dr. Mary Walker," *Oswego County Today*, May 13, 2012, https://oswegocountytoday.com/news/oswego/hundreds-turn-out-to-pay-tribute-to-dr-mary-e-walker/.

613. See "A Remarkable Woman Dead," *Emporia Gazette*, February 22, 1919, 1; "Dr. Mary E. Walker, Advocate of Dress Reform, Dies at 89," *New York Tribune*, February 23, 1919, 13; "Mary Walker Woman Surgeon Passes Away," *Alaska Daily Empire*, February 22, 1919, 8; "Dr. Mary Walker Dead," *Williams News*, March 14, 1919, 5. Some obituary information must be considered fanciful at best.

614. "Dr. Mary Walker Dead at 87," *Oswego Daily Palladium*, February 22, 1919, 4. In addition to the newspaper articles mentioned in the obituary, Dr. Walker was also the author of two books, *Hit!* (1871) and *Unmasked: The Science of Immorality* (1878). The first was addressed to women and the second, to men.

615. For a history of the 26th Regiment, see Paul Taylor, *Glory Was Not Their Companion: The Twenty-Sixth New York Volunteer Infantry in the Civil War* (Jefferson, NC: McFarlane and Co., 2005).

616. See Snyder, *Oswego County, New York in the Civil War*, 95–100.

617. Ulysses S. Grant, *Personal Memoirs* (New York: Modern Library, 1999), 462. See also 458–60. For a detailed account of the battle of Cold Harbor, see Ernest B. Furgurson, *Not War But Murder: Cold Harbor 1864* (New York: Vintage Books, 2000).

618. No headline, *Mexico Independent*, June 30, 1864.

619. No headline, *Oswego Commercial Advertiser*, June 16, 1864.

620. Crisfield Johnson, *History of Oswego County, New York, 1789–1877* (Philadelphia: L H. Everts, 1877), 347.

621. "Brought Home for Interment," *Oswego Commercial Times*, June 16, 1864.

622. John Joseph, who had only reenlisted to please his parents, returned to duty and was seriously wounded twice during the siege of Petersburg. Declared totally disabled, he was discharged on June 5, 1865, two days shy of the first anniversary of Granville's death and one day after the first birthday of his son, John Granville.

Bibliography

Newspapers

Alaska Daily Empire
Albany Argus
Albany Evening Times
Albany Morning Express
Albany Times
Albany Times-Union
Alexandria Gazette
Arkansas Gazette
Atlantic City Daily Tribune
Auburn Bulletin
Auburn Morning News
Auburn News and Bulletin
Auburn Weekly Democrat
Baldwinsville Gazette and Farmers' Journal
Boston Daily Advertiser
Boston Herald
Brooklyn Morning Eagle
Brooklyn Standard
Buffalo Daily Courier
Buffalo Evening News
Buffalo Morning Express
Buffalo News
Camden Advance-Journal
Cayuga Chief
Cazenovia Republican
Catskill Recorder
Chenango American

Chicago Daily Tribune
Corpus Christi Times
Dansville Advertiser
Elmira Telegram
Emporia Gazette
Evening Star
Fairport Herald-Mail
Franklin Gazette
Fulton Patriot
Fulton Evening Times
Fulton Times
Grand Rapids Herald
Great Bend Register
Herald of Progress
Hillsboro News-Herald
Homer Republican
Hudson Daily Register
Iola Index
Ithaca Daily Journal
Ithaca Daily News
Ithaca Morning Herald
Jefferson County Journal
Journal of Commerce Junior
Kansas Chief
Kansas City Star
Kenosha Evening News
Kingston Daily Freeman
Lancaster Intelligencer
Lawrence Daily Journal
Leavenworth Times
Lockport Union-Sun
Lowville Journal and Republican
Louisville Daily Journal
Maysville Evening Bulletin
Mexico Independent
Morning Star
Muskegon Chronicle
National Police Gazette
National Tribune
New Orleans Times-Picayune
Newport Mercury
New South Berlin Bee

New York Clipper
New York Daily Herald
New York Daily Reformer
New York Daily Tribune
New York Herald
New York Press
New York Reformer
New York Sun
New York Times
New York World
Niagara County News
Northern Christian Advocate
Ogdensburg Daily Journal
Oneida Dispatch
Oneida Morning Herald
Oregonian
Osage County Chronicle
Oswego Advertiser and Times
Oswego Commercial Advertiser
Oswego Commercial Times
Oswego Daily Press
Oswego Daily Times
Oswego Daily Times and Express
Oswego Daily Palladium
Oswego Morning Herald
Oswego Morning Post
Oswego Palladium-Times
Oswego Weekly Advertiser
Oswego Weekly Commercial Advertiser
Oswego Weekly Palladium
Philadelphia Inquirer
Phoenix Register
Pittsburgh Post-Gazette
Plattsburgh Sentinel
Potsdam Courier & Freeman
Poughkeepsie Daily Eagle
Pulaski Democrat
Richmond County Journal
Richmond Dispatch
Richmond Times Dispatch
Rochester Democrat and Chronicle
Rochester Evening Express

Rome Citizen
Rome Daily Sentinel
Rutland Daily Herald
Sacramento Weekly Union
Sag-Harbor Express
Saginaw News
Salem Register
Salina Semi-Weekly Journal
Sandy Creek News
Scranton Tribune
Seneca County News
Sugar Planter
Syracuse Daily Courier
Syracuse Daily Journal
Syracuse Daily Standard
Syracuse Herald-Journal
Syracuse Journal
Syracuse Morning Standard
Syracuse Post-Standard
Syracuse Sunday Herald
Syracuse Weekly Express
Terre Haute Weekly Gazette
Troy Daily Times
Troy Daily Whig
Troy Weekly Times
Utica Gazette
Utica Herald-Dispatch
Utica Morning Herald
Utica Morning Telegram
Utica Weekly Herald
Utica Weekly Herald and Courier
Valley News
Wall Street Journal
Washington Evening Journal
Washington Evening Star
Washington Sentinel
Washington Times
Watertown Daily Standard
Watertown Daily Times
Weekly Saratogian
Williams News

Periodicals

Allen, L. L. "Pioneer Granger Was Hero of Kearsarge Crew in Civil War Battle." *Watertown Daily Standard*, April 9, 1927, 9.
Delaney, Norman C. "Victory Has Perched on Our Banners." *Naval History* 28, no. 3 (June 2014), 32–38.
DeRousie, Anne. "The Rome-Oswego Plank Road." *Thirtieth Publication of the Oswego County Historical Society* (Phoenix, NY: Phoenix Press, 1969), 52–53.
Halpin, Lester A. "Only woman to win 'the medal' wouldn't give it back." *Oregonian*, June 30, 1974: 104.
"Improved Friction Clutch." *Scientific American* (May 17, 1873), 312.
Knox, Jay. "Do You Remember?" *Oswego Palladium-Times*, May 31, 1945, 15.
Levshiz, Ves. "Medal of Honor Recipient Remembered for Heroic Actions Aboard Union Ship." *Oswego Palladium-Times*, July 17, 2000: 1.
Lynch, Grace. "The Way It Used to Be." *Fulton Patriot*, March 21, 1963.
Snyder, Charles McCool. "The Antislavery Movement in the Oswego Area." *Eighteenth Publication of the Oswego County Historical Society* (Oswego, NY: Palladium-Times, 1955), 2–12.
Stimpson, George. "You'd Be Surprised." *Corpus Christi Times*, July 18, 1940: 6.
Wellman, Judith. "'Bound by Duty': Abolitionists in Mexico, New York, 1830–1842." *Thirty-Fourth Annual Publication of the Oswego County Historical Society* (Oswego, NY: Beyer Offset, 1974), 1–30.
Woodall, Natalie J. "Lost and Found: Captain Delos Gary's Grave." *Oswego Palladium-Times*, May 28, 2019: 1.
———. "On to Glory: Oswego's 147th Regiment at Gettysburg." *Oswego Palladium-Times*, July 1, 2019: 1.

Online Sources

www.Ancestry.com.
www.Familysearch.com.
www.Findagrave.com.
www.Fultonhistory.com.
www.NYSHistoricalNewspapers.org.
"Directory of Deceased American Physicians Card File." Ancestry.com, accessed January 18, 2022, https://www.ancestry.com/search/collections/7833/.
Gayley, Alice J. "Samuel Eliot—A Diary of Prison Life." PA Roots, accessed January 18, 2022, https://www.pa-roots.com/pacw/reserves/7thres/eliotdiary.html.
Graham, Chris. "More Steam Shovel History." Heritage Machines, March 20, 2021, https://heritagemachines.com/plant-machinery/more-steam-shovel-history/.

"Grasshopper Plague of 1874." https://www.kshs.org/kansapedia/grasshopper-plague-of-1874/12070#.

Hickox, Will. "The Civil War's 11th–Hour Soldiers." *New York Times Opinionator*, April 6, 2015, https://opinionator.blogs.nytimes.com/2015/04/06/the-civil-wars-11th-hour-soldiers/.

Hunter, G. Howard. "Unionist Troops in Louisiana." 64 Parishes, April 10, 2013, https://64parishes.org/entry/unionist-troops-in-louisiana.

Jones, Woody. "In their Own Words: Stephen Eliot 'That the Past May Be Vindicated.'" Roberson Project, March 24, 2020, http://www.meridiana.sewannee.edu/2020/03/24.

Kratz, Jessie. "Pieces of History." National Archives, March 22, 2019, http://www.prologueblogs.archives.gov.2019/03/22.

Lineberry, Cate. "The Boys of War." *New York Times Opinionator*, October 4, 2011, http://opinionator.blogs.nytimes.com/2011/10/04/the-boys-of-war.

"Mary Edwards Walker." *Civil War* (blog), November 21, 2013, http://civilwaref.blogspot.com/2013/11/mary-edwards-walker-born-november-26.html.

"Mexico Electric Light Heat and Power Company." Mexico Historical Society, accessed January 18, 2022, http://www.mexicohistoricalsociety.com.

"More Steam Shovel History." www.heritagemachines.com.

New York State Military Museum. "Home." New York State, accessed January 18, 2022, https://dmna.ny.gov.

"Oswego County Anti-Slavery Society Annual Meeting." Freethought Trail, January 17, 1839, https://freethought-trail.org/historical-events/event:1839-anti-slavery-meeting/.

"Pieces of History." www.prologueblogs.archives.gov.2019/03/22.

"Samuel Eliot—A Diary of Prison Life." www.pa-roots.com.

Caughey, D. C. "Samuel J. Crockett, 1st U. S. Cavalry." Regular Cavalry in the Civil War, January 15, 2021, https://regularcavalryincivilwar.com/2021/01/15/samuel-j-crockett-1st-u-s-cavalry/.

"Seneca, Oswego, Jefferson." *Impartial Citizen*, November 21, 1849, www.libraries.udmercy.edu.

"Unionist Troops in Louisiana." www.64parishes.org.

Vaticano, Patricia. *A Defense of the 63rd New York State Volunteer Regiment of the Irish Brigade*. Master's Thesis, University of Richmond, Richmond, Virginia, 2008, https://scholarship.richmond.edu/cgi/viewcontent.cgi?article=1702&context=masters-theses.

"23rd Wisconsin Infantry History." Wisconsin Historical Society, accessed January 18, 2022, https://www.wisconsinhistory.org/Records/Article/CS2332.

"Waterford Civil War Veterans." Wordpress, June 9, 2011, www.waterfordcivilwarveterans.wordpress.com.

"Wisconsin Genealogy Trails." Genealogy Trails History Group, accessed January 18, 2022, http://genealogytrails.com/wis/.

Yablonski, Steve. "Hundreds Turn Out to Pay Tribute to Dr. Mary Walker." *Oswego County Today*, May 13, 2012, https://oswegocountytoday.com/news/oswego/hundreds-turn-out-to-pay-tribute-to-dr-mary-e-walker/.

Books

Annual Report of the Adjutant-General of the State of New York. 43 vols. Albany, NY: Brandow Printing Co., 1893–1905.
Appendix of the Congressional Globe of the 25th Congress. Washington, DC: Blair and Rives, 1839.
Appleton's Cyclopedia of American Biography, 1600–1889. 6 vols. New York: D. Appleton & Co., 1889.
Blackmar, Frank W. *A Cyclopedia of State History, Embracing Events, Institutions, etc.* 2 vols. Chicago: Standard Publishing Co., 1912.
Cavanaugh, Michael. *Waterford Celebrities*. Waterford, Ireland: C. P. Redmond & Co., 1902.
Chadwick, Bruce. *1858: Abraham Lincoln, Jefferson Davis, Robert E. Lee, Ulysses S. Grant and the War They Failed to See*. Naperville, IL: Sourcebooks, 2008.
Churchill, John. *Landmarks of Oswego County, New York*. Syracuse, NY: D. Mason & Co., 1895.
Congressional Record Containing the Proceedings and Debates of the Forty-Ninth Congress, First Session. Vol. XVII. Washington, DC: Government Printing Office, 1886.
Conynham, Captain D. P. *The Irish Brigade and Its Campaigns*. Glasgow: Cameron & Ferguson, 1868.
Cook, Joyce. *Elmina Spencer: Oswego's Civil War Battlefield Nurse*. Syracuse, NY: Avalon Document Services, 2017.
Cooper, Lieut. A. *In and Out of Rebel Prisons*. Oswego, NY: R. J. Oliphant, 1888.
Cunningham, Edward. *The Port Hudson Campaign, 1862–1863*. Baton Rouge, LA: Louisiana State University Press, 1963.
DuMond, Dwight L. *Anti-Slavery: The Crusade for Freedom in America*. Ann Arbor: University of Michigan Press, 1961.
Ebert, Thomas J. *147th New York Volunteer Infantry: September 22, 1862–June 7, 1865: The Oswego Regiment: A Documentary History*. 3 vols. Clovis, CA: T. J. Ebert, 2009.
48th Congress, Second Session, Report No. 1371.
Furgurson, Ernest B. *Not War But Murder–Cold Harbor 1864*. New York: Vintage Books, 2000.
Grant, Ulysses S. *Personal Memoirs*. New York: Modern Library, 1999. Reprint of the 1885 edition.

Harris, Sharon. *Dr. Mary Walker: An American Radical, 1832–1919.* New Brunswick, NJ: Rutgers University Press, 2009.
Hendrix, Dorothy Kincheloe. *A Leaf from Army Life: Background and Experiences of a Civil War Soldier.* 2nd ed. Independently published, 1995.
Johnson, Crisfield. *History of Oswego County, New York, 1789–1877.* Philadelphia: L H. Everts & Co., 1877.
Kaminski, Theresa. *Dr. Mary Walker's Civil War.* Guilford, CT: Lyons Press, 2020.
King, W. C. and W. P. Derby. *Camp-Fire Sketches and Battle-Field Echoes of 61-65.* Springfield, MA: King, Richardson, & Co., 1888.
Ladd, David L. and Audrey J. Ladd, eds. *Bachelder Papers: Gettysburg in Their Own Words.* 3 vols. Dayton, OH: Morningside House, 1994–1995.
Lee, James. Unpublished Diary. Transcribed by Eva Hope Clark Place. Stored in the H. Lee White Maritime Museum, Oswego, NY.
Lord, Henry Dutch. *Memorial of the Family of Morse, Compiled from the Original Records for the Honorable Asa Porter Morse.* Cambridge, MA: Harvard Printing Co., 1896.
May, John Joseph. *Danforth Genealogy, Nicholas Danforth and William Danforth and Their Descendants.* Boston: Charles H. Pope, 1901.
McElroy, John. *A Story of Rebel Military Prisons.* Toledo, OH: D. R. Locke, 1879.
Northrop, John Worrell. *Chronicles From the Diary of a War Prisoner in Andersonville and Other Military Prisons in the South.* Wichita, KS: Published by the author, 1904.
Roberts, Edward F. *Andersonville Journey: The Civil War's Greatest Tragedy.* Shippensburg, PA: Burd Street Press, 2000.
Robinson, Wardwell G. *History of the 184th Regiment, New York State Volunteers.* Oswego, NY: R. J. Oliphant, 1895.
Sickles, Daniel E., William F. Fox, et al. *Monuments Commission for the Battlefields of Gettysburg and Chattanooga. Final Report on the Battlefield of Gettysburg.* Albany, NY: J. B. Lyon Co., 1900.
Snyder, Charles M. *Oswego From Buckskin to Bustles.* Port Washington, NY: Ira J. Friedman, Inc., 1968.
Snyder, Charles McCool. *Oswego County, New York in the Civil War.* Oswego, NY: Oswego County Historical Society, 1962.
Taylor, Paul. *Glory Was Not Their Companion: The Twenty-Sixth New York Volunteer Infantry in the Civil War.* Jefferson, NC: McFarlane and Co., 2005.
Walker, Mary E. *Unmasked: The Science of Immorality.* Philadelphia: Wm. H. Boyd, 1878.
Welch, Edgar Luderne. *Grip's Historical Souvenir of Camden.* Camden, NY: Camden Advance-Journal, 1902.
———. *Grip's Historical Souvenir of Mexico.* Syracuse, NY: Grip, 1904.
———. *Grip's Historical Souvenir of Phoenix.* Pulaski, NY: Seamans Press, 1902.
———. *Grip's Historical Souvenir of Pulaski.* Pulaski, NY: Seamans Press, 1902.

Woodall, Natalie Joy. *Men of the 110th Regiment: A Biographical Supplement.* Oswego, NY: Port City Printing, 2021.

———. *Men of the 110th Regiment: Oswego's Own.* Denver, CO: Outskirts Press, 2016.

———. *Of Blood and Battles: Oswego's 147th Regiment.* Denver, CO: Outskirts Press, 2019.

———. *Oswego County and the Civil War: They Answered the Call.* Charleston, SC: History Press, 2013.

Index

Abolitionists, 3, 7–10, 49, 233
Aeonian Lodge #679 F&AM, 198
Albert E. Lee Memorial Hospital, 105, 106–107
Alexander, John Barclay, 1, 17–22, 234–235
Alexander, Mary I. Place, 17–18, 20, 22, 235
Alger, Anna Slauson, 25–26, 29
Alger, Catherine, 23, 25, 27–29
Alger, Samuel, 22–29, 236
Ames, Leonard, 8
American Anti-Slavery Society, 6
American Colonization Society, 9, 233
Andersonville (Camp Sumter), 127, 155–157, 159, 161, 254

Baker, T. C., 8
Barnes, Burrit, 44
Barnes, Harriet Cooke, 44
Barnes, Frances Caroline Morse, 31, 32, 33, 237
Barnes, James, 29–33, 237
Battles:
　Antietam, 173
　Appomattox, 63, 91, 93, 116, 138, 201
　Brandy Station, 49, 183
　Cedar Creek, 73, 192
　Chancellorsville, 37, 95, 178, 182
　Charleston Harbor, 37
　Cold Harbor, 44, 39, 86, 168, 173, 229, 249, 265
　Fair Oaks, 44, 168, 173
　First Bull Run, 95, 229
　Fort Myers, 69
　Fort Wagner, 37
　Fredericksburg, 49, 95, 173, 178, 182, 257
　Gettysburg, 37, 39, 49, 54, 122, 124, 125, 134–135, 154, 173, 182–183, 187, 251, 253, 256
　Groveton, 37
　Hatcher's Run, 63, 201
　Kelly's Ford, 49
　Malvern Hill, 44
　Petersburg, 41, 44, 54, 86, 138, 173, 178
　Poplar Grove (Peebles' Farm), 168
　Port Hudson, 23, 30, 31, 68, 127, 237
　Quaker Road, 91
　Red River Campaign, 17, 23, 103
　Sailor's Creek, 201
　Second Bull Run, 37, 144
　South Mountain, 95
　Vicksburg, 103, 104

277

Battles (continued)
  Wilderness, 49, 54, 154–155, 173, 178, 229
  Williamsburg, 44
  Yorktown, 44
Beacon Light Lodge No. 464 IOOF, 160
Beebe, Asa, 8
Bird, Levi, 33–36, 238
Bird, Lizzie, 34–36
Brewster, Silas, 10
Brockman, Anna McNamara, 37–38, 40, 238
Brockman, John B., 1, 36–40, 238

Carpenter, Abigail Ann Stevens, 42–43
Carpenter, DeWitt Clinton, 41–44, 239
Castle Thunder, 116, 219, 249
Clark, Charlotte, 10
Clark, Edwin, 10
Clark, Starr, 8, 10
Clay, Henry, 9
Cleveland, Grover, 180, 257
Cleveland Lodge # 613 F&AM, 65, 242
Collins, Alonzo, 88
Cooke, Catherine "Kittie," 46–47
Cooke, Edward Austin, 1, 44–48, 239–240
Cooke, Harriet W. Griswold, 47, 48
Cooper, Alonzo, 168, 255
Copperheads, 14
Crockett, Frances Doolittle, 51, 52, 240
Crockett, Samuel James, 49–53, 240
Cross, Delia Gates, 54, 56, 57
Cross, Freeman Henry, 53–57, 241
CSS *Alabama*, 108–110

Danforth, Caroline Winters, 57, 59–60

Danforth, Horace Melvin, 57–62, 241
Danforth, Sarah P. Jersey, 60, 61, 241
Danville Prison, 49, 155, 158, 168, 169, 179
Darien Expedition, 30, 237
Davis, Edward, J., 29
Davis, Jefferson, 11
Deans, Ada Congdon Kime, 65, 66, 242
Deans, Claribel Houck Somer, 66, 242
Deans, Isabel Smith, 65, 66, 242
Deans, Thomas DeWitt, 1, 63–66, 241–242
Doyle, James, 67–72, 243, 250
Doyle, Margaret McCanna, 68, 72, 243
Dutcher, Gilbert C., 72–76, 243–244
Dutcher, Helen V. Forsyth, 74, 76, 244
Dutcher, Himan P., 72, 73, 74

Emancipation Proclamation, 14, 214
Enrollment Act of March, 3, 1863, 13

Falley, Lewis, 8
Ferguson, Helen A. Monroe, 77, 80, 81
Ferguson, William Dewey, 76–81, 244
Florence Prison Pen, 157–158
Fort Jefferson, 23, 68
Fort Sumter, 174
Frontier Lodge #422 F&AM, 46, 117
Fremont, John C., 38
Fugitive Slave Act of 1793, 10
Fugitive Slave Act of 1850, 9

Gallagher, Mason, 11
Gary, Catherine Martin, 83–84
Gary, Delos, 81–86, 245

Generals:
  Banks, Nathaniel, 31, 33, 68, 103, 105
  Burnside, Ambrose, 15, 245
  Butler, Benjamin, 23
  Grant, Ulysses S., 15, 63, 93, 154, 155, 168, 189, 212, 229, 265
  Hooker, Joseph, 15
  Lee, Robert E., 15, 63, 93, 138, 144, 246
  McClellan, George B., 15, 83, 245
  McClernand, John A., 102
  McDowell, Irvin, 15
  Meade, George G., 15
  Meagher, Thomas Francis, 173
  Pope, John 15, 143–144, 178
  Sheridan, Philip, 49, 73, 78, 192, 196
  Sherman William Tecumsah, 34, 70, 157
  Thomas, George H., 263
Gilbert, Hiram, 8
Gould, Joseph, 31, 86–88
Gould, Sarah L. Fuller, 87–88
Grand Army of the Republic (GAR), 1, 117, 141, 249, 254, 256
  Amos N. Kibbe No. 81, 160
  Andrew Jackson Barney No. 217, 34, 51
  Daniel F. Schenck, No. 271, 79, 177, 180, 205, 257
  Fairbanks No. 17, 181
  Garfield No. 25, 103
  Hiram Sherman No. 434, 163, 165
  Homer Lester Farmer No. 16, 65–66
  James Doyle No. 591, 193
  John D, O'Brian No. 65, 45, 59, 61, 70, 74, 92, 117, 123, 127, 174, 187, 198, 239
  Joseph Bradley Butler No. 111, 38, 39, 55, 134, 139

  Joseph Gould No. 145, 31, 33, 87
  J. Parson Stone No. 482, 60
  Lewis B. Porter No. 573, 117, 120
  May Humphrey Stacy No. 586, 198
  Melzar Richards No. 367, 96–98, 134, 193, 211, 246
  Merwin Olmstead No. 387, 42
  Rensselaer Bailey No. 19, 51, 70, 117, 240
  Ross No. 31, 60
  William C. Raulston 111, 179
Grange Movement "Grange," 111, 134, 193, 248, 249

Hiram Lodge #145 F&AM, 80, 236
Hirschbolz, Aletha Mary Kingsley, 91, 93, 246
Hirschbolz, Andrew J., 89–95, 246
Hirschbolz, Louise Eckl, 94–95, 246
Home for the Homeless (Ladies' Home), 199, 215–216, 262
Huntington, Edwin Lester, 95–101, 246–247
Huntington, Florence Adelle Allen, 96, 101
Huntington, Mary A. Turdot, 96, 101, 247

Ingersoll Gang, 127–128
Irish Brigade, 173

Jackson, James Caleb, 8

Keeler, Albert, 187, 258
Kent, Amos, 10

Lee, Albert Lindley, 101–107, 247–248
Lee, James H., 107–114, 248, 249
Lee, Julia Elizabeth Place, 110, 111, 113, 114, 249

Lee, Victorine Lind Foley, 103, 105, 106, 107, 248
Libby Prison, 116, 184
Lincoln, Abraham, 3, 12, 15, 83, 143–144, 155, 184, 193, 220, 234, 245
Littlefield, Hamilton, 8
Lockwood, Belva Ann Bennett, 224, 264
Lord, Edward, 12
Lyman, Henry Harrison, 147, 187

Mattison, Caroline A. Gillmore, 117–119, 250
Mattison, Lucius V. S., 114–121, 249
Mattison, Mary Sinclair Oliver, 120, 121, 250
McKinley, James A., 121–126, 250–251
McKinley, Jane Reid, 121, 126
McSweeney, Daniel, 126–131, 237, 251–252
McSweeney, Mary H. Sheridan, 128, 129–130, 131, 252
Mexico Lodge #136 F&AM, 99, 211
Miller, Albert, 218, 219
Missouri Compromise, 10, 11
Mowry, Ella Albertine Calkins, 133, 135, 137, 252
Mowry, Oliver Burrill, 131–137, 252
Muzzy, Alma P. Witt, 138–139, 141, 142, 253
Muzzy, Lawson Read, 137–142, 253

Old Settlers' Association, 117, 193
Olmstead, Elizabeth Crocker, 143, 144, 148
Olmstead, Julia A. Gilbert, 146, 148
Olmstead, Orimel Brown, 143, 144–145, 146–148, 253
Olmstead, Permilia Jane Palmer, 145, 148

Olmstead, Samuel Merwin, 1, 142–148
Oswego County Antislavery Society, 6
Oswego County Civil War Veterans' Association, 135, 179
Oswego Lodge #127 F&AM, 170–171

Parke, Clark Stewart, 148, 151–153
Parke, Harriet J. Stewart, 148, 150, 153
Parke, Smith, 1, 148–153
Pease, Catherine Lord, 159, 161, 162, 254
Pease, Francis M., 153–162, 254
Philanthropic Lodge #164 F&AM, 60
Pitcher, Margaret Blair, 162, 165, 166, 254
Pitcher, Peter, 162–166, 254
Place, John Albro, 17, 18
Preuss, Charles, 38–39, 238
Pulaski Lodge #415 F&AM, 42, 44, 139

Raulston, John, 166, 168, 169, 171
Raulston, William, C. 1, 166–171, 179, 254, 255
Reynolds, Lawrence, 1, 171–177, 255–256
Rice, Arvin, 10
Robinson, Ralph, 8
Robinson, Wardwell Green, 77, 83, 192

Sandy Creek Lodge #564 F&AM, 80
Schenck, Cornelia Smith Robinson, 180–181, 257
Schenck, Daniel Falley, 177–181
Schenck, William, 10, 177, 256
Schuyler, Anthony, 11
Search, Edward, 120

Selfridge, Thomas Oliver, 30
Seward, William H., 8
Slavery, 5–12, 234
Smith, Gerritt 6
Smith, Margaret Mary, 169, 255
Smith, Warren Douglas, 14–15
Snow, Horace, 13
Spencer, Elmina Pleiades Keeler, 2, 181–190, 230–231, 257, 258–259
Spencer, Ida Rosencraft, 187
Spencer, Robert H., 181, 182, 184, 185, 186, 189, 190
Squires, Francis C., 117, 190–195, 259
Squires, Maria Louisa Vanderbilt Coe, 193, 195
Squires, Sarah R. Rice, 191–192, 195
Stockwell, James K., 196–200, 259, 260
Stockwell, Margaret Fleming, 196, 198–199, 200, 260
Sykes, Elizabeth Ann Slaver Moore, 203–204, 205, 260
Sykes, Fannie A. Jones Whitaker, 202
Sykes, Hannah Lynch Glynn, 202
Sykes, Harriet C. Grotton, 202
Sykes, John Wilson, 200–205
Sykes, Mary Jane Guernsey Allen Oakes, 202–203

Taney, Roger Brooke, 10

Tillapaugh, Florence C. Murphy Huntley, 209
Tillapaugh, Harriet M. Tiffany, 209–210, 211
Tillapaugh, William A., 206–211, 260–262

Underground Railroad, 10, 177
Underwood, Edmund, 211–217, 262
Underwood, Mary Beardsley, 212–213, 214–217, 262
United States Sanitary Commission, 182
USS *Kearsarge*, 107–110, 113

Vallandigham, Clement Laird, 14–15, 83, 245
Veterans' Reunion Association, 45, 70, 71, 249

Walker, Mary Edwards, 2, 217–227, 262–264
Ward, Samuel Ringgold, 9
Waugh, William E., Jr., 27–28, 236
Wilder, John, 13
Woman's Relief Corps, 2, 43, 101, 187, 188
Woodall, Granville Sharp, 227–232, 265
Woodall, John Joseph, 227, 228, 229, 230, 265

www.ingramcontent.com/pod-product-compliance
Lightning Source LLC
Chambersburg PA
CBHW030734250426
43671CB00035B/340